WOMEN, MODERNISM AND PERFORMANCE

Women, Modernism, and Performance is an interdisciplinary study that looks at a variety of texts and modes of performance in order to clarify the position of women within – and in relation to – modern theatre history. Considering drama, fiction, and dance, as well as a range of performance events such as suffrage demonstrations, lectures, and a legal trial, Penny Farfan expands on theatre historical narratives that note the centrality of female characters in male-authored modern plays but that do not address the efforts of women artists to develop alternatives both to mainstream theatre practice and to the patriarchal avant garde. Focusing on Henrik Ibsen, Elizabeth Robins, Ellen Terry, Virginia Woolf, Djuna Barnes, Edith Craig, Radclyffe Hall, and Isadora Duncan, Farfan identifies different objectives, strategies, possibilities, and limitations of feminist–modernist performance practice and suggests how the artists in question transformed the representation of gender in art and life.

PENNY FARFAN is Associate Professor of Drama at the University of Calgary. Her work has appeared in such journals as *Text and Performance Quarterly*, *Modern Drama*, *Theatre Journal*, and *The Journal of Dramatic Theory and Criticism*. She has held fellowships at the Folger Shakespeare Library and the Calgary Institute for the Humanities, and her research has been funded by the Social Sciences and Humanities Research Council of Canada.

WOMEN, MODERNISM, AND PERFORMANCE

CAMBRIDGE
UNIVERSITY PRESS

CAMBRIDGE UNIVERSITY PRESS
Cambridge, New York, Melbourne, Madrid, Cape Town, Singapore, São Paulo

Cambridge University Press
The Edinburgh Building, Cambridge CB2 8RU, UK

Published in the United States of America by Cambridge University Press, New York

www.cambridge.org
Information on this title: www.cambridge.org/9780521837804

First published 2004
This digitally printed version 2007

A catalogue record for this publication is available from the British Library

Library of Congress Cataloguing in Publication data
Farfan, Penny.
Women, Modernism, and Performance / by Penny Farfan
p.   cm.
Includes bibliographical references and index.
ISBN 0 521 83780 4
1. Women in the theater – Europe – History – 19th century.   2. Women in the
theater – Europe – History – 20th century.   3. Women in the performing arts – Europe –
History – 19th century.   4. Women in the performing arts – Europe – History – 20th century.
5. Women in literature.   6. European drama – History and criticism.   I. Title.
PN1590.W64F37   2004
792′.082′094034 – dc22   2004045682

ISBN 978-0-521-83780-4 hardback
ISBN 978-0-521-04098-3 paperback

For my mother
Aurelie Wickham Farfan
and
in memory of my grandmother
Aurélie Vega Wickham

Contents

Illustrations

Abbreviations

The following abbreviations are used in parenthetical references within the text:

AROO	Virginia Woolf, *A Room of One's Own*
AS	Elizabeth Robins, *Ancilla's Share: An Indictment of Sex Antagonism*
BSC	Elizabeth Robins, *Both Sides of the Curtain*
"ET"	Virginia Woolf, "Ellen Terry"
IA	Elizabeth Robins, *Ibsen and the Actress*
ML	Isadora Duncan, *My Life*
"SA"	Elizabeth Robins, "Some Aspects of Henrik Ibsen: Lecture delivered before The Philosophical Institute, Edinburgh. October 27, 1908"
SML	Ellen Terry, *The Story of My Life*
TF	Elizabeth Robins, *Theatre and Friendship*
WH	Elizabeth Robins, *Whither and How*

Acknowledgments

I am indebted to a number of organizations and individuals for support that has been essential to the completion of this book. More specifically, I was very fortunate to be awarded a three-year Standard Research Grant from the Social Sciences and Humanities Research Council of Canada that facilitated every aspect of the project, from research travel to photocopying to graduate research assistance. Also, an annual fellowship at the Calgary Institute for the Humanities, with additional funding from the University of Calgary Department of Drama and Faculty of Fine Arts, provided teaching release time that enabled me to write chapter 4, and I am grateful to Gerry Dyer, Lorraine Ellert, and Denise Hamel for creating such a productive working environment at the Institute. A two-month fellowship at the Folger Shakespeare Library supported my research on Ellen Terry, and the staff at the Folger, as well as at the McKimmie Library at the University of Calgary, the Fales Library at New York University, the British Theatre Museum, and the Ellen Terry Memorial Museum, have all been extremely helpful to me in tracking down research materials relating to this project. I should add that in addition to sharing their expertise on Ellen Terry, Edith Craig, and the Barn Theatre, Margaret and Tony Weare of the Ellen Terry Museum kindly provided hot tea and a space heater on some very chilly December days in Terry's sixteenth-century farmhouse. Victoria Leacock has been extraordinarily hospitable on my various research trips to New York, and Dawn Ford saved me many, many hours of library time during her years as my research assistant. Christine Froula, Nancy Fraser, and Susan Manning read early versions of several chapters of the book and, together with Joseph Roach, have in different ways influenced my thinking about women, modernism, and/or performance. Thomas King, Eric Savoy, Jim Ellis, and Tracy Davis have all been supportive of my work, and I am grateful to Victoria Cooper of Cambridge University Press for her interest in the book, as well as to the two Cambridge readers who provided invaluable feedback on the manuscript. Finally, my very special thanks are due to Susan

Bennett, who has been as ideal a colleague as one could possibly wish for, and to Lory Wainberg, who has been a consistently amazing friend.

Unpublished writings by Elizabeth Robins are from the Elizabeth Robins Papers at the Fales Library, New York University, and are reproduced here by permission of the Royal United Kingdom Beneficent Association as Trustees of the Backsettown Trust. Ellen Terry's unpublished marginal comment on *Hedda Gabler* is reproduced by permission of the National Trust, Ellen Terry Memorial Museum, Smallhythe Place. Every effort has been made to obtain permission to reproduce copyright materials; I apologize for any omissions and would welcome these being brought to my attention.

Brief passages of the introduction and chapter 4 originally appeared in my article "Reading, Writing, and Authority in Ibsen's 'Women's Plays,'" *Modern Drama* 45.1 (Spring 2002): 1–8. An earlier version of chapter 1, "From *Hedda Gabler* to *Votes for Women*: Elizabeth Robins's Early Feminist Critique of Ibsen," was published in *Theatre Journal* 48.1 (March 1996): 59–78 (copyright ©1996 by the Johns Hopkins University Press). An earlier version of chapter 3 was published as "*Freshwater* Revisited: Virginia Woolf on Ellen Terry and the Art of Acting" in *Woolf Studies Annual* 4 (1998): 3–17. Chapter 5, "Writing/Performing: Virginia Woolf Between the Acts," was originally published by the National Communication Association in *Text and Performance Quarterly* 16.3 (July 1996): 205–215.

Introduction

Joan Templeton has pointed out that "[w]hatever particular meanings 'modernism' takes on when it is used to categorize different writers or genres, [. . .] its chief characteristic was a thoroughgoing revolt against the prevailing order" and that, "[i]ndisputably, the woman question had prime importance for the originators of modern drama."[1] Katherine E. Kelly has similarly noted that male authors of modern drama tended to "[represent] modernity in the figure of a woman in crisis."[2] Given the primacy of the "woman question" in such innovative and controversial plays as *A Doll's House* (1879), *Ghosts* (1881), *Rosmersholm* (1886), and *Hedda Gabler* (1890), "'Ibsenism' was," as Templeton states, "synonymous with modernism" throughout the late-nineteenth century.[3] Ibsen's "women's plays" in turn provided the inspiration – or provocation – for now-canonical plays featuring central female characters by younger male modernists such as George Bernard Shaw and August Strindberg. Yet in feminist–modernist Virginia Woolf's semi-autobiographical first novel *The Voyage Out* (1915), the central character Rachel reads Ibsen's plays and is changed by them, envisioning herself momentarily as "an heroic statue in the middle of the foreground, dominating the view," and acting his characters for days at a time afterward, but ultimately not finding in them a viable alternative to the conventional feminine roles that have been prescribed for her or the terms to imagine new roles that would make possible her survival.[4]

Notably, though it has commonly been suggested that the door-slam at the end of *A Doll's House* signaled the advent of both modern drama and the women's movement,[5] Nora's forgery of her father's signature is in fact the act of transgression that sets the drama in motion; and indeed, authorship and authority are linked throughout Ibsen's "women's plays," so that acts of writing, reading, or – in Hedda's case – manuscript-burning serve to signify the female protagonists' respective degrees of critical engagement with hegemonic cultural texts that deny women status as authoritative subjects.[6] Correspondingly, feminist artists in the late-nineteenth and early-twentieth

centuries engaged with the texts of the culture at large through their relationships to the texts of the theatre, so that their responses to dramatic
literature and theatrical practice in effect constituted feminist critical discourse both through theatre and about theatre itself. Such feminist discourse
was as much a defining feature of modernism as "the figure of [the] woman
in crisis" that pervaded modern drama, yet it has not been sufficiently
accounted for in narratives of modern theatre history that note the centrality of female characters in male-authored plays but do not address the
efforts of women artists to develop alternatives both to mainstream theatre
practice and to the patriarchal avant garde.

   Recent feminist research – for example, Katherine Kelly's edited anthology *Modern Drama by Women 1880s–1930s* (1996) and Sheila Stowell's *A
Stage of Their Own: Feminist Playwrights of the Suffrage Era* (1992) – has
begun to redress these omissions, recovering the work of neglected and forgotten women playwrights of the period, including, for example, Elizabeth
Robins and Djuna Barnes, both of whom are discussed in this study. Also
worth considering, however, are women artists primarily associated with
fields other than theatre whose work was nonetheless motivated at least to
some degree by their responses to particular aspects of theatre and drama.
Virginia Woolf's 1941 novel *Between the Acts*, for example, was informed
by her imaginative and actual engagement with the work of such theatre artists as Ellen Terry, Elizabeth Robins, and Edith Craig and, in it,
Woolf used theatrical performance to conceptualize the connection of art
to lived experience. On a different note, Isadora Duncan stated in her
autobiography that when she left Augustin Daly's renowned theatre company in 1897 to embark on her career as a solo concert dancer, she "had
learned to have a perfect nausea for the theatre: the continual repetition
of the same words and the same gestures, night after night,"[7] and that
when she went to see a musical comedy years later, she was moved to
tears, though the rest of the audience was laughing. "The waste was terrible to me," she said. "It was ghastly to see beautiful young girls come
out on stage saying meaningless words and making meaningless gestures,
when they could have been taught to be a force to the nation."[8] Thus,
the feminist–modernist aesthetics of key figures in the fields of dance and
literature developed in part out of their engagement with dramatic literature and theatrical practice, making their lives and work a part of theatre
history.

   As the examples of Duncan and Woolf suggest and as Bridget Elliot
and Jo-Ann Wallace contend in their interdisciplinary study *Women Artists
and Writers: Modernist (im)positionings*, "cross-disciplinary work, with its

tendency to 'make strange' or to 'defamiliarize' disciplinary assumptions, is of crucial importance in the production of feminist knowledge."[9] Tracy Davis has demonstrated the value of interdisciplinary methodologies for feminist theatre historical research in *Actresses as Working Women: Their Social Identity in Victorian Culture* (1991), and an interdisciplinary approach may similarly contribute to a fuller understanding of the history of women, modernism, and theatre. Thus, while the primary focus of this study is on theatre and drama, it also extends into the fields of literature and dance and is informed by an understanding of performance that encompasses not just the performing arts, but also suffrage demonstrations and pageants, lectures, a courtroom trial, a practical joke, the performance of gender in the practice of everyday life, and the performative act of producing feminist art and literature, theory and criticism.

Elin Diamond has noted that performance is always at once "a doing and a thing done" and that "[t]o study performance is not to focus on completed forms, but to become aware of performance as itself a contested space" in which "signifying (meaning-ful) acts may enable new subject positions and new perspectives to emerge, even as the performative present contests the conventions and assumptions of oppressive cultural habits."[10] Together with the range of performance modes considered here, this understanding of performance – and of theatre as performative practice – in terms of its potential to "[materialize] something that exceeds our knowledge, that alters the shape of sites and imagines as yet unsuspected modes of being,"[11] inflects my use of the word in my title: the chapters that follow consider the performative strategies, as much as the completed texts and performances, of a range of late-nineteenth- and early-twentieth-century feminist artists in order to clarify the position of women within – and in relation to – modern theatre history. Thus, though it is theatre-based, my analysis here is informed by the "interdiscipline" of performance studies.[12]

An interdisciplinary approach is supported by Rita Felski's proposal of the concept of a feminist public sphere as "a model for the analysis of diverse forms of [. . .] artistic and cultural activity by women in relation to the historical emergence of an influential oppositional ideology which seeks to challenge the existing reality of gender subordination."[13] As Felski explains it, "the feminist public sphere constitutes a discursive space which defines itself in terms of a common identity" – "the shared experience of gender-based oppression" – and which "needs to be understood in terms of a series of cultural strategies" intended to "convince society as a whole of the validity of feminist claims, challenging existing structures of authority through political activity and theoretical critique."[14] Felski's model thus enables an account of a feminist counter-public sphere working within and against the hegemonic counter-public sphere constituted by the male modernists who have typically dominated theatre historical narratives, but it can also accommodate the diverse and sometimes conflicting voices that together constituted feminist–modernist discourse through and about performance. It should be noted, for example, that although Ellen Terry's uncertainty about voting and ambivalence about militant suffrage activism have been taken as proof that she was not a feminist,[15] suffragism and feminism were not synonymous terms, so that while suffrage activism was of crucial importance to Elizabeth Robins and Edith Craig, other feminist–modernists – Duncan and Woolf, for example – were less interested in votes for women than in less directly political modes of social and cultural transformation. Duncan in fact believed that women's emancipation was not possible unless it began with women's bodies and so she remarked in her autobiography that her ideas about "the dance as an art of liberation" and "the right of woman to love and bear children as she pleased" were "considerably in advance of the Woman's Movement of the present day."[16] Elizabeth Robins, however, did not associate the sexual adventures recounted in *My Life* with any kind of political stance, remarking in her diary after reading Duncan's memoir, "If she'd been a feminist, she'd have been less unhappy. She allowed [men?] to devastate her."[17] Yet Robins had in common with Duncan an understanding of sex and gender as essentially unified, seeing no feminist value in the type of gender-play inherent in, for example, Sarah Bernhardt's portrayal of Hamlet[18] and remarking instead that she had been convinced by Bernhardt's performance that "women cannot 'do' men's parts" and that "[f]or a woman to play at being a man is, surely, a tremendous handicap in the attempt to produce stage illusion."[19] As Sheila Stowell has written of early-twentieth-century feminists in Britain more generally, Robins did not "seek to dissolve gender distinction" altogether, but, rather, "to intrude [her] own version of 'womanliness' into a male-dominated social and political system."[20] Such essential thinking about sex and gender was at odds with Virginia Woolf's theory of androgyny as articulated in *Orlando* and *A Room of One's Own*, as well as with Radclyffe Hall's representation of sexual inversion in her novel *The Well of Loneliness* and in her own public persona. By encompassing such diverse positions within feminism, as well as interdisciplinary cultural practice, and by situating feminist modernism in relation to both hegemonic modernism and mainstream theatre practice, the inclusive model of a feminist counter-public sphere can thus serve as a framework within which to represent more fully some of the different objectives and strategies – and ultimately, perhaps, the possibilities and limitations – of feminist performance practice in the modernist context.

In her introduction to *The Gender of Modernism*, Bonnie Kime Scott uses a diagram labeled "A Tangled Mesh of Modernists" to chart the myriad connections between the various writers included in her edited anthology,[21] thus rendering graphically visible the kind of discursive sphere that Felski describes. Although the representation of theatre and drama in Scott's anthology is minimal, her diagram could be extended or a similar diagram could be devised to establish the network of direct and indirect connections that existed between and among the central figures in this study, namely, Henrik Ibsen (1828–1906), Elizabeth Robins (1862–1952), Ellen Terry (1847–1928), Virginia Woolf (1882–1941), Djuna Barnes (1892–1982), Edith Craig (1869–1947), Radclyffe Hall (1880–1943), and Isadora Duncan (1877–1927). Terry, for example, was the mother of Duncan's lover Edward Gordon Craig, and she and Duncan were great admirers of each other's work. Robins met Terry in 1890, having seen her as Portia in *The Merchant of Venice* in the United States in the early 1880s and as a controversial Lady Macbeth in London in 1889. Like Terry's daughter Edith Craig, Robins became involved in suffrage theatre activities during the Edwardian period, and her essay *Ibsen and the Actress* was published by Virginia Woolf and her husband Leonard at the Hogarth Press in 1928. Robins later became friendly with Woolf, reading her novels *Night and Day*, *Orlando*, and *Between the Acts* and seeking her advice on a title for her own autobiography, published as *Both Sides of the Curtain* in 1940. Woolf herself reviewed fiction by Robins,[22] as well as a production directed by Edith Craig,[23] one of whose rehearsals she attended in 1922[24] and who may have been the model for the character Miss La Trobe in Woolf's final novel *Between the Acts*.[25] Woolf was also familiar with Duncan's autobiography, which Leonard Woolf reviewed favorably,[26] and she read Ellen Terry's memoirs and published letters, making her the central character in her play *Freshwater*, as well as the subject of one of her final essays. Shortly after Woolf's death in 1941, this essay was read by Woolf's friend and Craig's neighbor Vita Sackville-West at a memorial performance for Terry at the Barn Theatre that Craig established in the grounds of her mother's farmhouse-turned-museum in Kent.[27] Radclyffe Hall was Craig's friend and neighbor, as well as a subscriber to the Barn Theatre, and Woolf had been prepared to testify in defense of Hall's novel *The Well of Loneliness* when it was tried for obscenity in 1928. Djuna Barnes knew Hall in Paris in the 1920s and satirized her as Lady Tilly Tweed-in-Blood in her 1928 work *Ladies Almanack*; she may also have met Duncan in Berlin in 1921. Although Barnes was not directly involved in the suffrage theatre movement like Robins and Craig, she gave an extraordinary suffrage performance of a sort herself as a young journalist in New York in 1914, voluntarily undergoing forced feeding in order to be able to write about the experience of imprisoned British suffrage activists.[28] Barnes's 1923 play *The Dove* reads as a revision of Ibsen's *Hedda Gabler*, and indeed all the women considered here, with the possible though unlikely exception of Hall,[29] were familiar with Ibsen's work, whether as performers or as readers and spectators. Ibsen's pervasive influence is evident in this book, where *Hedda Gabler* is of particular and recurring interest.[30]

The chapters that follow stand on their own as independent essays combining biography, performance theory, theatre history and criticism, textual analysis, and feminist theory, but they are also related to each other in a kind of relay structure, with each chapter picking up on key questions raised by the preceding chapter. The political complementarities, strategic divergences, and thematic resonances that are thus cumulatively developed, as well as the actual personal and professional points of contact in the overlapping lives of the figures under consideration, demonstrate their cohesion within – and in fact their collective role in the formation of – a historic counter-public sphere in which modernist aesthetic concerns and first-wave feminist concerns productively coincided to infuse feminist subjectivity into public discourse on gender and culture.

In chapter 1 – "From *Hedda Gabler* to *Votes for Women*: Elizabeth Robins's Early Feminist Critique of Ibsen" – I consider Robins's evolving response to Ibsen – the "father" of modern drama – by tracing her progress from her work as an actress in the commercial theatre to her productions of his "women's plays" in London in the 1890s to her authorship of the 1907 suffrage drama *Votes for Women*. Viv Gardner has noted that the "New Woman" was popularly represented as having been "a devotee of Ibsen and given to reading 'advanced' books,"[31] yet Robins's interest in Ibsen appears to have been artistic rather than political. In comparison with most nineteenth-century theatrical fare, his drama, with its striking array of psychologically complex female characters, constituted a significant dramaturgical advance in terms of the representation of women and presented extraordinary acting opportunities for female performers such as Robins. By the early years of the twentieth century, however, Ibsen's plays no longer seemed to Robins to accurately reflect the full range of women's experience in that they neglected to represent its more progressive and constructive aspects, as evidenced, for example, in the organized women's suffrage movement. Increasingly politicized through her own suffrage activism, Robins attempted to compensate for this perceived deficiency in the Ibsen canon through her authorship of *Votes for Women*, in which she translated to the stage the real-life drama of the suffrage campaign. Yet while *Votes for Women* was highly successful with pro-suffrage audiences and inspired a series of similar propaganda pieces, including *A Pageant of Great Women*, with which Edith Craig was closely associated, Robins's melodramatic dramaturgy and reliance on the device of a "womanly woman" to articulate her pro-suffrage argument made her play complicit with the objectification of women that had motivated her to reject mainstream theatre in favor of Ibsen in the first place. In her quest for characters that were challenging theatrically yet acceptable within her developing political terms, Robins identified a crucial problem for feminist artists, but she did not definitively solve it.

Chapter 2, "Feminist Shakespeare: Ellen Terry's Comic Ideal," takes up from another perspective the problem crystallized in Robins's ultimately ambivalent response to Ibsen. Terry's hostility toward Ibsen's realist drama has generally been understood as evidence that she was essentially a Victorian actress, out of step with modern sociopolitical and artistic concerns, but Robins's re-evaluation of Ibsen from an emerging feminist perspective invites reconsideration of this conventional view of Terry's position in relation to Ibsen and, by extension, to feminist modernism. Terry's stated preference for Shakespeare's larger-than-life characters over Ibsen's realist characters and for comedy over tragedy, together with her claiming of Shakespeare as a proto-feminist whose female characters were more advanced than Ibsen's, indicate a transcendent utopian idealism at the heart of her aesthetic that was categorically opposed to realism, with its critical focus on exposing contemporary social problems. This expansive vision corresponded with Terry's endowment of her stage performances with a larger-than-life quality that was at the same time at odds with her own lived experience as the long-time leading lady of actor–manager Henry Irving, a contradiction borne out in the lectures on Shakespeare's female characters that she presented between 1910 and 1921. Not simply a Victorian figure who became "anachronistic" in the twentieth century,[32] Terry in fact embodied the contradiction between old and new that has been theorized as definitive of modern drama,[33] and in doing so, she posed the possibility of a more emancipatory if as-yet-unrealized alternative to the tortured and self-destructive heroines of Ibsen's tragic realism.

In chapter 3, "Unimagined Parts, Unlived Selves: Virginia Woolf on Ellen Terry and the Art of Acting," I consider Woolf's feminist–modernist fiction and literary theory in relation to the creative impasse that she saw in the

contradictory figure of the larger-than-life yet not fully realized Ellen Terry.
As her essays on the French actresses Rachel and Sarah Bernhardt make
clear, Woolf imagined acting in emancipatory terms, suggesting that in
impersonating dramatic characters, actresses are, in theory at least, afforded
unique opportunities for emotional exploration, heightened experience,
and self-discovery. In the case of Terry, however, Woolf suggested that this
expansive potential was not met because the existing dramatic repertory
failed to provide roles that would enable the actress to realize herself fully
in and through her art. In her own play *Freshwater*, in which Terry figures
as the central character, Woolf's concept of androgyny is implied as the
creative state of mind that cannot find expression in the corporeal and
therefore gendered art of acting. Thus, Terry signified for Woolf the value
of her own modernist fictional experiments, feminist theory, and literary
criticism as interventions in the historical entrapment of women in limiting,
male-determined roles, both on and off the stage.

Woolf's concept of androgyny was enabled in part by her relationship
with her friend and sometime lover Vita Sackville-West, who was the inspiration for the androgynous hero/heroine of her 1928 novel *Orlando*, and
by the more general establishment of modern sexual identities that coincided with the development of modernism in literature and the arts in the
late-nineteenth and early-twentieth centuries. The relationship between
representation and lived experience that is implied in Woolf's writings on
Terry and the art of acting is developed through the question of modern sexual identities in chapter 4, "Staging the Ob/scene." Here, Djuna
Barnes's play *The Dove* serves as a premise for an exploration of how the
hegemonic representational tradition has rendered autonomous female sexuality unthinkable and invisible – or as Barnes puts it, "obscene," by which
she implies both the conventional sexual sense of the word and a theatrical sense of off stage, out of sight, ob/scene. Barnes's staging of lesbian
sexuality in *The Dove* is analogous to the destruction of a canonical male
artist's painting of two courtesans that occurs at the end of the play. Her
metatheatrical intervention into the hegemonic representational tradition
in turn had real-life equivalents in the self-reflexive representational strategies of Edith Craig and Radclyffe Hall as they attempted to articulate an
emerging lesbian identity on the sociopolitical stage through such works as
A Pageant of Great Women and *The Well of Loneliness*, respectively. As the
intertextual referencing of *Hedda Gabler* in *The Dove* suggests, however,
Barnes also understood female homosexuality as a literalization of feminist
subjectivity, and in this way, her intention to stage the "ob/scene" of patriarchal culture in *The Dove* reflected the overarching project unifying the

various artists under consideration not only in this particular chapter but in the book as a whole.

Like *The Dove*, Virginia Woolf's self-reflexive final novel *Between the Acts* is concerned with the impact of art and literature on social actors. In chapter 5, "Writing/Performing: Virginia Woolf Between the Acts," I consider how the corporeality of performance enabled Woolf to theorize the connection of writing to material existence and to body forth her sense of how the work of women artists like herself – and like the other artists under consideration here – might function to transform gender norms that were, to her mind, debilitating in their effect on individuals and devastating in their social consequences. In *Between the Acts*, which incorporates a complete pageant of English literary history staged by the lesbian playwright–director Miss La Trobe, performance represents a liminal zone between art and life through which Woolf articulates her sense that literary texts are essentially cultural scripts which can operate in dominant and repressive capacities but which, by the same token, can put into play new modes of being by circulating alternative views of reality and devising new roles for social actors, who may see in them their "unacted part[s]."[34] Anticipating Tania Modleski's argument that feminist criticism is "performative and utopian, pointing toward the freer world it is in the process of inaugurating,"[35] *Between the Acts* suggests that writing was, for Woolf, a performative act with actual consequences and thus insists on the political implications of her work. This view was literalized through Woolf's highly selective public appearances in which she asserted through her physical presence the relation of her disembodied writing to feminist cultural politics.

Yet Judith Butler has noted the difficulty of "[determining] whether subversion has taken place,"[36] and while it is possible to extrapolate from *Between the Acts* a theory of performative writing, that is to say, a theory of writing as, in Butler's words, "authoritative speech" that "perform[s] a certain action and exercise[s] a binding power,"[37] the success of Woolf's performative intervention as a feminist–pacifist writing at the onset of World War II is left open to question by the ambiguous ending of *Between the Acts*. Chapter 6, "'Feminism, Tragedy, History: the Fate of Isadora Duncan,'" puts into question the possibility of transformation that Woolf theorized. More specifically, it considers Duncan's posthumous co-optation into a tragic master-narrative that depends upon the traditional gendering of hamartia – the tragic misstep or error in judgment – that Ibsen challenged in his "women's plays," where the tragedy develops out of the female protagonists' compliance with, rather than their departure from, the hegemonic cultural script that denies women status as authoritative subjects. The "fate" of Duncan thus reinforces the radical nature of Ibsen's dramaturgy even as it gave rise to subsequent feminist critique and modernist experiment, and underlines the interrelation and indeed the necessity of the diverse textual and corporeal strategies deployed by the artists who comprised the feminist–modernist counter-public sphere under consideration here.

CHAPTER I

From 'Hedda Gabler' *to* 'Votes for Women'*:*
Elizabeth Robins's early feminist critique of Ibsen

In Elizabeth Robins's preview of the Coronation Suffrage Pageant of 1911 – the largest and most spectacular demonstration of the British suffrage campaign – she announced that the Actresses' Franchise League contingent would be "led by Hedda Gabler, in the accomplished person of the Princess Bariatinsky on horseback."[1] The actresses' choice of a leader was at once fitting and incongruous. On the one hand, Hedda Gabler signified an anger that the actresses' professional reliance on popularity with audiences prohibited them from expressing more directly and assertively;[2] and Hedda's anger, together with her brilliance and desperation, had immediately established her as one of the great roles for women in the dramatic repertory. On the other hand, Hedda hardly qualified to marshal feminist followers toward their goal of emancipation, lacking the courage and conviction of the many suffragists who endured such hardships as jail sentences and forced feedings, and choosing to commit suicide rather than to confront in a more constructive manner the circumstances of her life that she finds so intolerable. Still, mitigating this apparently incongruous aspect of the actresses' choice of Hedda as their leader was the fact that though Ibsen included in his exposition the information that Hedda used to go riding in a long black skirt and with a feather in her hat prior to her marriage, she does not go riding within the time span of the play's action. Paradoxically, then, the recognizable figure whom the actresses were to rally behind was not the character that Ibsen depicted in his 1890 play but, rather, the character that they themselves imagined Hedda would have been had she somehow had existence outside of Ibsen's play.

This revisionist Hedda of the Coronation Suffrage Pageant encapsulates the challenges that faced early feminist theatre artists such as Elizabeth Robins as they attempted to create dramatic roles that were interesting theatrically yet acceptable within emerging feminist terms. Robins, who lived to the age of ninety, identified her performance of the title role in the English-language premiere of *Hedda Gabler* in London in 1891 as the defining moment of her long and varied career as an actress, writer, and suffragist. By her own account, this "epoch-making event," which won her fame as a daring theatrical innovator, caused her "to think of [her] early life as divisible in two parts 'before or after Hedda'"[3] and "was to remain the active principle/force shaping existence for [her] as long as life would last [. . .]."[4] Yet though Robins recognized Ibsen's impact on her career and claimed that "no dramatist [had] ever meant so much to the women of the stage,"[5] she was not simply uncritically admiring of the "father" of modern drama, whose notorious "women's plays," with their central female characters who defy prevailing standards of acceptable feminine behavior, had made him the darling of the late-nineteenth-century women's movement. On the contrary, Robins stated in her 1928 essay *Ibsen and the Actress*, "If we had been thinking politically, concerning ourselves about the emancipation of women, we would not have given the Ibsen plays the particular kind of wholehearted, enchanted devotion we did give"; what Ibsen offered in the 1890s "had nothing to do with the New Woman; it had everything to do with our particular business – with the art of acting" (31, 32–33). Thus, Robins did not hail Ibsen as a champion of feminism, but distinguished between his contribution to the cause of actresses and his non-contribution, by her standards, to the cause of women's emancipation. Her own 1907 suffrage play *Votes for Women* sought to redress Ibsen's failings, but as a revisionary effort was itself problematic: although it successfully broadened the scope of theatrical representation by bringing to the stage the real-life drama and spectacle of the suffrage campaign, it was at the same time heavily implicated in the ideas and practices that, to Robins's mind, had characterized the male-dominated commercial theatre prior to the advent of Ibsen and that had made his radical new drama so appealing to her in the first place. In thus clarifying the need to create characters that were challenging from an artistic perspective and yet acceptable within emerging feminist terms, Robins's theatre career, which became noteworthy with *Hedda Gabler* and ended with *Votes for Women*, serves as a useful starting point for a larger interdisciplinary consideration of women, modernism, and performance. This chapter will chart Robins's feminist critique of Ibsen as it developed over the course of her career and resulted in an unresolved tension not unlike that inherent in the figure of Hedda Gabler as suffragist icon.

As an actress, Robins was interested in Ibsen for several reasons. George Bernard Shaw wrote of Ibsen's modern prose dramas, "He gives us [. . .] ourselves in our own situations,"[6] and indeed, at a time when the standard theatrical fare was melodrama, in which stock characters were straight-forwardly differentiated as either good or bad, Robins was struck by the unprecedented realism of the characters peopling Ibsen's plays and of the situations in which they found themselves. In *Ibsen and the Actress*, she describes the impact that Janet Achurch and Charles Charrington's momen-tous production of *A Doll's House* had on her when she saw it in 1889, recalling the shock of seeing Achurch, costumed in the shabby but pretty "clothes of Ibsen's Nora," break the tacit rule of that period of theatre history "that an actress invariably comes on in new clothes, unless she is playing a beggar," and suggesting that "[t]he unstagey effect of the whole play [. . .] made it [. . .] less like a play than like a personal meeting – with people and issues that seized us and held us, and wouldn't let us go" (10–11). When, soon after, Robins had the chance to perform in Ibsen's drama herself, she found the complex and ambiguous character of Hedda Gabler incomparably exciting because she was so astonishingly "*alive*" (*IA* 31).

But if the psychological and situational verisimilitude and the realistic representational style of Ibsen's plays made them particularly compelling for Robins, the accompanying new demands that his drama made on per-formers was also extremely appealing, causing her to tell the London theatre critic and Ibsen opponent Clement Scott that she was

> very grateful to a dramatist who gives us real work to do and does us the honour to presuppose a little intelligence and imagination on the part of the actor. Ibsen doesn't seem to think it necessary to put all his intention into words; he leaves a generous share to the artist to interpret in subtler ways.[7]

As Gay Gibson Cima has explained, Ibsen's method of retrospective action resulted in the emergence of "critical actors" who developed new meth-ods of study and rehearsal in order to approach characters distinguished from those in melodrama by interpretive openness, subtextual depth, moral complexity, and gestural subtlety.[8] Meeting these new interpretive demands even when playing a secondary and considerably less dynamic role such as Mrs. Linde in *A Doll's House* enabled Robins to think of herself as Ibsen's partner in art and left her with a welcome feeling of "self-respect" (*IA* 15). "More than anybody who ever wrote for the stage," she claimed,

> Ibsen could, and usually did, collaborate with his actors. [. . .] [T]o an extent I know in no other dramatist, he saw where he could leave some of his greatest effects to be made by the actor, and so left them. It was as if he knew that only so could he get his effects – that is, by standing aside and watching his spell work not only through the actor, but *by* the actor as fellow-creator. (*IA* 52–53)

After Robins encountered the "glorious actable stuff" of Ibsen's challenging characters, the roles available to actresses in the commercial theatres where melodrama prevailed seemed to her like inconsequential and insipid "hackwork" in which she could not fully exercise her capacity for theatrical artistry (*IA* 31, 33). As she wrote of her mainstream theatrical prospects upon completion of *Hedda Gabler*, "there were plenty of 'parts' – but what sort? Not such parts as we had in mind – pretty little parts however much they were called heroines, or 'leading parts' – Heaven save us leading nowhere."[9]

Robins was also exhilarated by the critical attention that she received for her groundbreaking work in Ibsen's dramas. Her pre-Ibsen press notices were as bland as the plays she had appeared in: a reviewer of her 1889 performance in *Little Lord Fauntleroy*, for example, focused on her "sweet individuality, [. . .] refinement of manner, and [. . .] delicacy of style" and noted her "expression of chastened sorrow, [. . .] tenderness of manner [. . . and] fine sense of dignity,"[10] while commentators on her performance in *Forget-Me-Not* that same year remarked in passing that she was "pleasing and tender," "tender and graceful," and "very sympathetic and charming."[11] With *Hedda Gabler*, both the quality and quantity of critical attention that Robins attracted changed radically. Finally at center stage in a performance variously described as "brilliant," "dazzling," and "graphic and finished," the actress also found herself at the center of a heated critical controversy over the merits of Ibsen, causing denouncers to temper their criticism of him with praise for her "misdirected talent."[12] Perhaps most notably, the anti-Ibsen critic Clement Scott conceded that Robins had

> done what no doubt she fully intended to do. She has made vice attractive by her art. She has almost ennobled crime. She has stopped the shudder that so repulsive a creature should have inspired. She has glorified an unwomanly woman. She has made a heroine out of a sublimated sinner. She has fascinated us with a savage.[13]

After the genteel commentary that her work had inspired in the past, these reviews of *Hedda Gabler* were, in Robins's words, "a palpitating excitement." "[W]hether we met abuse or praise," she stated in *Ibsen and the Actress*, "in the end it was all grist to our mill. It was tonic to be attacked" (18, 32).[14]

In order to have the opportunity to be a "fellow-creator" of art rather than a mere "hack" actress and to gain the full and serious attention of the critics, Robins had been obliged to undertake staging *Hedda Gabler* herself, in collaboration with her friend Marion Lea. Robins had realized as she struggled to break into the theatre scene upon her arrival in London in the late 1880s that, while being an American newcomer certainly exacerbated the difficulty of finding decent work with a reputable company,

[n]ot even actresses who by some fluke had proved their powers – had any choice as to what they should act. Not Ellen Terry herself, adorable and invaluable as she was, had any choice of parts, nor choice of how the parts chosen for her should be played. The only one who had a choice was the Actor-Manager or the Actress-Manager. . . .[15]

Eager to determine both what roles she would play and how she would play them, Robins approached various London actor–managers about the possibility of producing *Hedda Gabler* in their West End theatres, with herself and Marion Lea in the roles of Hedda and Thea respectively. At the time, however, the lead role in most scripts was the one to be played by the actor–manager so that "[m]en who wrote plays for women had long been seeing that they simply had little or no chance of being acted" (*WH* n. pag.). Not surprisingly, then, Robins and Lea's attempts to interest an actor–manager in *Hedda Gabler* were met with such forthright exclamations of amazement as:

"There's no part for *me*!"
"But this is a woman's play, and an uncommon bad one at that!"
"What you can *see*. . .!" and so on. (*IA* 16)

Undaunted, the two actresses rented a theatre and produced the play themselves, using jewelry and a wedding present as collateral on a loan of £300.

This bold and unconventional move on Robins and Lea's part intensified the controversy that *Hedda Gabler* generated of itself, for though they were not the first women to try their hands at management, their choice of play caused their initiative in assuming control of their careers to be seen by some to be as transgressive as Hedda's attempt to control a human destiny. One anonymous but presumably male critic concluded an indignant review by wondering why

actresses of the approved artistic intelligence and mental refinement of the Misses Robins and Marion Lea [. . .] should demean their quality by worshipping at the feet of such an earthy Dagon [Ibsen]; and the marvel of his notorious influence over the feminine rather than the masculine mind becomes the greater when it is considered that his characterisations of womankind deny her the purest and highest attributes of her nature, whether as maiden, wife, or mother.[16]

There was, to this reviewer's mind, a tacit connection between art and life in Robins and Lea's production of *Hedda Gabler*; in willfully producing and performing such a provocative piece of drama, the actresses had, he implied, gone as far beyond the pale of accepted standards of femininity as Ibsen's title character herself.

This suggestion of a correspondence between the unorthodox circumstances of the production and the disturbing content of the play was indirectly substantiated by Robins in *Ibsen and the Actress* when she stated that she "did not see Hedda as she was described by any critic," but as "a bundle of unused possibilities, educated to fear life; too much opportunity to develop her weakness; no opportunity at all to use her best powers" (18–19). Electing to play this repressed, thwarted woman in a controversially sympathetic production for which she and her female collaborator were entirely responsible, Robins introduced the subjectivity of the actress into the formula of theatre production, communicating her dissatisfaction with characters constituted of what the above-quoted critic saw as "the purest and highest attributes of [womankind's] nature, whether as maiden, wife, or mother," but also inevitably calling attention to her own previously "unused possibilities" in the mainstream actor–manager-controlled theatre and making apparent her rebellion against her consignment to the status of what Jirí Veltrusky called "human [prop]" in the "hierarchy of parts."[17]

But if there were similarities between Robins and Hedda, whom Jane Marcus has romantically described as "the universal of the unawakened female artist,"[18] there was also a great difference in that where Hedda's creative potential remained untapped to the point of implosion, Robins's did not. Producing and performing *Hedda Gabler* was an exhilarating and incredibly liberating experience that confirmed her sense that to be a leading lady in the commercial theatre was to be in "leading-strings" (*TF* 149); that while men and women alike might suffer "[t]he strangulation of this rôle and that through arbitrary stage management" by actor–managers showcasing themselves at the expense of both the drama and the rest of the company,

freedom in the practice of our art, [. . .] the bare opportunity to practise it at all, depended, for the actress, on considerations humiliatingly different from those that confronted the actor. The stage career of an actress was inextricably involved in the fact that she was a woman and that those who were masters of the theatre were men. These considerations did not belong to art; they stultified art. (*TF* 33–34)

Working on Ibsen's drama, Robins tried to overcome these stultifying conditions and forge for herself an exciting and successful career. She played a total of six other Ibsen characters besides Hedda and Mrs. Linde: Martha Bernick in *The Pillars of Society*, Hilda Wangel in *The Master Builder*, Rebecca West in *Rosmersholm*, Agnes in *Brand*, Asta in *Little Eyolf*, and Ella Rentheim in *John Gabriel Borkman*. She was, in addition, responsible for staging all of these productions except *The Pillars of Society* and *A Doll's House*, and the experience of having her own company and the "freedom of judgement and action" which that entailed left her with next to no taste for participating in mainstream theatrical enterprises (*TF* 33, 149).[19]

At some point, however, the scope of Robins's cultural critique expanded to include not just the commercial theatre but Ibsen's drama as well, and though it is not possible to ascertain precisely when and why she began to "think politically" about the man whose work had meant so much to her as an actress, her horrified response to his final play *When We Dead Awaken* (1899) is significant. In her memoir *Raymond and I*, Robins states that *When We Dead Awaken* "was matter almost for tears" and that, with it, "the Master hand had weakened, the Master voice was failing."[20] In a letter to her friend Florence Bell, she expressed her disappointment in even stronger terms:

The interest of 10 years is ended and as I think of the nightmare the play really is, with its jumble of Hilda, Hedda, Borkman, Peer Gynt, etc.; it's as tho' in the loosening of that mind from its moorings one kept seeing swept by on the flood marred pieces of mighty work done in days of vigor – wreckage on a giant scale.[21]

When We Dead Awaken clearly appalled Robins in a way that no Ibsen play had done before, though not simply by its aura of symbolism or by its technically problematic finale, which requires that the two main characters be buried under an avalanche: *Brand* also ends with an avalanche and works such as *The Master Builder*, *Rosmersholm*, and *John Gabriel Borkman*, all of which Robins had staged, presage the combination of realism and symbolism that marks Ibsen's last play. Rather than in its style, its staging difficulties, or its purported lack of originality – an evaluation with which such notable contemporary readers as James Joyce and George Bernard Shaw did not concur[22] – the explanation for Robins's intensely negative response to *When We Dead Awaken* should perhaps be sought in the play's content and the implications of this content in view of the actress's statement that she saw floating about in it "marred pieces of mighty work done in days of vigor."

When We Dead Awaken is, in Adrienne Rich's words, "about the use that the male artist and thinker – in the process of creating culture as we know it – has made of women, in his life and in his work; and about a woman's slow struggling awakening to the use to which her life has been put."[23] This theme was not an entirely new one for Ibsen; as Michael Meyer has observed, "the man who sacrifices the happiness of his wife or the woman he

loves for the sake of a cause or a personal ambition" had already been seen
in such plays as *Brand, An Enemy of the People, The Master Builder*, and *John
Gabriel Borkman*.[24] Moreover, the companion to this theme – the woman
who seeks a male channel for her ambition and creativity – had come up
with equal persistence in such works as *Hedda Gabler, Rosmersholm*, and
The Master Builder. Confronted with *When We Dead Awaken*, Robins may
have suddenly become aware of this commonality among Ibsen's works,
for though she later recalled how she used to be struck with "wonder at
the absolute newness of the mintage" of every one of his characters and
how each of his plays seemed "an absolutely fresh attack upon th[e] raw
stuff of existence" ("SA" 36), she also connected Ibsen's earlier plays not
only to his last work but to each other when she lamented in her letter to
Florence Bell that she saw them all "jumbled" up together in *When We Dead
Awaken*.

In her significantly titled anonymous feminist tract *Ancilla's Share: An
Indictment of Sex Antagonism* (1924),[25] Robins discusses how women's
"inventiveness, [. . .] humour, [. . .] intellectual passion, [. . .] vision, [and]
poetry" have traditionally been subsumed into the art of the men in their
lives.[26] Her description in this tract of the general experience of becoming
sensitized to the widespread existence of "sex antagonism" suggests how the
stark presentation of a male artist's devastation of his female model's life in
When We Dead Awaken may have triggered in Robins a flash of recognition that caused her to perceive variations of the same theme everywhere
in Ibsen's drama and to critically reevaluate his work as a consequence of
her new insight. "Much as passages of doubtful propriety pass the juvenile
reader unnoticed," Robins writes,

> women of all ages seldom consciously register the judgments slighting or condem-
> natory meted out wholesale to her sex. Little short of amazement is in store for
> women who re-read their poets and historians with a view to collecting evidence
> of man's account of her character and of her place in the scheme of things. [. . .]
>   As from day to day [a woman] reads the papers, skims through current fiction,
> or turns the pages of biographer or poet, she will repeat a common experience: that
> of coming upon some word as she thinks for the first time, or upon some truth
> never in her own mind formulated before – and thereafter finding the new word,
> or newly apprehended fact, re-appear with a frequency, an insistence, that leaves
> her marvelling how it contrived so long to escape her. (49–50)

Ancilla's Share further suggests how the recurrence in the Ibsen canon of
the idea that is played out so explicitly in the relationship between the
model Irene and the sculptor Rubek in *When We Dead Awaken* may have
led Robins to believe that this idea must surely have been sanctioned by

"the Master" himself, for as she states in criticizing H. G. Wells for his sexist attitudes,

To impute to a writer an opinion which he has put in the mouth of one of his characters is, of course, not defensible. But when a writer through a long series of books has consistently expressed through many mouths a certain idea, we know that idea has for him the validity and importance which alone could justify such emphasis, or indeed lend a writer such tireless patience in repetition. (*AS* 83)

Though in *Ancilla's Share* Robins was critical of her associates Henry James and George Bernard Shaw as well as of H. G. Wells, she did not mention Ibsen, perhaps out of concern for the preservation of her anonymity or perhaps because her personal investment in his work was as great as that of Irene in Rubek's sculpture in *When We Dead Awaken*. In any case, Robins's disappointment with Ibsen's last play put an end to her decade of work staging his drama, and though she went on to perform in a couple of unmemorable commercial productions of plays by other authors, she had long before lost heart for "hack-work." She devoted herself increasingly to writing and gave up acting altogether in 1902, by her own account "without bitterness, without even the decency of sharp regret" (*TF* 212).[27]

Whatever the process by which Robins came to critical consciousness with regard to Ibsen, in 1908 she demonstrated a clear movement away from her earlier enthusiasm for his work when she presented a lecture entitled "Some Aspects of Henrik Ibsen" at the Philosophical Institute in Edinburgh.[28] The "aspects" of Ibsen under consideration in this unpublished lecture are his philosophy and his poetry, and Robins's main premise is that though the playwright has been regarded by some "as first and foremost a thinker," he was, as he himself realized, more than anything else a poet ("SA" 11).[29] As such, she argues, he was unsurpassed, and if his plays have seemed at times to present "material towards a retrial of old conclusions, it was chiefly because of the value of an independent witness of unflinching veracity who precisely had no doctrinal axe to grind" ("SA" 12). His desire as a dramatist was not to teach or to philosophize; rather, as he once remarked with reference to *Hedda Gabler*, he wanted "'to <u>depict human beings</u>, human emotions, and human destinies upon a groundwork of certain of the social conditions'" of his day.[30] If he had not "left conclusions to shift for themselves – if he had not given us drama rather than moralizing," then, to Robins's mind, "we should be more disposed to quarrel with him as a thinker" ("SA" 15).[31]

But Robins was not *in*disposed to quarrel with Ibsen's limitations in her lecture, and the first that she singled out for critical attention was what she

saw as his glorification of the individual will, epitomized in his character
Dr. Stockmann's notion "that the strongest man is he who stands most
alone" ("SA" 15). This theme of *An Enemy of the People* "makes a capital
play," Robins states, but it is obviously seriously flawed as "a philosophic
dictum": "A man should be sure enough of his faith to be *ready* to stand
alone – but if he continue to stand alone he proves the valuelessness of his
faith except for one man out of all the populations of the world. [He is then
'strong' only for himself and for his fellows the weakest of weak reeds]" ("SA"
15).[32] In Robins's opinion, "Ibsen's bias towards individualism leads him
into that pitfall of the incurable hero-worshipper, belief in the Superman,
which is nothing but a revamped Romanticism returned to us in another
guise" ("SA" 16).

   This naive and retrograde belief of Ibsen's in turn has a negative effect
on his dramaturgy, Robins maintains, because "he does not correct and
r[a]tionalize his vision [of the powerful individual will] by relating it scien-
tifically to other wills" ("SA" 16–17). In *Brand*, for example, the character
Agnes submits to the wishes of her superman–husband at the expense of
their dying child. Robins acknowledges that there is "a strong dramatic
idea in the situation of a mother in whom the wifely instinct is stronger
than the maternal; who sees her duty to the child and yet sacrifices it to the
husband." She reminds us, however, that this idea was not Ibsen's concern
in *Brand*. Rather, his concern was with "the complete dedication of life
to the service of the highest," and for this reason, Agnes's fatal decision
"[outrages] reason and dramatic probability" ("SA" 17). Preoccupied with
his title character, Ibsen failed to recognize that "not only the tender Agnes,
but any mother worthy of the name" would have taken her child away to
recuperate and then rejoined her husband at a later time ("SA" 17). This
solution, so much more credible to Robins than the one Ibsen actually
scripted, would not necessarily have contravened his theme but "would
have stopped his particular drama" ("SA" 17). Saving his play, Ibsen unwittingly "[arraigned . . .] the woman's love for her child – which [he] thought
he was presenting as without a flaw" – and thus in effect undermined his
own theme ("SA" 18).

   After taking issue with Ibsen's individualism and its problematic dramaturgical consequences, Robins goes on to dismiss the notion that his
"profound understanding of women" earned him the "right to be considered as a thinker" ("SA" 18). She concedes that his female characterizations
evolved over time and states that, though in an early draft of *The Pretenders*,
Ingeborg defines "woman's saga" as being "[t]o love, to sacrifice all and be
forgotten,"[33] Ibsen was too astute an observer to "look at life and fail to

see that that is but one aspect of the matter" ("SA" 18), and he therefore revised the line to read as the individual character's saga rather than as that of all women. Moreover, Robins continues, Ibsen did more in his later plays "than any writer of the age to give the coup de grace to the old conception of a heroine as a creature half angel, half idiot" ("SA" 18); to familiarize the world "with the fact that woman's soul no less than her brother's is the battleground of good and evil" ("SA" 23); and "to disembarrass women from the ignoble shackles of sentimentalism" ("SA" 24). Regardless of these advances, however, Ibsen remained, in Robins's opinion, "[f]ar [. . .] from realizing what is called the feminist point of view" ("SA" 24). With the exception of Nora in *A Doll's House*, Robins argues, Ibsen was "not so much profound in his judgements of women as vivid in his power of transferring materials for judgement to the mimic scene." Indeed, she suggests, he "often [. . .] does not himself realize the far-reaching implications in [his] flashes of actuality; as in Brand where he sermonizes the mother for living according to a base standard which was not of her raising and which had been forced upon her as an unwilling bride" ("SA" 24).

Robins draws further examples from *Brand* to illustrate her sense of Ibsen's "failure or [. . .] indifference to arriving at the implicit conclusion" of his insights into the workings of women's minds ("SA" 24). In an early epic poem dealing with the same characters, Brand's mother slaps the face of her dead husband, whom she was forced to marry, and cries out that he has wasted her life. In revising this poem into dramatic form, Ibsen wrote what Robins found to be a "feeble unrationalized corresponding scene" ("SA" 27) in which the mother no longer expresses righteous indignation, but instead demeans herself by rooting about the corpse in search of money that will compensate her for having sacrificed her life in a loveless marriage. Still more unfortunately from Robins's point of view, Ibsen failed to realize in the course of his revisions that Brand's wife Agnes might have the same sort of critical insight as the mother in the epic poem and might consequently "look back at the end and say with stinging scorn: 'Take my loathing for that you not only sacrificed our child's life to your pride of Will, but you bound upon my back the burden of knowing that my criminal submission to you was in sort a murder of my child'" ("SA" 27). Thus, Robins seems to imply, though Ibsen had opportunity, through Agnes and through Brand's mother, to pronounce judgment on a society in which women were forced to marry men they did not love and to obey even the most unsanctionable demands of their husbands, in both instances he let the opportunity pass. Robins concludes, therefore, before extolling Ibsen's genius as "the supreme dramatic poet of the age," that if he has been heralded foremost as a thinker, it is not because of the soundness of his ideas but because his ideas are easier to translate from Norwegian than his poetry or because the critics have been so overcome "with surprise at [his] discovery of how poignant could be the drama of ideas" that they have neglected to evaluate the soundness of these ideas in themselves ("SA" 27).

Robins's argument in "Some Aspects of Henrik Ibsen" is somewhat convoluted, perhaps because of the difficulty of navigating between her celebrity and authority as one of Ibsen's main proponents in England on the one hand and her subsequent feminist critique of his work on the other. Nevertheless, it is possible to infer from the text of the lecture that feminism was associated in Robins's mind with women's recognition and transcendence of subordination, and that because Ibsen's Hedda, for example, does not articulate a feminist critique of her life circumstances or do anything constructive about them, Ibsen could not, according to Robins's taxonomy, be classified as a feminist. Robins, then, would not have agreed with Jane Marcus that "[t]he feminist critical consciousness has no need to remake Hedda into a suitable propagandistic model" because "[s]he exists, as Ibsen created her, as a horrifying example of the personal and social consequences of neglecting to give women useful and interesting work of their own."[34] On the contrary, Robins quite clearly came to feel a need to "remake Hedda into a suitable propagandistic model" and, in her 1907 suffrage play *Votes for Women*, had already attempted to do so.

Since 1906, the suffrage movement had increasingly been played out in the streets, parks, and public buildings of London, and this real-life drama must certainly have clarified for Robins the omissions of Ibsen's plays with respect to the representation of women and the limits his characters posed to the enactment of female subjectivity. Unlike Hedda Gabler, who, as noted earlier, was, in Robins's words, "a bundle of unused possibilities, educated to fear life" (*IA* 18), the women who bodied forth their desire for the vote by participating in mass suffrage demonstrations came from all walks of life and applied their abilities and talents in a range of different occupations. These women risked censure and harassment by demonstrating and speaking in public, but in the courage of their convictions, they rose admirably to the occasion. Casting about for a topic for a play, Robins seized on these women, and over the course of her research, she was converted to their cause.[35]

Robins had initially taken up writing to make money while looking for work as an actress during her early days in London, but, "loving The Stage ever the best," had regarded it then as a somewhat tedious "way out" rather than as "a way in, or a way up" (*BSC* 232, 21). Her commitment to writing grew as she achieved increasing success as a novelist, but it was only with *Votes for Women* – the first work she had "written under the pressure of a strong moral conviction" and among her earliest active involvements in the suffrage campaign – that she found her niche as a writer.[36] By 1909, she was president of the newly formed Women Writers' Suffrage League, advocating "the use of the pen" to obtain the vote and "to correct the false ideas about women which many writers of the past have fostered."[37] The chief writer in Robins's own past was of course Ibsen, and *Votes for Women* was indeed intended as a revision of his drama, as the author herself wittily signaled in the novel version of the play, *The Convert* (1907), in which one character describes a suffragist character as "Hilda [Wangel of *The Master Builder*], harnessed to a purpose."[38]

Classified by Robins as a "dramatic tract,"[39] *Votes for Women* concerns a woman named Vida Levering, who, prior to the action of the play, was involved with the wealthy Geoffrey Stonor and became pregnant out of wedlock. Persuaded by Geoffrey to have an abortion in order to safeguard his patrimony, Vida consequently lost her love for him and without explanation severed their relationship. Ten years later, at the start of the play, she is a beautiful, unmarried, and somewhat mysterious suffragist and he is an important politician running for re-election and recently engaged to a pretty and politically naive young heiress. In Act I, the former lovers meet unexpectedly at a weekend house party but pretend not to know each other, while Geoffrey's fiancée Jean develops an interest in the hotly debated issue of women's suffrage and chances to learn the secret of Vida's past, though not the identity of her lover. As the act ends, Vida leaves for London and Jean persuades Geoffrey to take her to a suffrage rally at Trafalgar Square that she has heard about from Vida. Act II is set at the rally, where Vida turns out to be making her debut as a platform speaker. Deeply committed to eradicating "[t]he helplessness of women," which she sees as "the greatest evil in the world" (49), Vida details in an impassioned speech the suffering of a working girl who was sexually exploited by her married employer, became pregnant, killed her newborn baby, and was hanged for infanticide, while her master, whom she identified before the court as the father, was censured by the coroner but could not be held legally responsible and so went scot-free. Watching Geoffrey listen to this terrible story and to Vida's expression of sympathy for the desperate girl driven to act on a "half-crazed temptation" by the harrowing experience of childbirth, Jean realizes that he is the man in Vida's past and deserts him to offer her services to Vida and the suffrage cause (72). All the principals converge at Jean's house in the final act, and Jean insists that Geoffrey make amends to Vida by offering to marry her. Vida refuses his reluctant proposal, having long ago dedicated her life to the common good rather than to her own personal happiness. Instead, using her influence over Jean as a weapon, Vida tries to force Geoffrey to pay his debt to her by lending his political support to the suffrage campaign. Though he notes that this attempt at coercion threatens to compromise his already intended endorsement by giving it "an air of bargain-driving for a personal end" (86), Geoffrey is persuaded by Vida's selfless passion to commit himself to the cause of women's suffrage. At the play's conclusion, Vida confides that maternity is the true source of feminine happiness and that Geoffrey need not worry about Jean's interest in suffrage if she has a child because "from the beginning, it was not the strong arm – it was the weakest – the little, little arms that subdued the fiercest of us" (87). She adds that though she herself will never be a mother, she will try to make the world a better place for all children by devoting herself to the suffrage cause more fully than women with children are free to do.

Votes for Women compensates for each of the failings outlined in "Some Aspects of Henrik Ibsen." For example, where, in Robins's opinion, Ibsen occasionally subordinated dramatic probability to dramatic effect, she herself carefully developed her suffrage theme as the logical and perhaps inevitable outcome of her heroine's past circumstances. Unlike Ibsen's Agnes, who passively allows her child to die and then loses the will to live herself, Robins's no less remorseful Vida Levering survives her heartbreaking experiences of pregnancy and abortion and makes them the starting point of her service to the suffrage cause and of her determination to put an end to the helplessness of women. Moreover, where Ibsen allowed only Nora of all his female characters to speak out against the injustices they have suffered as women, Robins provided Vida with the opportunity not only to pronounce judgment on men and on patriarchal society throughout *Votes for Women*, but also to demand – and get – political compensation for women from Geoffrey Stonor in the final act.[40] Finally, where Ibsen appeared to Robins to espouse a retrograde and problematically elitist philosophy of individualism, she herself promoted the grass-roots feminism of the suffrage movement, dramatically actualizing this contrast in the suffrage rally in Act II of *Votes for Women*, which differs significantly from the meeting in Act IV of *An Enemy of the People* at the same time that it recalls it.[41] Thus, where Ibsen's scene is constructed so that Dr. Stockmann predominates even when he is not speaking, Robins did not bring Vida Levering on stage until two-thirds of the way through the act, giving the floor first to several other speakers representative of the class, gender, and age diversity of the suffrage ranks. Further, where the self-proclaimed intellectual aristocrat Dr. Stockmann uses the meeting platform to express his dissent from "the plebs, the masses, the mob" that he sees as "nothing but raw material which may, some day, be refined into individuals,"[42] Robins's genteel Vida Levering uses the rally platform to express solidarity with women of all classes and to argue the necessity of organization and co-operation. In these respects, *Votes for Women* was a considerable revisionary achievement.[43]

The Court Theatre production of Robins's play, directed by Harley Granville Barker, drew extensive critical attention, with most reviewers commenting on the impressive realism and dramatic excitement of the suffrage rally scene. The reviewer for *The Clarion*, for example, described the rally as "the sensation of the theatrical season,"[44] while the *Times* reviewer called it "an admirably managed 'living picture' with as realistic a crowd as we have ever seen manoeuvred on the stage"[45] and the reviewer for *The Era* believed that it was "some of the most striking stage-management that we have ever seen on the boards of a theatre."[46] Beyond this widespread appreciation of the rally scene, the production as a whole met with the approval of pro-suffrage spectators, who, as several reviewers reported,[47] were generous in their applause, while for audience members who were less certain of the merits of the case for women's suffrage, *Votes for Women* was at least informative and thought-provoking. The reviewer for *The Pall Mall Gazette*, for example, valued the play's "revelations of suffragette psychology,"[48] and the reviewer for *The Era* remarked that "[i]f *Votes for Women!* does not have the effect of altering opinions as to the question of female suffrage, it will, at any rate, show the women's side of the question in a fresh light to most playgoers."[49] Such appreciative comments on the part of reviewers who were not suffrage advocates indicate the didactic value of Robins's expansion of the scope of theatrical representation to encompass the suffrage movement. Another more literal political value of the play derived from Robins's donation of part of her earnings from it to leading suffrage organizations.

But while *Votes for Women* compensated for the omissions and limitations that Robins perceived in the Ibsen canon and while it was successful in generating awareness of and affirming pro-suffrage arguments, the reviewer for *The Era* remarked that Robins had "taken care to give the women all the best parts in the piece,"[50] and this statement invites consideration of the play in relation to what Robins had herself most valued during her career as an actress. Robins's primary goal during her days on the stage was to play complex and challenging female roles and therefore, unlike the German actress who would not perform the final act of *A Doll's House* as written because she herself would never leave her children,[51] she did not feel any desire "to whitewash General Gabler's somewhat lurid daughter," "to try to make her what is conventionally known as 'sympathetic,'" or to otherwise "mitigate Hedda's corrosive qualities." On the contrary, far from being a deterrent to her as an actress, "[i]t was precisely the corrosive action of those qualities on a woman in Hedda's circumstances that made her the great acting opportunity she was [. . .]" in the first place (*IA* 20–21) and that made her seem so incomparably "*alive*" (*IA* 31). The fact that Hedda, like so many of Ibsen's other female characters, demanded intelligence and artistry of actresses rather than the usual good looks and charm[52] further enhanced her appeal. To Robins's mind, one of the most objectionable and humiliating conditions for women in the commercial theatre was the chronic emphasis on conventional feminine attractiveness, an emphasis Robins experienced even in her work on *The Master Builder* when, after a dress rehearsal, her friend Henry James pressured her to alter Hilda Wangel's characteristically utilitarian and negligent costume to something "*pretty*, [. . .] agreeable, in the right key" (*TF* 99–100). Coupled with the common practice of casting according to line or type, which Robins deplored as harmful to actresses (*BSC* 252), this emphasis on appearance effectively cut short the theatrical careers of many talented women, among them possibly Robins herself, who retired from the stage when she was forty and later noted of the theatre that "[for] the middle-aged performer – the hold had to be a sentimental one or a family tie."[53]

At the same time that *Votes for Women* presented a central female character who exemplified what Robins understood to be "the feminist point of view" by recognizing women's subordination in patriarchal society and doing something constructive about it, certain aspects of Robins's characterization of Vida Levering directly contravened the theatrical and dramatic reforms that she had worked so diligently to institute over the course of her career as an actress and producer and that were so definitively advanced in her work on *Hedda Gabler*. Described in the stage directions as "an attractive, essentially feminine, and rather 'smart' woman of thirty-two, with a somewhat foreign grace; the kind of whom men and women alike say, 'What's her story? Why doesn't she marry?'" (46), Vida Levering is ultimately a melodramatically conventional victim who has, by her own admission, come to terms with her emotional conflict long before the action of the play and whose demands on the actress portraying her – beyond physical

beauty – are consequently relatively simple: an occasionally superior know-
ingness tinged with remembered pain in Act I, genteel reticence gradually
overcome by passionate commitment in Act II, and fiercely righteous indignation in Act III.[54] The conventionality of Robins's characterization of her
heroine caused Max Beerbohm to remark in his review of *Votes for Women*,
"The scorn with which Miss Levering rejects [Geoffrey Stonor's] offer [of
marriage] I may safely leave to your imagination; you will have already
foreseen it,"[55] while, under the subtitle "The Bathos of the Plot," reviewer
Alex Thompson wrote in *The Clarion*,

it is notable that [Vida Levering], the most conventional stage figure in the crowd,
is, despite [actress] Miss Matthison's intense sincerity and rare emotional power,
perhaps the least impressive. In her character, we return to the normal, the chronic.
It is of the stage, stagey. The Niobe of the conventional drama, all tears, is less
tolerable at the Court than in any other theatre, because we are accustomed there
to take our sentiment with the saving salt of humour. The very excellence of Miss
Matthison's performance tells against her here. The deep sadness of her declamation
of her wrongs, the dramatic fervour of her indictment of man's injustice to woman,
would bring down the house in any conventional play. But here, surrounded by
realities, her dolorous heaviness produces an effect of artificiality.[56]

Thompson's disappointment with the melodramatic sentimentality of
Robins's portrayal of Vida Levering and his opposition of such sentimentality to the usual, more ironic fare of the innovative Court Theatre would
seem to support Suzanne Clark's contention that male modernism was
premised upon a rejection of the sentimental as feminine,[57] and indeed,
citing Clark, Sue Thomas has pointed out that the hegemonic modernist
denigration of the feminized sentimental was a factor in other negative
critical reactions to *Votes for Women* as well.[58] But while Clark's corrective
feminist insight that "the sentimental has" in fact "successfully functioned to
promote women's influence and power"[59] may certainly be applicable to the
strategic dimensions of the melodramatic dramaturgy of *Votes for Women*,
it is worth remembering that, as noted earlier, shortly after the Court
production, in her 1908 lecture "Some Aspects of Henrik Ibsen," Robins
herself explicitly praised Ibsen for doing more than any other writer "to
disembarrass women from the ignoble shackles of sentimentalism" ("SA"
24). One notable instance of Ibsen's anti-sentimentalism in the representation of women is Hedda Gabler's resistance to becoming a mother, but
while such "corrosiveness" was particularly valued by Robins as an actress,
and while she herself is believed to have been childless,[60] she nevertheless
framed her heroine Vida Levering's commitment to suffrage activism in

sentimental maternal terms and "[insisted] on," in one reviewer's words, "the natural glory of motherhood."[61] Thus, Vida tells Geoffrey Stonor in the final moments of *Votes for Women*,

You will have other children [. . .] – for me there was to be only one. Well, well – (*she brushes her tears away.*) – since men alone have tried and failed to make a decent world for the little children to live in – it's as well some of us are childless. (*Quietly taking up her hat and cloak.*) Yes, *we* are the ones who have no excuse for standing aloof from the fight. (87)

The contradiction between the suffragist Robins's sentimental valoriza- tion of motherhood and the actress Robins's appreciation of the dramatic power of the non-maternal Hedda's "corrosiveness" had its correlative in Robins's strategic deployment of desirable female bodies in *Votes for Women*, despite her objections as an actress to the exploitation of beautiful women in mainstream theatre. Cautioning against ahistorical feminist critiques of suf- frage dramas such as *Votes for Women*, Sheila Stowell has argued that Robins, writing within a patriarchal dramatic tradition, was attempting with Vida Levering both "to reconstruct the woman with a past as a figure of absolute integrity, one who firmly believes in the life she lives," and to "counter prevailing stereotypes of suffrage supporters as 'unnatural' masculinized women poaching on male preserves."[62] Lisa Tickner, moreover, enables Robins's strategy to be situated within a broader representational context, noting that suffrage artists in various media commonly employed conven- tional images of femininity in order to "[invite] identification and [offer] reassurance, both to potential converts and to suffragists themselves."[63] Whatever the reasoning behind the suffragists' representational strategy, however, the problems inherent in it are evident in some of the reviews of the Court Theatre production of *Votes for Women*. A reporter for *The Irish News*, for example, remarked that "Miss Edith Wynne Mathison [sic] in the leading part of Vida, is a very charming suffragette, and one must confess bears very little resemblance to the genuine 'woman's righter.'"[64] Similarly, having duly reported "Miss Levering's" assertion that men are wrong to assume that all women long to be married, the critic for *The Times* lead- ingly wondered why the character herself "[takes] such care to make the best of her good looks and pretty figure and wear such charming frocks? Is it to please other women?" Then, patronizingly exempting the central figure of Robins's play from the general contempt he feels for suffragists on the grounds that she is atypical, the *Times* reviewer concludes that the suffrage cause would undoubtedly "make much more headway [. . .] if all its advocates were as fair to look upon, as agreeable to hear, and as beautifully dressed as Miss Wynne Matthison."[65] The reviewer for *The Clarion* responded in similarly erotic terms to actress Dorothy Minto's portrayal of the suffragist character Ernestine Blunt, described by Robins in the stage directions of *Votes for Women* as "better turned out than the rest [of the women speakers at the rally, excluding Vida Levering], [. . .] quite young, very slight and gracefully built, with round, very pink cheeks, full, scarlet lips, naturally waving brown hair, and an air of childish gravity" (61). In the *Clarion* reviewer's account,

Most fascinating of all the fascinating figures in this fascinating tableau is pretty little Dorothy Minto as a young Suffragette, a sweet and comely maiden in neat, shop-girl attire, with a wisp of nut-brown hair straggling in attractive carelessness from under her toque. A wonderfully winning little figure in her childishness, her daintiness, her utter unconsciousness of self. Very pathetic are her good-tempered earnestness, and the wistful, precociously wise smile with which she receives the jeers and comments of the not too-mannerly crowd. No wonder that she conquers their hostility. I think she nearly converted us all. So graceful, so naïve, so girlishly frail, so free from affectation and coquettishness. No air or note of theatricalness in her pleading. A plaintive, winning, memorable little figure. It was a stroke of genius to engage Miss Dorothy Minto, and make her describe herself as "a female hooligan." A volume of Swift's satires could not have answered the Yellow Press more effectively than the deprecatory and appealing smile with which, in quoting the expression, she fills the air as with a fluid caress.[66]

While such comments as these from *The Clarion*, *The Times*, and *The Irish News* may arguably indicate that Robins's tactic of employing the figure of the "womanly woman" to score feminist points achieved a certain measure of qualified success, they also underline the dramatist's implication in the very attitudes and practices that had been so oppressive and demeaning to her as a theatre artist. This implication is made even more apparent by the unfortunate resonance of these critics' language and tone with those of the quintessential actor–manager Henry Irving, whom Robins sardonically quoted in *Both Sides of the Curtain*, her autobiographical account of her struggle to break into London theatre, as having stated that "women have an easy road to travel on the stage. They have but to *appear* and their sweet feminine charm wins the battle" (241).

Rather than in its problematic usage of the image of the womanly suffragist or in its compensatory dramaturgical approach, the more fundamental and effective way in which *Votes for Women* challenged male dominance was by virtue of its status as a "dramatic tract." While Robins admired Ibsen for his poetry rather than for his philosophy, reviewers of the Court Theatre production pointed out that by classifying her own play as a

ELLIOTT & FRY   Copyright.   55, BAKER STREET. W.
AND AT 7, GLOUCESTER TERRACE, S.W.

Figure 1 A studio portrait of Elizabeth Robins as Hedda Gabler (1891), apparently
destroying the manuscript.

Figure 2 An anti-suffrage postcard (circa 1914), by Donald McGill.

"dramatic tract," she "deprecat[ed] merely aesthetic criticism"[67] and that by "sacrific[ing] that precious thing, her art" for the sake of a transitory cause, she "willfully miss[ed]" writing "a very fine play."[68] Indeed, Robins made no claims for *Votes for Women* as a work of art, and so, as well as employing the melodramatic techniques she had deplored as an actress to forward the plot and enlist sympathy for her suffragist heroine, she incorporated into her "tract" long passages of undisguised propaganda that she may have transcribed from actual suffrage meetings.[69]

In addition to conveying her position on the immediate issue of women's suffrage, however, Robins's politically expedient dramaturgy communicated her much broader and less topical sense of the need to create – even at the temporary expense of art – conditions conducive to the development of women's potential, the possibility of which is denied in Ibsen's plays, where female characters repeatedly channel their energies through male characters. Thus, when a contemptuous heckler calls out during the suffrage rally in *Votes for Women* that there has never been a woman Beethoven, Plato, or Shakespeare, Vida Levering spoke for the largely sympathetic and predominantly female audience at the Court Theatre,[70] as well as for Robins as actress-qua-playwright claiming the avant-garde stage for the purpose of feminist propaganda, by replying:

Since when was human society held to exist for its handful of geniuses? How many Platos are there here in this crowd? [. . .]

How many Shakespeares are there in all England today? [. . .]

I am not concerned that you should think we women can paint great pictures, or compose immortal music, or write good books. I am content that we should be classed with the common people – who keep the world going. (70–71)

Were that equal classing achieved, Robins was to claim years later in an argument that anticipated Virginia Woolf's in *A Room of One's Own*,[71] a great step would have been taken toward creating an environment in which female genius might for once have a chance to flourish (*AS* 102). *Votes for Women* was a contribution to the creation of such an environment. Rejecting the patient and orderly but ineffectual proceedings of the Constitutionalist suffragists in favor of a more radical and spectacular activism,[72] Robins's play mediated constructively, through its pointedly political artlessness, between Hedda Gabler's furiously impulsive destruction of Eilert Løvborg's manuscript (figure 1) and the acts of vandalism that were perpetrated by increasingly desperate militants in the final phase of the suffrage campaign and that included an attack on Velázquez's masterpiece, the *Rokeby Venus*, in the National Gallery in early 1914 (figure 2).

This connection between Hedda's inarticulate rage at her inability to control her own destiny and the suffragists' indignation at not having their rights recognized was confirmed in the use of Hedda Gabler as the rallying figure for the Actresses' Franchise League in the Coronation Suffrage Pageant of 1911. In the process of reforming the original Ibsen character into a dashingly self-assured and righteously outraged feminist leader, however, the actresses had necessarily to suppress Hedda's more desperate and cowardly aspects and, in so sanitizing and idealizing her, they implicitly emptied her of the "corrosive" qualities that, in Robins's opinion, had made her such a wonderful acting opportunity to begin with, turning her instead into a character more along the lines of Robins's own Vida Levering. Thus, the ambivalent image of Hedda on horseback leading the beautifully attired actresses in the suffrage parade bodied forth the central tension of Robins's long and complex relationship with Ibsen by pointing both toward the limitations of even the most sophisticated male-authored characterizations of women and toward the continued attraction of early feminists in the theatre to these characters, even as they struggled, with mixed success, to develop new roles for themselves. In foregrounding this figure in spite of her ambivalence, the actresses, like Robins through her authorship of *Votes for Women*, claimed not only literal space on the political stage but also figurative space in the imaginative realm of art and drama. This dual claim was a crucial premise for the development of feminist–modernist performance practice.

CHAPTER 2

Feminist Shakespeare:
Ellen Terry's comic ideal

According to George Bernard Shaw, Ellen Terry was "the most modern of modern women" – an "ultra-modern talent" wasted by Henry Irving "on pre-Ibsenite plays which were by [Shaw's] standards womanless" and among which he included the works of Shakespeare.[1] Terry herself responded negatively to Ibsen's plays, however, most notably in an essay entitled "Stray Memories" that was published in 1891 around the time when Elizabeth Robins was making waves in London as the first English-language Hedda Gabler and in the same issue of *The New Review* as Henry James's article "On the Occasion of *Hedda Gabler*," in which James remarked on the theatrical power of Ibsen's dramas and on the extraordinary acting opportunities they presented to actresses.[2] In her 1891 essay, Terry wrote:

[. . .] I am very loth to dogmatise on any point. But I have received so many letters lately from people asking me to state my views on *Hedda Gabler* that I cannot resist the temptation of speaking my mind outright, though it seems to me that everybody has said everything that can be said about Ibsen's plays. Well, to be frank, I should not myself care to act in them. I consider myself very happy and fortunate in having nearly always been called upon to act very noble, clear characters, since I prefer that kind of part, and love Portia and Beatrice better than Hedda, Nora, or any of those silly ladies. Yet Ibsen is attractive to actors and especially to actresses. I think it must be that Ibsen is so extraordinarily easy to act. For instance, how much easier it is to ask *naturally* for a dirty bonnet to be removed from a chair than to offer, *naturally*, a kingdom for a horse. [. . .]

Ibsen's characters are drawn in plain, straight strokes which makes it very easy for actors to personate them, and "dress" them as it were. If only he were more true to reality and held the mirror up to Nature – as she is, streaked white and black, not all black – then I should like to act in his plays, for they give actors immense opportunity.

I hear it often said that his plays are so *real – natural –* true to nature. Very odd this! They have always struck me as being preposterously *unreal – untrue to nature.* Ibsen makes his characters *converse* naturally, and that seems their sole source of strength. But enough of Ibsen!

Figure 3   Ellen Terry in her study, by Miss K. Dunham.

"Autumn days come quickly like the running of a hound upon the moor." One can scarcely do everything. I prefer presenting to an audience, and living familiarly with, Queen Katherine and Imogen rather than with Dr. Ibsen's foolish women.[3]

When, many years later, Terry saw Eleanora Duse perform the role of Mrs. Alving in *Ghosts*, she remarked in her diary, "Ghosts. A horrible play, but Duse superb."[4]

In view of the close relationship between modern drama and the "woman question," Terry's seemingly reactionary statements about Ibsen's female characters would initially appear to situate her in opposition to both feminism and modernism and to problematize Shaw's claims about her status as a quintessentially modern woman. Terry was a figure of considerable significance for such feminist–modernists as Isadora Duncan and Virginia Woolf, however, and Shaw exempted her from the "senior generation" of "ignoramus"–actresses that he believed could not play Ibsen because they were so "inveterately sentimental," "schooled in the old fashion if at all, born into their profession, quite out of the political and social movement around them – in short, intellectually *naïve* to the last degree."[5] Instead, Shaw accounted for Terry's dismissal of Ibsen by suggesting that "[s]uch a play as [. . .] Ghosts had no mission for her, because she had not had to break Mrs. Alving's chains, never having worn them,"[6] while more recently, Nina Auerbach has similarly attributed Terry's unreceptiveness to "the power of Ibsen's heroines" to "[h]er inability [. . .] to imagine a good wife's sedate seclusion" and to the fact that "she could conceive of no restraint strong enough to generate Nora's inspired flight, Hedda's ferocity of destruction."[7] Yet while Terry's off-stage life indeed differed radically from the lives of the central female characters in Ibsen's controversial "women's plays," her negative reaction to these plays and her unfavorable comparison of Ibsen's female characters to Shakespeare's may perhaps merit consideration as more than what Michael R. Booth has called "a striking misjudgement,"[8] particularly given that as prominent an Ibsen actress as Elizabeth Robins eventually qualified her initial enthusiasm for Ibsen on feminist grounds.

Whereas Robins framed her critique of Ibsen in terms of the omissions of his dramatic canon, including realist and non-realist works alike, Terry's opposition to Ibsen was explicitly targeted at his realist plays; and although her understanding of realism was somewhat limited, her rejection of it was informed by her preference for a transcendent idealism that to her mind was exemplified in Shakespeare's comic heroines and that she believed was more appropriate to a feminist vision than Ibsen's tragic realism. Terry's idealism regarding the representation of women corresponded with the larger-than-life dimensions of her work as an actress, and her general quality of expansiveness in turn accounts in large measure for her influence on the creative visions of feminist–modernists such as Duncan and Woolf. Rather than situating her in opposition to both feminism and modernism, then, Terry's view of the comparative merits of Ibsen and Shakespeare, which I will trace out in this chapter, in fact constituted an alternative to Elizabeth Robins's perspective on and response to the limitations of the Ibsen canon for feminism. As such, Terry's perspective represented an important aspect of feminist–modernist discourse through and about theatre, while the powerful yet ambiguous figure of Terry herself was productive of further feminist–modernist re-imaginings of gender.

It is worth noting that late in 1888, just prior to the appearance of Ibsen's "women's plays" on the London stage, Terry made her first appearance as a controversial Lady Macbeth,[9] a character who, with her infamous "unsexing" speech, was as much a lightning rod for nineteenth-century gender anxiety as more contemporary "unwomanly woman" characters such as Nora Helmer, Hedda Gabler, and Rebecca West. The critical controversy over the Lyceum *Macbeth* began before the production even opened, in part because the role of Lady Macbeth was seen as unsuitable for Terry, who was, for many, quintessentially feminine[10] and whose established strengths as an actress were not in the "heavy" line[11] but, as Michael Booth has stated, "in playing innocence, romantic love, and pathos."[12] Thus, Frederick Hawkins reported late in 1888 that "[s]peculation is already rife as to how the only Beatrice and Ophelia of our time will treat this formidable character" and wondered whether Terry would "try to emulate the majesty and heartlessness and grim determination which the great actresses of old imported into it."[13] The "actress of old" most associated with the part was Sarah Siddons, who, a century earlier,[14] had set a standard by playing Lady Macbeth as a physically imposing virago of such "turbulent and inhuman strength of spirit" that she completely dominated her husband, turning him "to her purpose, [making] him her mere instrument, [guiding], [directing], and [inspiring] the whole plot," an "evil genius" of such overwhelming presence that she effectively usurped Macbeth's position as the main character in the play.[15] Despite this influential stage portrayal, however, Siddons stated in a written analysis that Lady Macbeth was "of that character which I believe is generally allowed to be most captivating to the other sex, – fair, feminine, nay, perhaps, even fragile [. . .]."[16] Terry accounted for the "difference [. . .] between the great actress's theory and practice" by explaining that

[i]t is not always possible for us players to portray characters on the stage exactly as we see them in imagination. Mrs. Siddons may have realized that her physical appearance alone – her aquiline nose, her raven hair, her flashing eyes, her commanding figure – was against her portraying a fair, feminine, "nay, perhaps even fragile" Lady Macbeth. It is no use an actress wasting her nervous energy on a battle with her physical attributes. She had much better find a way of employing them as allies.[17]

Using her own attributes as allies – the attributes that caused journalist Austin Brereton to identify "true womanliness" as the dominant note in her acting[18] – Terry set out to "[a]dapt the part to [her] own personality,"[19] drawing inspiration and support from Sarah Siddons's unrealized vision of the character as other than, in Joe Comyns Carr's words, "a sexless creature [. . .] with the temper of a man and the heart of a fiend."[20] If Lady Macbeth was as bad as tradition would have it, Terry reasoned, then she had no need of spirits to "unsex" her.[21] Instead, Lady Macbeth was, in Terry's view, "a <u>woman</u> – a mistaken woman – & <u>weak</u> – not a Dove – of course not – <u>but first of all</u> **a wife**"[22] whose "ambition is all for her husband," whom she discovers to be both weaker and more evil than she knew.[23] As with Nora's crime of forgery in *A Doll's House*, then, Lady Macbeth's crime of complicity in murder was, as Terry saw it, a logical extension of wifely devotion.[24] That she is subsequently "haunted by the horror of the murder," that "[i]t preys upon her mind, and saps her physical strength" until "[s]he dies of remorse," was, for Terry, "good evidence that she is not of the tigress type, mentally or physically."[25]

Anticipating the uncomprehending responses to Ibsen's female characters of many nineteenth-century critics, exemplified by Clement Scott's inability or unwillingness to reconcile the happy wife of the start of *A Doll's House* with the woman who becomes so "absolutely inhuman" as to walk out on her husband and children at the end of the play,[26] some critics of Terry's performance as Lady Macbeth were reluctant to acknowledge that the character could be a beautiful and loving wife rather than, in the words of one reviewer, "a six-foot termagant."[27] Austin Brereton, for example, wrote that Terry's "[. . .] Lady Macbeth, interesting as it was, lost from [the] very charm of gentleness, [the] pathetic stop, [the] womanly feeling with which the actress is so endowed," adding, however, that "if the stage has lost a Lady Macbeth – as we understand the character – it has found in her the absolute realisation of more than one Shakespearean part."[28] From a critical perspective such as Brereton's, Terry's purported failure as Lady Macbeth was, as journalist Olive Weston caustically but nonetheless perceptively remarked, "her virtue and not her shame,"[29] yet Brereton's qualification – "as we understand the character" – is significant, for as Nina Auerbach has stated, "if Lady Macbeth was not a monster, she exposed a side of woman's nature that most men and many women did not want to know about."[30] Indeed, as one reviewer suggested, what some critics regarded as the actress's failure could as easily be seen as the critics' own refusal to accept the fact of the character that Terry presented to them:

On the one hand, Miss Terry's performance is so entirely novel as to take the would-be critic aback. On the other, her version of the erstwhile wicked woman is allowed on all hands to be more natural and more feminine than it has ever been, as played by our greatest actresses of past days. But then comes the difficulty – could a woman so gentle, so full of grace, and so charming in every way, be guilty of such crimes? The answer is supplied by Miss Terry herself, who, by her winning grace, defies criticism, and presents a living character to her astonished audience.[31]

For her own part, Terry expressed concern that her "methods [were] not right" but remained convinced of the rightness of her interpretation, asserting that Sarah Siddons's stage portrayal of Lady Macbeth was "her Lady M. not Shakespeares [sic]"[32] and that, in contrast, she herself was aiming for "a true *likeness*,"[33] one in which the character functioned "as part of a *whole*" rather than "as a single, forceful dramatic figure."[34]

Though costumed in a ravishing Pre-Raphaelite gown rather than the "blue woollen dress" of Ibsen's Nora,[35] Terry's Lady Macbeth was not unrelated to the realistic female characters in the "women's plays" by Ibsen that were beginning to appear on the London stage as the Lyceum production of *Macbeth* came to the end of its run in June 1889.[36] Whereas Sarah Siddons had achieved a magnificent grandeur in the part, Terry's portrayal of Lady Macbeth as "a determined, managing wife" was, according to critic Edward Russell, without "attempt at majesty of demeanour"[37] but was instead characterized, particularly in the early scenes, "by an audacity of realism which in high tragedy [had] never been seen before"[38] and which perhaps accounted for another critic's assertion that at the Lyceum, *Macbeth* had been "cleverly and ingeniously transposed into the key of domestic drama."[39] Indeed, in written remarks on *Macbeth*, Terry occasionally used terms that resituated Shakespeare's tragedy within the domestic context of middle-class marriage that was the focus of so much of Ibsen's realist drama: somewhat comically, for example, she referred to "the Macbeths," to "Mrs. McB," and to "that damned party in a parlour – 'Banquet Scene' as it is called."[40] As Roger Manvell has stated, Terry's revisionist interpretation of Lady Macbeth "broke the hitherto inflexible mould in which the part had been confined, that of the cruel and bitter-tongued virago,"[41] and humanized the character so that she was, in Nina Auerbach's words, "no longer beyond the pale of womanhood."[42] In her misguided resolve to fulfill her husband's desire for power and attain what Russell called "the consort's dream of the golden round,"[43] Terry's Lady Macbeth shared the quality of moral ambiguity characteristic of Ibsen's women[44] and, as Auerbach has noted, "[placed] the bourgeois wife in the same sinister perspective the malevolent Hedda does."[45] Thus, where Ibsen actresses such as Elizabeth Robins wanted to get away from playing "womanly women," Terry's "fair, feminine, [. . .] fragile" but nonetheless murderous Lady Macbeth cast the "womanly woman" in a disturbing new light and invited the world to see her differently, thus contributing to the challenging of contemporary gender ideology that made Ibsen's work so provocatively disturbing to nineteenth-century audiences.

The experience of playing Lady Macbeth marked a turning point in Terry's career, causing her to divide her years at the Lyceum into "*before* 'Macbeth', and *after*," just as Elizabeth Robins thought of her early life in terms of "before or after Hedda."[46] In her 1908 autobiography *The Story of My Life*, Terry accounted for this division in terms of "the amount of

preparation and thought" that the production involved and the discussion that it generated, suggesting as well that it was after or even perhaps
because of *Macbeth* that the Lyceum began its gradual decline (111, 194). In
a letter to William Winter, however, she confided that she was "so excited
at playing the horrid part,"[47] and indeed, the passionate intensity evident
in her notes, letters, and public statements on the part of Lady Macbeth
is without parallel in her body of work. Like Robins, who reveled in the
critical controversy that *Hedda Gabler* generated, Terry wrote in her diary
of the response to her performance in *Macbeth*, "Some people hate me in
it; some, Henry among them, think it my best part, and the critics differ,
and discuss it hotly, which in itself is my best success of all! [. . .] Oh, dear!
It is an exciting time!" (qtd. in *SML* 197). And once again like Robins, for
whom the melodramatic roles available to women in the mainstream theatres seemed like "hack-work" after she had played Hedda Gabler,[48] Terry's
disenchantment with the roles assigned to her at the Lyceum appears to
have increased after *Macbeth*: she wrote of the period immediately following the production, "Here I was in the very noonday of life, fresh from
Lady Macbeth and still young enough to play Rosalind, suddenly called
upon to play a rather uninteresting mother in 'The Dead Heart'" (*SML*
198), while of the part of Rosamund in Tennyson's play *Becket*, which was
staged at the Lyceum in 1893, she remarked, "I don't know what to do with
her. She is not there. She does not exist. I don't think that Tennyson ever
knew very much about women, and now he is old and has forgotten the
little that he knew. She is not a woman at all."[49]

But if Terry's innovative portrayal of Lady Macbeth offset her seemingly
reactionary response to Ibsen and suggested that she was not as far removed
from feminism and modernism as her 1891 statement made her seem, she
nevertheless rejected realism, which she perhaps did not fully understand as
being concerned with contemporary individuals at odds with verisimilarly
represented determining environments, but instead more superficially associated with prosaic characters and dialogue and a fixation on the more base
and unpleasant facts of life – in the case of Ibsen's "horrible play" *Ghosts*,
for example, sexually transmitted disease, incest, and prostitution. Thus,
she commented at the foot of a page of dialogue between Hedda and Thea
in her copy of *Hedda Gabler*, "All this is mere commonplace cackle,"[50] and
stated in a 1908 issue of her son Edward Gordon Craig's journal *The Mask*,

I dislike realism as the word seems to be understood today. Reality seems to be
ill-expressed by means of Realism, for reality seems to me to be more than mere
brutality, and Realism is often only this. It is called "Holding the mirror up to

Nature" whereas, it seems to me to be lowering the mirror so as to reflect the inferior details of human nature. Acting should not be a frank representation of *human* nature.[51]

Terry, of course, had connections to the aesthetic movement[52] and her negative view of realism corresponded with that of key aesthetic theorist Oscar Wilde, who argued in his 1889 essay "The Decay of Lying" that "Art takes life as part of her rough material, re-creates it, and refashions it in fresh forms, is absolutely indifferent to fact, invents, imagines, dreams, and keeps between herself and reality the impenetrable barrier of beautiful style, of decorative or ideal treatment."[53] In Wilde's view, realism represented the decadence of art because in it, "life gets the upper hand, and drives Art out into the wilderness."[54] Far better for life to imitate art than for art to imitate life.[55]

In view of Terry's connection to the aesthetic movement, with its commitment to creative idealism and rejection of imitative realism in art, it may be worth noting Lady Colin Campbell's remarks in a 1902 issue of the women's magazine *Madame* on Terry's stated preference for Shakespeare's female characters over Ibsen's:

Few people will blame such a choice, for Ellen Terry belongs to the ideal few among the human race, great-souled, great-hearted, great-bodied, built in body and mind on generous lines that satisfy both eye and heart and brain, when she moves across the stage with her long, graceful stride, the exquisitely characteristic movements of her hands emphasising and underlying the music of her lovely voice, in which tears and laughter are ever breaking in on one another in a way that makes her audience thrill with sympathy, hardly knowing why. To think of her embodying the morbid, hysterical, narrow-minded, neurotic degenerates whom Dr. Ibsen draws, alas! so truthfully, would be a sacrilege. It is not that such portraits are unreal or untrue, as she in her healthy optimism declares them to be; they are but too numerous unfortunately; but Ellen Terry's splendid personality, her superb animal magnetism, her broad humanity and bubbling humour, could never be cramped into such pitiful outlines.[56]

Terry herself believed that many of the modern plays proposed to Henry Irving for production at the Lyceum were "on too small a scale for the theatre" (*SML* 233; see also 205), and though she did eventually act in modern dramas by Shaw and James M. Barrie, she found these plays too small for her style[57] – in the words of her "literary henchman,"[58] biographer, and editor Christopher St. John, "bad fits, far too small for a great actress."[59] Thus, though Terry wrote in an undated letter to Elizabeth Robins that she had had a beautiful dream of the two of them acting together, she added that "[t]he dream [was] only a dream & will not turn out true after all";[60]

Terry's dream was for something larger, less "cramped," more capacious and transcendent than the modern female characters of the realist drama that Robins made her name playing.[61]

But in addition to rejecting realism in favor of a more idealized, larger-than-life vision of the human condition, Terry preferred comedy to tragedy, identifying herself as primarily a comic actress despite her passionate engagement with the part of Lady Macbeth[62] and admiring particularly the comic heroines of her "sweetheart" Shakespeare.[63] In her lecture "The Triumphant Women" – the most popular of the four lectures on Shakespeare that she presented in Great Britain, the United States, Australia, and New Zealand between 1910 and 1921 – Terry remarks on "how much we all, and women especially, owe to Shakespeare for his vindication of woman" through his comic heroines, and she argues that these "fearless, high-spirited, resolute and intelligent" characters owe their "virile" attributes not to the fact that "they were always impersonated by men," but to Shakespeare's attunement to "the liberal ideas about the [female] sex which were fermenting in [his] age." She then goes on to explain that "[t]he assumption that 'the woman's movement' is of very recent date – something peculiarly modern – is not warranted by history. There is evidence of its existence in the fifteenth century. Then as now it excited opposition and ridicule, but still it moved!" By way of example, she cites Erasmus and Vives on the need to educate women and points out that "[t]he scholarship of Lady Jane Grey, who at thirteen could read Plato in the original; of Mary Stuart, who at sixteen delivered an extempore oration in Latin; of Queen Elizabeth who made translations of the classics, was not exceptional in the class of society which received any education at all." She notes, however, that "[t]hen, as now, some people thought [educating women] most undesirable. What use was learning to a woman? It might even have the dreadful result of making her less attractive to a man!"[64] When Terry punctuated this part of her lecture by laughingly quoting the critic of Vives who said, "From a gray mule and a girl who speaks Latin may heaven defend us," she was, according to a review in *The New York Times*, "rapturously applauded" by her primarily female audience.[65]

Of course, not all of Shakespeare's comic female characters readily illustrated Terry's reading of their creator as proto-feminist and so, in her lecture entitled "The Pathetic Women," she admitted that "Helena in *All's Well that Ends Well*, and Julia in *Two Gentlemen of Verona* belong to the 'doormat' type" who "seem almost to enjoy being maltreated and scorned" by the men they love.[66] Despite occasional exceptions such as Helena, however, Terry saw Shakespeare's later female characters as mostly "great-hearted,

great-minded, lovable women,"[67] and she accounted for this fact by suggesting that when Shakespeare first arrived in London, he was "still smarting
under the disillusionment of his [. . .] unfortunate marriage" and had not yet
taken up with Mistress Mary Fitton, whose positive influence, she believed,
resulted in "many of those touches of aristocratic pride, of brilliant spirits,
of witty speech" that distinguish his female characters.[68] But while Terry
acknowledged the feminist failings of a few of Shakespeare's comic heroines,
in the case of Portia in *The Merchant of Venice*, she expressed impatience
with the view that "it is strange that a woman of this type, in the habit of
directing herself and directing others, should be willing to be directed by a
man so manifestly inferior to her as Bassanio." Instead, Terry suggested, "if
we take the trouble to enquire into the motives at the back of the famous
speech of surrender, it will not strike us as either strange or repellent" but,
rather, as "a 'beau geste'" on the part of a great lady "and little more," "[t]he
proof [being] that she retains her independence of thought and action"
and, immediately following her marriage, sets "her own plans for saving
Antonio's life, without so much as a 'with your leave or by your leave' to her
lord and master!"[69] Thus, Terry would have not have agreed with Susan
Carlson's contention in her 1991 book *Women and Comedy* that the freedom from prevailing gender norms enabled through the device of comic
inversion is typically curtailed through the comic resolution of marriage as
it coincides with a return to the traditional social order.[70]

In an essay published in 1910 around the time when she was beginning
to tour her Shakespeare lectures, Terry wrote that with the exception of
those of George Meredith, "all nineteenth-century heroines seem singularly
'backward' and limited" in comparison with those of Shakespeare, who
"seems to have loved *resolute* women, gallant, high-spirited creatures ever
ready for action, a hundred times more independent than the heroines
created by writers in these later days."[71] Terry's reference to Meredith in
establishing the comparative feminist merits of nineteenth-century writers
and Shakespeare is significant, given that, in his 1877 essay on comedy,
Meredith had equated comedy with equality of the sexes, arguing that
"there will never be civilization where Comedy is not possible" and that
comedy is not possible where there is "a state of marked inequality of the
sexes."[72] In Meredith's view, "[. . .] Comedy lifts women to a station offering
them free play for their wit,"

[exhibiting . . .] their battle with men, and that of men with them: and as the two,
however divergent, both look on one object, namely, Life, the gradual similarity
of their impressions must bring them to some resemblance. The Comic poet dares

to show us men and women coming to this mutual likeness; he is for saying that when they draw together in social life their minds grow liker; just as the philosopher discerns the similarity of boy and girl, until the girl is marched away to the nursery.[73]

Meredith further states that, because of its tendency toward equality of the sexes, comedy thrives "where women are on the road to an equal footing with men, in attainments and in liberty – in what they have won for themselves, and what has been granted them by a fair civilization [. . .]."[74] In contrast, where women "have no social freedom, Comedy is absent," and for this reason, Meredith calls on "cultivated women to recognize that the Comic Muse is one of their best friends."[75]

In the same way that the influence of the aesthetic movement may have informed Terry's rejection of realism in favor of a more idealized form of representation, a Meredithian view of the progressive nature of comedy appears to have informed her understanding of Shakespeare's comic heroines and contributed to her higher regard for them than for either his tragic female characters or Ibsen's tortured modern women. But just as there was a utopian dimension to Meredith's thinking about comedy, there was a dimension to Terry's thinking about Shakespeare's comic heroines that did not correspond exactly with her lived experience of them. The critic of *The Daily Telegraph* wrote of Terry's presentation of "The Pathetic Women" in 1911,

It was as if the record of those brilliant Shakespearean seasons at the old Lyceum, extending over a period of years, had been compressed into two brief hours, and memory flew back to the days when Henry Irving and Ellen Terry reigned supreme at that theatre, and by their marvellous art created a gallery of portraits which no one who had the privilege of looking upon will ever permit to lapse into oblivion.[76]

Another reviewer wrote of a presentation of "The Triumphant Women" that "[c]ontinually in her illustrative acting she visualises memories of old Lyceum days, and bygone performances of Shakespearean heroines whom she herself made truly triumphant. In the brief hours one has the compressed and fragrant essence of a whole Shakespearean season."[77] Strictly speaking, however, while Terry's lectures on Shakespeare's female characters may have recalled her famous Lyceum performances, they were not simply "epitomes," as Christopher St. John suggested,[78] but in fact revised those performances in a number of different respects. Most obviously, whereas most Lyceum productions were orchestrated around the central figure of actor–manager Henry Irving, who, according to Terry, "never spent much time on the women in the company" (*SML* 108) and, according to Shaw, "composed his parts [. . .] without the least consideration for the play as a whole,"[79] Terry's lectures approached the plays by way of the female characters and then contextualized demonstrations of these characters within a feminist-flavored discourse that combined historical background, character analysis, and autobiographical anecdote. This contextual discourse included critical reflection on her Lyceum experiences, as, for example, in her discussion of *Much Ado About Nothing*, where she objected to Irving's insistence on a "traditional 'gag' at the end of the church scene" that she found demeaning to Beatrice:

I had omitted this gag, "Kiss my hand again," when I had first played Beatrice in the provinces, and I was appalled at finding that I was expected to say it at the Lyceum. My tongue refused to utter the obnoxious words, impossible to the Beatrice of my conception, for many rehearsals. Then one day Henry said: "Now I think it is about time to rehearse this scene as we are actually going to play it, so, Miss Terry, we must please have the gag." I did not like to show any insubordination before the company, so with a gulp, I managed to obey, but I burst into tears! Henry was most sympathetic, I remember, but would not budge. I went home in a terrible state of mind, strongly tempted to throw up my part! Then I reflected that for one thing I did not like doing at the Lyceum, there would probably be a hundred other things I should dislike doing in another theatre. So I agreed to do what Henry wished, under protest.[80]

Terry also lamented that, as Beatrice, "I was never swift enough, not nearly swift enough at the Lyceum where I had a too deliberate, though polished and thoughtful Benedick in Henry Irving."[81]

Christopher St. John regarded Terry's Shakespeare lectures as compensatory acting opportunities for an actress whose advancing age prevented her from playing the parts in which she had made her reputation,[82] but the lectures on Shakespeare's women had something of the quality of feminist events when Terry began touring them during the suffrage campaign. When she first presented "The Triumphant Women" in New York in November of 1910, for example, she was, according to *The New York Times*,

greeted with obviously sincere warmth by a packed house of women, who had braved the torrents of rain in order to hear and see her. For half an hour before the matinée Forty-fourth Street was practically blocked with taxis, hansoms, and motor cars. When nearly half an hour after the announced time of the matinée Miss Terry appeared the enthusiasm was enormous.[83]

When she presented "The Pathetic Women" at the same theatre a week later, the "well-filled house" again "consisted chiefly of women who listened intently and were free in their applause of the several dramatic scenes she read."[84] In London the following year, "The Triumphant Women" was presented as part of the first season of the Pioneer Players, a woman-centered, feminist-oriented company that had grown out of the suffrage theatre activities of Terry's daughter Edith Craig; and a notice in *The Vote*, entitled "Shakespeare as Suffragist," reported Terry to have declared that "Shakespeare was one of the pioneers of women's emancipation" and that Portia, Beatrice, and Rosalind "were prototypes of modern suffragists."[85] Thus, Terry's Shakespeare lectures were not simply consoling exercises for an aging actress whose day had passed but in fact contributed to emergent feminist discourse through and about theatre and to the formation of a feminist counter-public sphere that coincided with and indeed was precipitated by the emergence of modern drama.

Notably, the pro-Lyceum, anti-Ibsen critic William Winter was unimpressed with Terry's performance as a lecturer when he attended a presentation of "The Triumphant Women" in New York in 1910. Whereas the reviewer for *The New York Times* reported on the predominance of women in attendance and quoted Terry as having stated that "[. . .] Shakespeare's women have more in common with our modern feminine revolutionaries than is ordinarily supposed,"[86] Winter made no reference to the feminist dimensions of Terry's lectures. Instead, describing her "method" as "experimental," he discounted her authority as a Shakespearean commentator, dismissed her views as "flimsy," "often incorrect, generally commonplace, and, in the manner of thought, superficial," and suggested that "the particular truth which has been disclosed by her advent here as a lecturer" is "that while she is important as an *impersonator* of Shakespeare's heroines she is not at all important as an *expositor* of them." In Winter's opinion,

The wiser course [. . .] for Miss Terry to pursue, as a Shakespearean entertainer, would have been to read or recite Scenes [sic] from Shakespeare [. . .]. The most illustrious of her female predecessors on the platform, Fanny Kemble and Charlotte Cushman, took that course and were brilliantly successful in it. To *act* is one thing: to *expound* is another [. . .].[87]

On the issue of "expounding," Susan Sontag has argued that

[i]nterpretation [. . .] presupposes a discrepancy between the clear meaning of the text and the demands of (later) readers. It seeks to resolve that discrepancy. The situation is that for some reason a text has become unacceptable; yet it cannot be discarded. Interpretation is a radical strategy for conserving an old text, which is thought too precious to repudiate, by revamping it. The interpreter, without actually erasing or rewriting the text, *is* altering it. But he [sic] can't admit to doing this. He claims to be only making it intelligible, by disclosing its true meaning.[88]

On the flyleaf of the heavily annotated copy of her Shakespeare lectures that she used most often, Terry wrote, "To act, you must make the thing written your own. You must steal the words, steal the thought, and *convey* the stolen treasure to others with great art."[89] In the lectures that were at once like and not like her Lyceum performances and that William Winter found so objectionable, Terry "stole" Shakespeare's words and "conserved" them within a feminist–modernist context by resituating them within her interpretive "discourses."[90] Her lecture–demonstration format signaled the utopian dimension of her Meredithian comic vision in that the Shakespeare she advocated on feminist grounds was not the Shakespeare she had actually played but an altered, rewritten Shakespeare underpinned by her rejection of what she saw as Ibsen's "realism of low-down things" in favor of an alternative "realism," redefined as "real feeling, real sympathy,"[91] and – to adapt the words of Oscar Wilde – "the telling of beautiful" if larger-than-life and as yet "untrue things."[92]

In his 1888 manifesto of modern drama "Preface to *Miss Julie*," August Strindberg argued that because modern characters "[live] in a transitional era," they are not simple and unified but, rather, "torn and divided, a mixture of the old and the new," "conglomerations from various stages of culture, past and present,"[93] while in his 1909 study *The Sociology of Modern Drama*, Georg Lukács similarly observed that with the advent of modern drama, the stage "turned into the point of intersection for pairs of worlds distinct in time" and that "the realm of drama is one where 'past' and 'future,' 'no longer' and 'not yet,' come together in a single moment."[94] As a theatrical presence, Terry shared the quality of inherent doubleness and contradiction associated with modern character as theorized by Strindberg and Lukács,[95] perhaps accounting for her status as Shaw's "most modern of modern women." In an explanation of his concept of the "not/but" as a strategy for alienating social contradictions and enabling the conceptualization of change, Bertolt Brecht wrote that

[w]hen [an actor] appears on the stage, besides what he is actually doing he will at all essential points discover, specify, imply what he is not doing; that is to say he will act in such a way that the alternative emerges as clearly as possible, that his acting allows the other possibilities to be inferred and only represents one out of the possible variants.[96]

Terry was "not" the "new woman" associated with Ibsen's modern realist drama, "but" she was not the "old woman" either. Instead, alienating social contradictions about gender ideology and inspiring feminist thinking not only beyond the limits of the Lyceum Shakespeare but also beyond the realist "women's plays" that marked the beginnings of modern drama, she pointed, through a kind of Brechtian "not/but," toward another type of feminist heroine and a more perfect future, both on and off the stage. Perhaps for this reason, while Terry signified for Elizabeth Robins the limited possibilities for actresses in actor–manager-controlled theatres,[97] she was, for Isadora Duncan, "my most perfect ideal of woman!"[98] and caused Virginia Woolf, for whom she held considerable imaginative importance, to remark in her diary in 1930, "I've read Q[ueen] V[ictoria]'s letters; & wonder what wd. happen had Ellen Terry been born Queen. Complete disaster to the Empire?"[99]

CHAPTER 3

Unimagined parts, unlived selves:
Virginia Woolf on Ellen Terry and the art of acting

Several days before her play *Freshwater* was performed at a Bloomsbury party on 19 January 1935, Virginia Woolf noted in her diary that she planned to "hire a donkeys head to take [her curtain] call in – by way of saying This is a donkeys work."[1] Woolf took none of her writing lightly, however, and despite her self-deprecating attitude and the play's buoyant comic tone, *Freshwater* was not simply "a joke" entirely without connection to her other work, as has often been assumed.[2] Indeed, Woolf had the project in mind for a very long time, mentioning an idea for a play about her Victorian relations Julia Margaret Cameron and Charles Hay Cameron as early as 1919,[3] drafting one version of the play in 1923, and revising it for the Bloomsbury performance more than a decade later. As Lucio Ruotolo has noted, "even a casual study of the text shows how fully Virginia had researched the subject of her great-aunt Julia Margaret Cameron."[4]

But if Woolf set out with the idea to write a play about the Camerons, she ended up writing one about the actress Ellen Terry, a change in focus most apparent in Act II of the 1935 version of *Freshwater*. This act, which is not included in the one-act 1923 version, is set not at the Camerons' Freshwater home but at the rocks called the Needles off the Isle of Wight, and only Terry, John Craig, and a porpoise appear in it. Terry's prominence in this middle section indicates that she is literally the "central" character of *Freshwater* and that *her* departure rather than the Camerons' is the play's central action. So, whereas Woolf felt in 1923 that she "could write something much better, if [she] gave up a little more time to it,"[5] when she redrafted *Freshwater* in 1935, it was the centrality of the Terry character that she chose to refine.[6]

Terry was a figure of considerable significance for Woolf, who wrote about her not only in *Freshwater* but in a 1941 essay that she worked on while she was completing her self-reflexive final novel *Between the Acts*, in which performance functions as a central metaphor. Read together with her early

49

essays on the French actresses Sarah Bernhardt and Rachel, these writings on Terry clarify Woolf's sense of the historical entrapment of women in restrictive, male-determined roles and of the need to put into play previously "unacted parts"[7] through feminist cultural critique and literary experiment. Woolf's use of the figure of the actress, particularly Terry, thus establishes a connection between her own feminist–modernist fiction, theory, and criticism and the questions raised in the preceding chapters about the feminist possibilities and limitations of the male-authored dramatic canon, including the works of Shakespeare and Ibsen. Indeed, in using the figure of Terry to literalize the restrictions that conventional gender roles impose on human creativity and to conceptualize the potential of her own writing to articulate alternative and more emancipatory modes of subjectivity, Woolf implied that the needs for roles that are at once challenging theatrically and acceptable within feminist terms are in fact indistinguishable. Woolf's writings on Terry thus establish a connection between her own feminist–modernist literary project and the dramaturgical explorations of pioneering feminist playwrights – Elizabeth Robins and Djuna Barnes, for example – and underline her sense of the very real importance of such explorations in terms of actual lived experience. In doing so, these writings on Terry and the art of acting complement Woolf's use of theatrical performance as a device by which to represent the repressive and transformational possibilities of art for social actors in *Between the Acts*.

Woolf idealized the stage as a potential site for expansive and liberating self-expression whereon performers could both form and themselves be formed by fictional beings and could experience *through* their art new aspects of themselves which they would at once express *in* their art. In her 1908 review of Sarah Bernhardt's memoirs, for example, Woolf states that she expects actresses to lead fuller, richer, more interesting and complicated lives than people who do not exist in co-productive relationship with dramatic characters, the fictional vessels of distilled human feeling and experience. Each part that an actress plays, she writes, "deposits its own small contribution upon her unseen shape, until it is complete and distinct from its creations at the same time that it inspires them with life."[8] For this reason, Woolf believed that Bernhardt, one of the most celebrated actresses of all time, should have had "more strange things" to tell "of herself and of life" than perhaps any other woman alive (201). In reading the memoirs, however, she found that an overwhelming self-centeredness prevented Bernhardt from permitting any part she played to "deposit" in turn "its own small contribution" upon her and that, as a consequence, she failed to fulfill the potential for expanded experience through creative relationship that Woolf saw as the special privilege of actresses.

Woolf's ideas about acting are further developed in her 1911 review of Francis Gribble's biography *Rachel: Her Stage Life and Her Real Life*, in which she takes issue with Gribble's distinction between the French actress's on-stage and off-stage lives, as well as with his attribution of Rachel's melancholy to a realization that she had spent her days living the lives of her characters and had therefore had no opportunity to live her own life. "[W]hat, after all, is one's 'own life'?" Woolf asks.

Why should we draw these distinctions between real life and stage life? It is when we feel most that we live most; and we cannot believe that Rachel, married to a real man, bearing real children, and adding up real butcher's bills, would have lived more truly than Rachel imagining the passions of women who never existed.[9]

Gauging real life according to range and intensity of emotional experience, Woolf viewed acting not as the loss of self within a character but as the expression of previously unexplored aspects of the self, newly discovered through the process of giving shape to invented dramatic beings. For this reason, she doubted that Rachel was any more "real" in her extravagant social performances than she was on stage in the theatre. Indeed, for Woolf, the "others" whose lives Rachel lamented having lived were not her characters, as Gribble argued, but the obsequious, distracting, and finally exhausting social roles that the actress of humble origins had to learn to play when, before the age of twenty, she was caught up in "the blaze of sudden and violent celebrity" (155). "The truth," Woolf suggests,

seems to be that one does not stop acting or painting or writing just because one happens to be dining or driving in the Park; only trying to combine the two things often ends disastrously. Perhaps disaster is more common among actresses than among other artists, because the body plays so large a part upon the stage. (155)

Rachel's particular "disaster" was to "[die] of exhaustion at the age of thirty-seven, having kicked her body round the world, secured no permanent happiness, and outlived her success" (155). The pressures of off-stage life had required her to expend precious creative energy, which should have been channeled into her on-stage acting, in "a great deal of pose and bad art," and "the seed of that melancholy lay in the thought, not that she had been an actress, leading an unreal life, but that she might have been a greater actress, leading a still more real life" (155). Prevented from realizing herself fully by her obligatory social performances, the Rachel of this 1911

review is not unlike the doomed heroine Rachel Vinrace in Woolf's first
novel *The Voyage Out*, which she was in the process of writing at around
the same time.[10]

The possibilities and limitations of acting that Woolf outlined in these
early essays on Bernhardt and Rachel informed her understanding of the
artistic potential and ultimate failure of her quintessential actress Ellen
Terry, who, unlike Bernhardt, was not inordinately egocentric but could
both shape and be shaped by the characters she played and, unlike Rachel,
did not have to waste herself performing socially but could devote her
entire creative energy to her on-stage art. In *Freshwater*, a youthful Terry
and her aging husband, the painter George Frederick Watts, are guests,
together with Alfred Tennyson, at the summer home of the photographer
Julia Margaret Cameron. Tired of posing for Watts as Modesty at the foot
of Mammon, Terry steals away for a rendezvous with a stranger who, earlier,
tossed her a note as he leapt, on horseback, across a lane where she was
picking primroses. After she has gone, Watts discovers with horror that
he has inadvertently painted Modesty wearing a veil that symbolizes the
fertility of fish. In Act II of the 1935 version, the scene shifts to the seashore,
where Terry has met up with the stranger, a young naval officer by the
name of John Craig. When Terry confides to Craig that she is unhappy
as her husband's model, immortalized in paintings, he proposes marriage
and a life completely different from the one she knows now. She accepts
and throws her wedding ring to a porpoise. Watts has been spying on the
lovers and in Act III he returns to the house to tell Cameron and Tennyson
that his wife is dead. Tennyson immediately sets to work on a poem about
the drowned Ellen Terry, but then the actress re-appears to announce that
she is leaving Watts to live with Craig in Bloomsbury. Cameron and her
husband depart for India, and Watts and Tennyson are left alone with their
art until they are visited by Queen Victoria, who awards the painter the
Order of Merit and the poet a peerage.

Freshwater's few commentators have tended to read Woolf's seventeen-
year-old Terry as wanting to escape from all art when she leaves Watts
for Craig,[11] but this interpretation is problematic in several respects. First,
Craig's Bloomsbury address was Woolf's address after her father's death in
1904 and the address at which the Bloomsbury group came into being.[12]
In sending her character off to this address, Woolf projected her own experience onto Terry, and Woolf's residency in Bloomsbury – her first room
of her own – was, in a sense, her liberation into art. Secondly, describing
the end of her six-year sojourn in the country with architect and occasional

theatrical designer Edward Godwin, the lover she ran off with after her marriage to Watts, the real Ellen Terry told in her autobiography of being stuck
in a lane with a broken cartwheel when the playwright Charles Reade, out
fox-hunting, leapt over the hedgerow, recognized her, and lured her back
to a lifelong career on the stage with a £40-a-week part in his latest play.[13]
This autobiographical account of Terry's return to the theatre was clearly
the source of Woolf's image of her character Terry's first encounter with
John Craig and so further problematizes the notion that she is rejecting
art by leaving Watts to take up with him. Finally, although John Craig's
last name is that which Terry and Godwin's two children Edith Craig and
Edward Gordon Craig adopted for themselves as they embarked on what
were to be distinguished careers as theatre artists,[14] he is the only character
in *Freshwater* who does not appear to be based on an actual historical per-
sonage. Thus, although he has been described as a "healthy [Philistine],"[15]
instead of functioning in opposition to art, John Craig in effect embodies
art as a figure created to serve an imaginative function. This fictitious status
is reinforced by the fantasy quality of Act II, in which Craig first appears:
set "on a rock in the middle of the sea" (23) rather than in the Victorian
interior of Cameron's studio, this act also features a hungry porpoise –
played by a human – who swallows Terry's wedding ring. In *Freshwater*,
then, Terry does not divorce herself from art altogether. Rather, her art as
an actress, to be resumed after her flight from Freshwater to Bloomsbury, is
aligned with Woolf's own literary project and is opposed to the Victorian
artistic tradition that Woolf herself was writing against. Indeed, prompted
by a fictitious male whose surname is that of her two artist–children, Terry's
return to the stage is associated with a more fertile creativity than is possible for her at the Victorian bastion of Freshwater and is endowed with the
promise of the birth of modernism.

In Watts's paintings, Cameron's photographs, and Tennyson's poetry,
Terry is the reluctant model for a range of feminine images that are essentially variations of the same Victorian ideal of womanhood that Woolf
called "the Angel in the House" and regarded as the mortal enemy of
women artists.[16] In her "Speech of January 21 1931," Woolf describes this
angel as "the woman that men wished women to be" – sympathetic, charming, unselfish, without "a wish or a mind of her own," and, above all, pure
(xxix–xxx) – and she recalls how she felt the pressure of this ideal early in her
own career when she began to write literary reviews in which she expressed
her opinions on the work of male authors. Then, "[t]he shadow of [the
angel's] wings fell upon the page" and she would hear a voice counselling
her to make whatever she wrote "pleasing to men" (xxx–xxxi). Killing the

angel in the house was, she felt, one of the definitive moments in her career as a woman writer.

In *Freshwater*, Woolf farcically signifies the artificiality of this ideal of self-abnegating femininity when her character Terry is required to pose for Cameron as the Muse to "Poetry in the person of Alfred Tennyson" (10) by standing on a chair, throwing out her arms, directing her eyes upwards, and wearing turkey wings. Yet despite this comic treatment, the pressure to conform to the role of the angel is no less deadening for Terry than it was for Woolf: Cameron demands that she "keep perfectly still" for fifteen minutes as the Muse (14); Watts requires her to "[k]eep perfectly still" for four-hour stretches as Modesty (6); and Tennyson finds "something highly pleasing about the death of a young woman in the pride of life" (40).[17] Indeed, Tennyson's ludicrously self-involved disappointment when Terry destroys his "immortal poem" in the making by turning up alive (44) makes evident Woolf's sense of the reliance of Victorian art on dead or immobile women. Moreover, Cameron's participation in the entrapment of Terry in a limited range of male-determined female roles gives comic expression to Woolf's insight that the cultural tradition is bound up with patriarchal ideology and that women artists must adapt and transform existing modes of representation if their art is to communicate a fuller range of women's experience.[18] Shedding her wings to run off to Bloomsbury with her ficti-tious lover, Woolf's young actress-character resists sacrificing herself to the artistic standards of the Victorian old-guard at Freshwater and replicates Woolf's own escape from her Victorian heritage. Cameron was, after all, Woolf's great aunt and had photographed her mother Julia Duckworth Stephen; and Woolf's father Leslie Stephen was a prominent man of letters who was first married to William Makepeace Thackeray's daughter and whose influence on his own daughter Virginia was so overwhelming that she wrote in her diary twenty-four years after his death, "Father's birthday. He would have been [. . .] 96[,] 96, yes, today; & could have been 96, like other people one has known; but mercifully was not. His life would have entirely ended mine. What would have happened? No writing, no books; – inconceivable."[19]

Against the immobilization of the lively young actress by Victorian artists creating "immortal" art, Woolf sets Terry's desire to swim. In the 1923 draft of *Freshwater*, Terry confides that she wants to quit posing, become an actress, and have someone fall in love with her (70). In the 1935 version, she states instead that she wants to quit posing and go for a swim and that she would rather swim than hang "in the Tate Gallery for ever and ever" (27). Woolf's revision of her character's longings to act and to fall in love into a single, seemingly unrelated desire to swim is not a transmutation but a symbolic abstraction in the spirit of her parodic treatment of the Freshwater artists' obsession with symbolization. Indeed, through the desire to swim, Woolf situated her character between her own feminist–modernist artistic vision and the patriarchal ideology and aesthetics of the Victorian artists in her play.

The activity of swimming – especially as it replaces wanting to make art and be in a love relationship – is a symbol that resonates with figures Woolf employed elsewhere in her writings on women artists, imagination, and androgyny. In the "Speech of January 21 1931," for example, Woolf describes her professional experiences with what she calls "that very shy and illusive fish the imagination" by presenting the woman writer

<in an attitude of contemplation, like a fisherwoman,> sitting on the bank of a lake with [. . .] <her> fishing rod <held over its water.> [. . .] She was not thinking; she was not reasoning; she was not constructing a plot; she was letting her imagination down into the depths of her consciousness while she sat above holding on by a thin <but quite necessary> thread of reason. She was letting her imagination feed unfettered upon every crumb of her experience; she was letting her imagination sweep unchecked round every rock and cranny of the world that lies submerged in our unconscious being. (xxxvii–xxxviii)

The imagination does not swim free for long, however. Instead, it surfaces lethargically for lack of interesting life materials to feed on or is yanked out of the water for swimming too deeply and dangerously into the woman writer's experience, especially of her female body. Only in another fifty years, Woolf predicts, will conventions permit the woman writer to make use of the insights that the fish at the end of her imagination's line is ready to bring her (xxxviii–xxxix).

Woolf used the figure of a fish in her earlier essay *A Room of One's Own* as well, this time in connection with her concept of an androgynous and fully expressive artistic imagination that remains as yet primarily in the realm of the ideal, attained only by the rarest few. At the beginning of this essay, as she sits on a river bank pondering the subject of women and fiction and watching an undergraduate row through the reflections on the water's surface, Woolf feels the tug of an idea at the end of her metaphorical line and pulls it up for examination:

Alas, laid on the grass how small, how insignificant this thought of mine looked; the sort of fish that a good fisherman puts back into the water so that it may grow fatter and be one day worth cooking and eating. I will not trouble you with that thought now, though if you look carefully you may find it for yourselves in the course of what I am going to say.[20]

At the end of *A Room of One's Own*, Woolf refers back to this moment on the river bank (104–105) and in doing so implies that the fish she tossed back then was her not-yet-developed idea of a state of androgynous creativity wherein "the mind is fully fertilized and uses all its faculties" without gender-related impediment, inhibition, or self-consciousness (98).

Woolf's concept of creative androgyny is implicit in *Freshwater* as the state that Terry wants to attain in swimming beyond the static, imprisoning experience that the Victorian artists impose on her. Midway through painting Modesty as personified by Terry in a starry white veil signifying the Milky Way, Watts is devastated to discover that he has made a terrible error in symbolism:

Horror! Horror! I have been most cruelly deceived! Listen: (*He reads* [from a book on ancient Egyptian mythology].) "The Milky Way among the ancients was the universal token of fertility. It symbolized the spawn of fish, the innumerable progeny of the sea, and the fertility of the marriage bed." Horror! Oh Horror! I who have always lived for the Utmost for the Highest have made Modesty symbolise the fertility of fish! (19)

In his distress that he has unwittingly undermined the Victorian ideal of feminine purity in his painting, Watts serves as a ludicrous example of what Woolf would have classified as an entirely masculine and therefore ultimately sterile artist whose conscious gender bias obstructs and corrupts his creative expression. In *A Room of One's Own*, she argued that when an artist uses art to assert ego or to protest against the equality (or inequality) of the other sex, the art

is doomed to death. It ceases to be fertilized. Brilliant and effective, powerful and masterly, as it may appear for a day or two, it must wither at nightfall; it cannot grow in the minds of others. Some collaboration has to take place in the mind between the woman and the man before the act of creation can be accomplished. Some marriage of opposites has to be consummated. The whole of the mind must lie wide open if we are to get the sense that the writer is communicating his experience with perfect fullness. (104)

There is nothing fertile or collaborative about Watts or his art as presented in *Freshwater*. Instead, he suppresses his own vital artistic impulses for the sake of an abstract and exclusionary ideal and requires of his model silence, immobility, and self-effacement in exchange for an immortality that for Terry does not actually transcend death but is, in effect, death's equivalent.

John Craig, on the other hand, as the only entirely fictitious character
in the play, is at once the imagined product and the actual embodiment of
the masculine aspect that promises to animate Terry's immobilized androgynous creativity. His enlivening and unselfconscious virility and his gen-
erative function, as suggested by the derivation of his name from Terry's
artist–children, contrast sharply with Watts's determined sterility, and his
union with Terry provides an alternative not only to her sexless marriage
to the aging painter, rumored in real life to have been impotent, but also to
the artistic self-centredness and consequent barrenness that Watts's work
and that of his Victorian friends apparently represented for Woolf. Kissing
Terry, Craig opens her up to "dreadful thoughts" of "beef steaks; beer; standing under an umbrella in the rain; waiting to go into a theatre; crowds of
people; hot chestnuts; omnibuses – all the things I've always dreamt about"
(28–29). Unrepresented in the art of Watts, Cameron, and Tennyson and
made visible to Terry through her intercourse with Woolf's invented navy
man from Bloomsbury, these London activities may be read as indicators
of a desire not to live a life free of art, but, rather, to live – and to make
art of – a full life encompassing the total range of human experience and
dismissing no detail as invalid, improper, or beneath her artistic dignity. In
a complicated parodic gesture, Woolf's Terry divorces Watts by throwing
her wedding ring to a porpoise, who then takes her place in marriage to
Watts's art and whose indeterminate sex will not "matter a damn" (35) to the
painter so concerned with transcendence that he has lost touch with what
Woolf elsewhere called "things in themselves" (*AROO* 111).[21] Liberated from
her immortal symbolic burden into the breadth, freshness, and vitality of
the vision that her new, fictitious male partner has awakened in her, Terry
contrasts with Watts and is instead allied artistically with Woolf herself,
with her androgynous poet Orlando, who pursues the elusive "wild goose"
of poetry right into the present moment,[22] and with Mary Carmichael, the
invented author of *Life's Adventure* whom Woolf encourages in *A Room of
One's Own* to observe and write, "as a woman who has forgotten that she is
a woman," about those obscure lives and those aspects of human existence
that male writers have traditionally ignored (93).

As Nina Auerbach has argued, however, in *Freshwater* Woolf may have
been "[t]rying to write a comedy about material she [feared was] tragic."[23]
In the 1923 version of the play, Terry runs off dressed in checked trousers
that recall a costume the actress actually wore in a favorite boy role of
her childhood days on the stage. In the 1935 version, however, she departs
dressed "not as a boy, but as a fallen woman,"[24] deplored by Watts for being
"painted, powdered – unveiled" (47). The replacement of the earlier visual

image of an androgynous female artist with that of a rebellious but finally conventional Victorian heroine presaged Terry's fate as Woolf described it in her 1941 essay–portrait of the actress, in which Terry is presented as having died without ever having found a stage on which to fully realize her creative promise. So too did the association of the fluid young actress who wants to swim away from Freshwater with the under-developed, thwarted, and premature fish of *A Room of One's Own* and the "Speech of January 21 1931." In her essay on Rachel, Woolf attributed the prevalence of "disaster" in the lives of actresses to the important part that the body plays upon the stage. This contention, now implicitly gender-related, underlies her essay "Ellen Terry."

In this essay, Woolf describes Terry's life as having been governed by an overarching quest for an elusive and unknown something within herself that was her artistic genius. "There was a self she did not know," Woolf states, "a gap she could not fill."[25] In returning to the stage after a six-year interlude with her lover Edward Godwin, Terry was seeking to fill that gap through her art as an actress.

The voice she heard in the lane was not the voice of [the playwright] Charles Reade; nor was it the voice of the bailiffs [to whom she and Godwin owed money]. It was the voice of her genius; the urgent call of something that she could not define, could not suppress, and must obey. So she left her children and followed the voice back to the stage, back to the Lyceum, back to a long life of incessant toil, anguish, and glory. (70)

Ultimately, however, none of Terry's many roles was large enough to animate, contain, and express the fullness of her androgynous imaginative genius.

The role of Lady Cecily in George Bernard Shaw's *Captain Brassbound's Conversion* serves as a case in point. In Woolf's account, Terry was not past her prime and losing her memory when she came on stage as Lady Cecily, forgot her lines, put on her glasses, and read from cue-notes pinned to the back of a settee, causing the entire stage illusion of Shaw's play to "[collapse] like a house of cards" under the power of her presence (67). Rather, she was, in Edward Gordon Craig's terms, a "conscientious objector," effectively undermining a second-rate role that was unsuited to her.[26] As Woolf reminds us, Craig believed that his mother "only forgot her part when there was something uncongenial in the words, when some speck of grit had got into the marvellous machine of her genius" (67). "When the part was congenial," Woolf states in comparison, when [Terry] was Shakespeare's Portia, Desdemona, Ophelia, every word, every comma was consumed. Even her eyelashes acted. Her body lost its weight. Her son, a mere boy, could lift her in his arms. "I am not myself," she said. "Something comes upon me. . . . I am always-in-the-air, light and bodiless." (67)

Such "golden moments" (71), Woolf explains, were achieved partly through intensive textual study but mostly through imagination. As she summarizes Terry's creative process,

Visit mad-houses, if you like; take notes; observe; study endlessly. But first, imagine. And so she takes her part away from the books out into the woods. Rambling down grassy rides, she lives her part until she is it. If a word jars or grates, she must re-think it, re-write it. Then when every phrase is her own, and every gesture spontaneous, out she comes on to the stage and is Imogen, Ophelia, Desdemona. (71)

This account of Terry's creative process, in which the dramatic role is integrated into the actress's off-stage life, resonates with the ideas about the mutually productive relationship between role and self that underlie Woolf's earlier essays on Rachel and Sarah Bernhardt. Yet though Terry experienced in Shakespeare those swimmingly buoyant moments "when she [became] bodyless [sic], not herself" ("ET" 71), Woolf argued in *A Room of One's Own* that in Shakespeare's plays, as in the male-dominated literary canon more generally, the women characters exist primarily in relation to men and are therefore ultimately oversimplified (82–84). "Suppose," she suggests,

[. . .] that men were only represented in literature as the lovers of women, and were never the friends of men, soldiers, thinkers, dreamers; how few parts in the plays of Shakespeare could be allotted to them; how literature would suffer! We might perhaps have most of Othello; and a good deal of Antony; but no Caesar, no Brutus, no Hamlet, no Lear, no Jaques – literature would be incredibly impoverished, as indeed literature is impoverished beyond our counting by the doors that have been shut upon women. (*AROO* 83)

Even in Shakespeare, then, there are limits to the potential for expansive self-discovery that Woolf saw as the special privilege of actresses, and these limits are linked, through the insights of *A Room of One's Own*, to the omissions of the male-dominated literary canon that are the effect of its traditional exclusion of women writers, who could bring to literature previously unrepresented aspects of women's experience.

But if Woolf saw Shakespeare's plays as more fully representative of male than of female experience, he nevertheless exemplified her ideal of a state of androgynous creativity wherein "the mind is fully fertilized and uses all its faculties" in the expression of art (*AROO* 98). As she wrote of Shakespeare in *A Room of One's Own,*

All desire to protest, to preach, to proclaim an injury, to pay off a score, to make the world a witness of some hardship or grievance was fired out of him and consumed. Therefore his poetry flows from him free and unimpeded. If ever a human being got his work expressed completely, it was Shakespeare. If ever a mind was incandescent, unimpeded, [. . .] it was Shakespeare's mind. (57)

Christine Froula has discussed Woolf's perception of Shakespeare's plays as autobiography "not [. . .] in the ordinary sense, but rather" in the sense of "the self (or selves) [being] 'completely expressed'" in and through the work.[27] As Froula points out, in Woolf's view this autobiographical self-expression resulted in a paradoxical anonymity or impersonality that leaves the reader free of the desire to know more about Shakespeare because he was so fully expressed in his work, "perfectly present and by the same token invisible."[28] Shakespeare's anonymity was, moreover, closely related to his androgyny in that both qualities entail a freedom "from every kind of constraint" and "historical contingency" that Woolf herself sought to achieve, most deliberately in writing *The Waves*.[29] To attain this state of creative autobiography, Woolf tried to write "as a woman who has forgotten that she is a woman" and so is free to write about "things in themselves."

This creative state in which the androgynous self is fully and freely expressed in and through art was that which Woolf saw Terry as having been unable to achieve in her career as an actress:

Each part seems the right part until she throws it aside and plays another. Something of Ellen Terry it seems overflowed every part and remained unacted. Shakespeare could not fit her; nor Ibsen; nor Shaw. The stage could not hold her; nor the nursery. But there is, after all, a greater dramatist than Shakespeare, Ibsen, or Shaw. There is Nature. Hers is so vast a stage, and so innumerable a company of actors, that for the most part she fobs them off with a tag or two. They come on and they go off without breaking the ranks. But now and again Nature creates a new part, an original part. The actors who act that part will always defy our attempts to name them. They will not act the stock parts – they forget the words, they improvise others of their own. But when they come on the stage falls like a pack of cards and the limelights are extinguished. That was Ellen Terry's fate – to act a new part. And thus while other actors are remembered because they were Hamlet, Phèdre, or Cleopatra, Ellen Terry is remembered because she was Ellen Terry. ("ET" 71–72)

Far from enabling the type of artistic self-realization through co-creative relationship that Woolf theorized in her essays on Bernhardt and Rachel, Terry's art form, in the limited roles it offered to women, was not yet a medium in which she could fully discover and express herself. "[C]aught and tangled in a woman's body" (*AROO* 48) that restricted her to impoverished female characters, Terry could not, as an actress, rewrite the destinies of these prescripted characters, but could only register her distance from and resistance to them by refusing to remember her lines and asserting her charismatic stage presence so that it overrode the world of the play. In the "Speech of January 21 1931," Woolf wrote that it would be another fifty years before women writers would be able to make use of the "very queer knowledge" about "womens bodies [sic]" and "passions" that the fish of the imagination discovers in the "dark pool of extraordinary experience" it visits before being yanked back to the surface for going further than convention permits (xxxviii–xxxix). Paradoxically, characters that explored women's bodies and passions more deeply than those in the male-authored dramatic canon might have enabled Terry's figurative disappearance from the stage by allowing her to cease functioning as a "conscientious objector" and concentrate herself more fully in her art. However, through the "disaster" of her female body on a historical rather than an ideal stage, the androgynous swimmer/actress of *Freshwater* became in Woolf's 1941 essay–portrait a woman artist who could never forget that she was a woman and who consequently remained overwhelmingly present as such in all her art, unable to make of drama a vehicle that would enable the type of autobiographical yet anonymous self-expression that Woolf saw as Shakespeare's great accomplishment and that she strove to achieve herself.

By 1941, Woolf had disengaged herself from the creative affinity with Terry that she established in *Freshwater* and the reasons for her disengagement are reflected in the play's relatively conventional and ultimately defeating dramatic form. What attracted and allied Woolf to Terry in *Freshwater* was a perception of her apparent containment within herself of "the innumerable progeny of the sea" and an intimation of the attendant potential for artistic expression implicit in such an infinitely various yet nonetheless integrated being. The Milky Way, after all, in which Watts mistakenly clothes Terry is, as a symbol of "the fertility of fish" and "the innumerable progeny of the sea," an androgynous body composed of countless male and female parts that cohere to form a fluid whole. If the character Watts does not himself entirely succeed in suppressing this subversive androgynous reality by confining his young wife within the traditionally feminine role of Modesty, the real Terry's historical moment and chosen art form did. Notably, in the second act of the 1935 *Freshwater*, Terry sits with Craig on a rock in the middle of the sea looking at the water but not yet swimming in it. Woolf's play thematically implies but does not dramaturgically actualize the notion of a self composed of multiple selves which actresses, by the nature of their work, should be more privileged than most to embody. In *Freshwater*, then, as in the essay "Ellen Terry," Woolf functioned finally as a sympathetic biographer powerless to transform history and her subject's already lived experience.

Woolf did not act in *Freshwater* when it was staged at her sister Vanessa Bell's studio in Bloomsbury in 1935, but the donkey's head that she planned to wear for her curtain call is suggestive of Shakespeare's mechanical-qua-man of the theatre Bottom, whose head is magically metamorphosed into that of an ass. Certainly, in writing drama, Woolf was, like Bottom, "translated" into an unfamiliar realm in which she was a gauche though happy intruder; but Bottom is also remarkable for his desire to play man, woman, and beast in the mechanicals' production, and in taking her bow in a donkey's head, Woolf identified writing as a position from which, as a woman artist, she could experience all the parts at once, anonymous yet fully expressed in her work.

Because the woman writer's body was not present in her art, she was not disastrously confined, as the actress was, to impoverished female roles. Nevertheless, the fact of literary convention remained, and the task of the woman writer was, as Woolf saw it, to imagine and script new and different roles, a task which, working at a physical remove, she might be at greater liberty to accomplish than an actress weighed down by the "deposits" of existing female roles. At the peak of her career when Terry died in 1928, Woolf was able to begin to transform conventional plots and characters to enable the type of artistic autobiography that she envisioned for herself. In her formally innovative works of fiction, she communicated, among other things, the idea that the female body contains within it the multiple contingent and variously gendered selves that Watts seeks to suppress in *Freshwater*. In *The Waves*, for example, her narrative voice flows in and out of six consciousnesses, male and female, homogeneously integrated "in the rhythm of the waves,"[30] simultaneously dissolving and expanding identity. In *Orlando*, a fantasy–biography of a transhistorical androgyne–author, she states that each person is "what is called, rightly or wrongly, a single self, a real self,"[31] and that this self is "compact of all the selves we have it in us to be," which include, in Orlando's case,

the boy who sat on the hill; the boy who saw the poet; the boy who handed the Queen the bowl of rose water; [. . .] the young man who fell in love with Sasha; [. . .] the Courtier; [. . .] the Ambassador; [. . .] the Soldier; [. . .] the Traveller; [. . .] the

Gipsy; the Fine Lady; the Hermit; the girl in love with life; the Patroness of Letters; the woman who called Mar (meaning hot baths and evening fires) or Shelmerdine (meaning crocuses in autumn woods) or Bonthrop (meaning the death we die daily) or all three together – which meant more things than we have space to write out [. . .].[32]

Through the formal innovations of such works as *Orlando* and *The Waves*, Woolf realized in fiction liberating notions of the self that were thematically implied but not dramaturgically actualized in *Freshwater* as it set aside modernist "fragmenting [of] unities of plot and character"[33] in order to parody Woolf's Victorian precursors, and that later informed Woolf's suggestion that Terry was ultimately unable to achieve her full creative potential due to the limitations of the existing dramatic canon. Cumulatively, then, Woolf represented Terry as historical proof of the necessity and value of her own feminist–modernist literary innovations and, by implication, of the corresponding explorations of women playwrights such as Elizabeth Robins and Djuna Barnes as they worked in very different ways to achieve more emancipatory representations of gender both on and off the stage.

The day after *Freshwater* was performed, Woolf wrote in her diary, "I have an idea for a 'play' Summers night [sic]. Someone on a seat. And voices speaking from the flowers."[34] The only play that Woolf wrote other than *Freshwater* was the pageant of English literary history that she incorporated into her final novel *Between the Acts* (1941), and a connection in her mind between these two works is suggested by her *Freshwater*-inspired diary images of an outdoor summer setting, unidentified characters, and dislocated voices, all of which are prophetic of *Between the Acts*.[35] Woolf was certainly thinking about Terry as she worked on her last novel. She researched and wrote her essay on the actress in the fall of 1940 and published it in February of 1941, shortly before completing *Between the Acts*. Also, several scholars have suggested that the character of Miss La Trobe may have been modeled after Terry's daughter Edith Craig, an experimental feminist theatre artist who was active in the suffrage theatre movement, staged historical pageants in various towns, and produced plays in a converted barn on the country property where her mother had lived and where a memorial to her was later established.[36] In *Between the Acts*, Woolf's use of performance as a metaphor to represent her understanding of literary texts as cultural scripts reflects and advances the ideas about acting and actresses that she outlined in her essays on Sarah Bernhardt, Rachel, and Ellen Terry. Moreover, whereas Woolf's representation of Terry as thwarted genius implicated her own feminist–modernist literary practice – and that of similarly minded women writers, including playwrights – as a response to the actress's confinement in male-determined roles that replicated those to which women were confined off stage, her use of performance in *Between the Acts* provided a model for how to read her own body of work and that of the other feminist artists considered in this study in terms of its potential to engender change through its articulation of alternative cultural scripts relating to gender.

CHAPTER 4

Staging the ob/scene

While Michel Foucault argued in *The History of Sexuality* that the nine-teenth century saw the disciplinary establishment of modern sexual iden-tities through such strategies as the "hysterization of women's bodies," the "socialization of procreative behavior," and "the psychiatrization of perverse pleasure,"[1] others have linked this historical formation of modern sexuali-ties, including homosexuality, with the development of literary modernism, focusing particularly on the issue of obscenity as a locus of this linkage. Leigh Gilmore, for example, has suggested that "obscenity is constitutive of rather than corollary to modernism,"[2] while Dianne Chisholm has noted, with reference to the obscenity trials of such works as James Joyce's *Ulysses* (1922), D. H. Lawrence's *Lady Chatterley's Lover* (1928), and Radclyffe Hall's *The Well of Loneliness* (1928), that "[m]odernist art is produced at the same historical moment and in the same social space as 'obscene' art,"[3] and that the "transgression" of these works of literary modernism

was made visible through the legal spectacularization of "obscene" sexuality. [. . .] Or, to put it another way, modernist sexuality became generally recognizable through the law's censorious focus on "corruptive" speech and verbal image. [. . .] Legal prosecutions led the way in shaping public knowledge about the obscene practices of modernist art; through legal mediation, the reader was directed to construe modernist transgression, favorably or unfavorably, as outlawed sexual representation.[4]

A corresponding relationship between the emergence of theatrical and dramatic modernism and the developments in the history of sexuality described by Foucault is suggested in a reference in a review of the 1889 London production of Ibsen's *A Doll's House* to a "scant audience of unnatural-looking women [and] long-haired men," as well as "atheists, socialists, and positivists";[5] and the charge of obscenity – or as the journal *Punch* wittily put it, "Ibscenity"[6] – loomed over Ibsen's rise to notoriety as a pioneer of modern drama whose works were sometimes staged before private subscription audiences in order to circumvent censorship or out-right banning as they addressed such controversial issues as the sexual double standard, marital failure, incest, and syphilis. Still, despite the connection between the purported obscenity of Ibsen's work and his sustained dramatic interest in issues associated with "the woman question," the interrelation-ship between the emergence of modern sexualities, theatrical and dramatic modernism, obscenity, and feminism has been insufficiently explored, and in this regard, American novelist and playwright Djuna Barnes's 1923 one-act play *The Dove* is of particular significance.

In the preceding chapter, I discussed Virginia Woolf's exploration in her "Speech of January 21 1931" of the challenges that face women writ-ers who seek to represent previously unrepresented truths about "womens bodies [sic]" and "passions," given that the rational, self-censoring part of the woman writer's mind may be telling her that "conventions are still very strong" and that "'My dear you were going altogether too far. Men would be shocked.'"[7] In staging the possibility of lesbian sexuality in *The Dove*, Djuna Barnes engaged with the representational challenge that Woolf was to identify, broadening the range of the dramatic canon beyond the "obscene" truths about women that Ibsen had dramatized in *Hedda Gabler*, which *The Dove* parodies, but also deliberately and explicitly challeng-ing the "conventions" of the male-dominated cultural tradition that had previously rendered such truths invisible and unthinkable. Through the self-reflexive dimensions of *The Dove*, Barnes posited a co-productive rela-tionship between representation and lived experience that corresponded with the ideas about the emancipatory potential of feminist literary, dra-matic, and theatrical practice that inform Woolf's writings on actresses and her novel *Between the Acts*. This interplay between art and life was liter-alized through the contiguities of character and artist in actual historical enactments of emergent modern sexual identities by such figures as Edith Craig and Radclyffe Hall. In this chapter, *The Dove* serves as a premise for a consideration both of the feminist redefinition of obscenity as an integral aspect of the development of modern theatre and drama, and of the relation of this feminist–modernist staging of the "obscene" to the performance of sexual identity on the sociopolitical stage and in the practice of everyday life.

Described by one early reviewer as "a crisp little essay into abnormality, filled with Freudian significances and probably [. . .] completely incom-prehensible to most of the audience,"[8] *The Dove* concerns two aging and unmarried sisters, Amelia and Vera Burgson, who live, together with a young woman they have taken in called the Dove, in an apartment that, according to Barnes's stage directions, they have decorated in "garish [. . .] reds and pinks" and with reclining furniture in "an evident attempt to make the place look luxuriously sensual."[9] One of the sisters, Amelia, is described by Barnes as "vitally hysterical," and the play is generally pervaded by a claustrophobic atmosphere of sexual repression, made dangerous by the fact that "[t]here are firearms everywhere," swords on the walls, and "a pistol or two [lying] in chairs" (149). This threat of a violent eruption of repressed sexuality is heightened by Vera's account of a daydream she once had: "I dreamt I was a Dresden doll and that I had been blown down by the wind and that I broke all to pieces – that is, my arms and head broke all to pieces – but that I was surprised to find that my china skirt had become flexible, as if it were made of chiffon and lace" (153–154). Just out of sight off stage, in what would be the entry to the apartment, is a reproduction of the painting *Two Venetian Courtesans*[10] by the Renaissance artist Carpaccio that seems to signify for the sisters the wickedness of their illicit fantasy lives: thus, Vera tells the Dove, "It's because of that picture of the Venetian courtesans that I send Amelia out for the butter, I don't dare let the grocer call" (158). Yet while the Carpaccio painting represents what have tradition-ally been understood to be two courtesans sitting waiting for their male patrons, there are hints in the play that what the sisters are repressing is in fact lesbian desire: Vera, for example, mentions finding in her sister's bed "some Parisienne bathing girl's picture stuck full of pin holes" (152), while Amelia reports an odd yet somehow flirtatious encounter with a woman selling fish at the market (159) and says with reference to the Dove, "Ah, God, it's a sin, truly it's a sin that I, a woman with temperament, permit a young girl to stay in the same room with me!" (159). For her part, the Dove tells Vera that she loves Amelia (152), and she seems to function in the world of the play as a kind of opposite to a repressive force, frighteningly provoca-tive in what Vera describes as her quality of "[wanting] to prevent nothing" (154). Toward the end of the play, Amelia, wearing red shoes, begins to dance hysterically and with mounting anger and desperation until finally she drops to her knees in front of the Dove. At first, it seems that she will reach for the sword that the Dove has been polishing throughout the play, but instead she takes hold of the Dove's hand and "clutches it convulsively" (161). At this point, the Dove slowly bares Amelia's left shoulder and breast and, according to the stage directions, "[leans] down" and "sets her teeth in" (161). The Dove then exits carrying a pistol and a shot is heard off stage. Amelia goes out to investigate and "[reappears] in the doorway with the

picture of the Venetian courtesans, through which there is a bullet hole"
(161). In the play's final line, Amelia says "slowly, but with emphasis," "*This
is obscene!*" (161).[11]

Anne B. Dalton's reading of *The Dove* as part of "Barnes's lifelong writing
cure"[12] as an incest survivor exemplifies a critical tendency to read Barnes's
work as autobiography, yet Dalton's biographical analysis of a play that
is so clearly concerned with representation diminishes the gestic critical
impact of Barnes's closing image and the feminist challenge that it poses to
hegemonic representational practices. In developing an alternative reading,
it is worth noting that a central feature of much of Barnes's writing is its
verbal complexity. Indeed, Barnes's biographer Phillip Herring reports that
at one point while T. S. Eliot was editing her 1958 play *The Antiphon*,
he "surrounded himself with three dictionaries in order to deal with lexical
obscurities,"[13] while Barnes's one-time assistant Hank O'Neal has noted that
a prominent feature of the tiny, cluttered Greenwich Village apartment in
which Barnes spent the last forty-two years of her life was "[a] set of English
dictionaries, very old and very large."[14] Shari Benstock has described Barnes
as "the one woman Modernist whose writing consistently turns on classical
sources of English words,"[15] and as James B. Scott has noted, Barnes's "most
imaginative efforts look both backward to a vocabulary old-to-archaic,
as well as forward, to constantly reinvent a language, challenging in its
metaphors and images, yet at once precise and elegant."[16] Given Barnes's
characteristic interest in the lexical particularities of words, the final line of
The Dove – "*This* is obscene!" – invites closer consideration.

In his *Encyclopedia of Word and Phrase Origins*, Robert Hendrickson
writes that

[a]ccording to one theory, *obscene* originally meant "off the stage" in ancient Greek
drama, deriving from the Greek *ob*, "against," and *scaena*, "stage." What was kept
off the stage in Greek drama was violence [. . .], not sex, of which there was plenty
in comedies and satyr plays [. . .]. Obscenity wasn't associated with sex until the
word made its appearance in England toward the end of the 17th [sic] century.
However, *obscene* is of obscure origin, and another theory, less likely, derives the
word from the Latin *caenum*, "mud." Shakespeare was the first to use *obscene* in the
sense of offensive to the senses, that is, disgusting, filthy, foul, etc., in *Richard II*:
". . . so heinous, black[,] obscene a deed." The Bard probably based the word on
the French *obscene*, meaning the same, which came from the Latin word *obscenus*.
Within five years or so, *obscene* was being used to mean "indecent and lewd" as
well.[17]

While the idea that the word "obscene" derives "from the Greek *ob*, 'against,'
and *scaena*, 'stage'" is not proven or unanimously credited,[18] this sense

of the word was in circulation in the late-nineteenth and early-twentieth centuries. The sexologist Havelock Ellis, for example, whose 1897 work *Sexual Inversion* was tried for obscenity, used the word "obscene" "in a colourless and technical sense to indicate the usually unseen or obverse side of life, the side behind the scenes, [. . .] and not implying anything necessarily objectionable,"[19] while D. H. Lawrence similarly suggested in his 1929 essay "Pornography and Obscenity" that the word might have been "derived from *obscena*: that which might not be represented on the stage."[20] The possibility of a theatrical derivation continues to inform some current usage[21] and literalizes Mary Caputi's recent association of obscenity with "the transgression of boundaries."[22] However doubtful in terms of veracity, this theatrical etymological tradition is significant for a reading of *The Dove*, where, in the final image, Amelia stands at the threshold of the stage, holding the destroyed picture of the two Venetian courtesans that has until this point remained out of sight off stage and asserting emphatically, "*This* is obscene."

At a time when homosexuality was equated with obscenity and when its explicit representation on the stage was generally prohibited,[23] the image of the Dove biting Amelia's shoulder or breast that immediately precedes the destruction of the off-stage painting was unquestionably provocative; to borrow a turn of phrase from Christopher Craft's queer reading of the cucumber sandwich scene in Oscar Wilde's *The Importance of Being Earnest*, at this moment in *The Dove*, "the obscene becomes the scenic."[24] Not surprisingly, misquoting the play's final line as "It is obscene! It is obscene!" one reviewer of the 1926 production of *The Dove* added, "And probably it is." This same reviewer also complained of the play's "decadent talk of most atrocious significance," "frequent references to nasty Parisian lithograph pictures hanging on the wall,"[25] and over-reliance on "the fine points of Freudian symbolism," and described Amelia as "one of the esoterically sensual sisters" who "[voices] her strange ecstasies in a long, jumbled monologue" before being bitten on the shoulder by "the girl who is in love with her."[26]

Yet while Barnes extended the field of the "scenic" beyond the gay male and heterosexual obscenities of two of her primary literary influences, Oscar Wilde and James Joyce, to encompass the unrepresented transgression of lesbian desire, she was not simply concerned with the act of making visible on stage that which had previously been considered obscene and unfit for representation. Rather, as the comparative implicit in Amelia's emphatic "*this*" makes clear, *The Dove* constituted a larger critique of the representational tradition exemplified by Carpaccio's *Two Venetian Courtesans*, which was described by Victorian art critic John Ruskin as "the best picture in the world."[27] Indeed, the emphasis in Amelia's closing line suggests a revaluation that shifts the charge of obscenity from the on-stage action to the painting and the cultural tradition that it represents, a tradition that is not limited to the visual arts but, as Barnes's wordplay with the theatrical "ob/scene" insists, encompasses the theatre as well.

The on-stage sisters Amelia and Vera double the two figures in Carpaccio's painting (figure 4), who resemble each other closely enough to seem to be related, with one appearing to be somewhat older than the other. In the painting, the two women are seen in profile, looking outward beyond the frame of the image. Though the painting has commonly been known as *Two Venetian Courtesans* (or simply *Two Courtesans*), art historian Jan Lauts has noted that this title "has little to justify it" as "[t]he costume does not differ from that customary in bourgeois circles during the period,"[28] while Vittorio Sgarbi has explained that the painting was in fact originally one part of a two-panel decoration of a door that, taken as a whole with the other panel depicting a hunting scene, represents the theme of *Waiting* and should more properly be known by that title.[29] Thus, Sgarbi interprets the painting as depicting two "noble, highly moral ladies [. . .] awaiting the return of their men from a leisurely hunt" and writes that

[t]he subject's essentially domestic and "feminine" nature, with its tones of intimacy and its marked sense of psychological depth, makes *Waiting* truly exceptional among Carpaccio's works. The rigid dignity of appearance and bearing that the painter attributes to the two women [. . .] (the young one, deadened by boredom, stares into space; the older one attempts futilely to enliven the melancholy atmosphere), [. . .] reveals an unusual level of understanding of the sacrifices and silent worries of the housewife's life.[30]

Whether Carpaccio's painting represents courtesans or respectable wives, its subject is two passive women who look not at each other or at their immediate environment but beyond the frame of the painting as they await the animating force of absent men.

Sister-characters in drama often function as devices by which to signify difference,[31] but the doubling of the sisters in *The Dove* with the two unidentified but clearly related figures in the Carpaccio painting suggests an interest in sameness rather than difference – in *homo* rather than *hetero* – so that the painting functions as a dramaturgical device by which Barnes can articulate a critique of compulsory heterosexuality and of the assymetrical power dynamics of the gender relations upon which it insists. With the destruction of this ob/scene – off-stage – canonical painting at the end of

Figure 4 *Two Venetian Courtesans* (circa 1495–1510), by Vittore Carpaccio.

a play that might be considered obscene by conventional standards for its suggestion of lesbian desire, and with the emphatic "*This*" of the play's final line, Barnes anticipated charges of obscenity that might be leveled at *The Dove* and redirected them toward a male-dominated representational tradition that precluded the possibility of autonomous female sexuality, thus redefining the obscene from a feminist perspective.

Leigh Gilmore has explained that, according to the Obscene Publications Act introduced in England in 1857, obscenity was "an effect rather than a cause or an inherent wrong"[32] and that, as specified in the Hicklin doctrine of 1868, "'The test of obscenity is this, whether the tendency of the matter charged as obscenity is to deprave and corrupt those whose minds are open to such immoral influences and into whose hands a publication of this sort may fall.'"[33] Thus, Gilmore argues, "throughout its historical development in British common law," the essence of which was heavily influential in the United States, "obscenity function[ed] as a legal name for what can be described as a broadly and loosely conceived threat to an emerging modern social order. In the absence of a legal definition of what obscenity *is*, obscenity's criminality exists wholly in relation to what it threatens."[34] Modern censorship of the sexually obscene is in this sense connected to the earlier censorial focus on religion and politics, so that sexual obscenity can be understood as a challenge to the prevailing moral and political order, while obscenity charges function as, in Gilmore's terms, "a legal form of social control."[35] In calling Carpaccio's painting obscene, then, Barnes calls attention to the relativity of perceptions of obscenity and suggests that the representational tradition for which the painting stands, underpinned by conventional gender politics, has a "depraving and corrupting" effect – witness the hysterical sisters in *The Dove*, for whom the painting functions as a repressive delimiter of experience. Barnes's own making scenic of ob/scene lesbian sexuality thus supports Dianne Chisholm's suggestion that "artistic obscenity [is] a particular practice of transgression that shocks and disperses the reactive forces of the sexual status quo while mobilizing radical, historical, and political insight."[36] The comparative "*This*" of *The Dove*'s final line extends such insight beyond the immediate world of the play to redefine and intervene in a larger representational tradition.

Nicholas de Jongh has suggested that the roots of early-twentieth-century British and American dramatic representations of homosexuality may be located in the "modern theatre movement of social analysis, dissent and nonconformity that Ibsen inaugurated" and in the somewhat earlier genre of "'Woman with a Past' society dramas" that Ibsen's realist plays revised,[37] while Laurence Senelick has observed that in late-nineteenth- and early-twentieth-century drama, "lesbians were largely subsumed under the categories 'hysterical women,' 'emancipated women' or '*femmes fatales*' when they made rare appearances on the dramatic stage."[38] With its hysterical women, guns, off-stage courtesans, and thematically significant portrait, *The Dove* suggests familiarity with Ibsen's 1890 play *Hedda Gabler*, as does the fact that Barnes spoke on more than one occasion of committing suicide "beautifully,"[39] an idea borrowed from Ibsen's title character. But while such thoughts of beautiful suicide suggest identification with Hedda Gabler, Barnes also expressed annoyance with what she described as Ibsen's "sort of matrimonial symbolism always throwing itself off high mountains or getting wind blown at some fjord."[40] Barnes's critique of the tragic heterosexuality of Ibsen's dramatic world was admittedly facetious.[41] Still, conjoined with her apparent parodic revisioning of *Hedda Gabler* in *The Dove* and the historical association of modernist representations of homosexuality with the realist dramatic tradition pioneered by Ibsen, it invites consideration of *Hedda Gabler* – one of the central texts of modern drama – in relation to the feminist redefinition of the obscene that Barnes's 1923 play proposes.[42]

In early reviews of *The Dove*, references to the play's "Freudian significances" and "Freudian symbolism" seem to function as coded references to homosexuality, and given Barnes's description of her character Amelia as "vitally hysterical," it is worth noting, as have many recent feminist critics and theorists, that hysteria – or "the daughter's disease," as Elaine Showalter has called it[43] – has historically been associated with homosexuality and bisexuality, as well as with feminism. In his "Fragment of an Analysis of a Case of Hysteria," also known as "Dora," for example, Freud wrote that "masculine or, more properly speaking, *gynaecophilic* currents of feeling are to be regarded as typical of the unconscious erotic life of hysterical girls,"[44] while in his "Hysterical Phantasies and Their Relation to Bisexuality," he wrote that "an hysterical symptom is the expression of both a masculine and a feminine unconscious sexual phantasy."[45] The resistance toward normative gender roles implied in the repressed homosexual desires and bisexual identifications of turn-of-the-century hysterics linked them to the emergent feminist movement, so that, as Showalter has suggested, "hysteria and feminism" can be seen to have "exist[ed] on a kind of continuum."[46] Indeed, in Hélène Cixous's postmodern revision of Freud's case history of Dora in her 1976 play *Portrait of Dora*, the hysteric is figured as protofeminist, a quintessentially modern woman walking out on Freud on 1 January 1900, signaling the dawn of a new age for women.[47]

As Gail Finney and Elin Diamond have demonstrated,[48] Ibsen's *Hedda Gabler* supports the notion of a relationship between hysteria, transgressive female desire, bisexual identification, and feminism. In some peculiar but telling stage directions, for example, Ibsen differentiates Hedda and her old acquaintance Thea Elvsted in terms of their hair, noting that Hedda's "hair is an attractive medium brown, but not particularly abundant," whereas Thea's "is remarkably light, almost a white-gold, and unusually abundant and wavy."[49] Thea's hair is an object of fascination for Hedda, who, in what has been read as an aspect of "hysterical discourse,"[50] alternately strokes it or threatens to burn it off; and while I don't want to suggest that Hedda's symptomatic fascination with Thea's hair is evidence of homosexual desire, it does make visible her simultaneous attraction to and rejection of the conventional ideal of femininity that Thea represents and thus it signifies the incapacitating ambivalence of the hysteric's simultaneously resistant masculine identification and compliant feminine submission.

In his working notes on the play, Ibsen himself described Hedda as a repressed hysteric who "wants to live a *man's* life wholly" but has "misgivings" due to "[h]er inheritance, what is implanted in her,"[51] while in an 1890 letter, he explained that by entitling his play with the character's maiden name, he intended "to indicate that Hedda as a personality is to be regarded rather as her father's daughter than as her husband's wife."[52] The importance of Hedda's father General Gabler in the dynamic of the drama is clear from the opening stage directions, where Ibsen positions his painted image as a sort of "vanishing point"[53] in Hedda's realistic stage world. As Kay Unruh Des Roches has written, "the framed portrait of General Gabler on the back wall is balanced midstage by the framed entrance into the back room and downstage by the frame of the proscenium: a frame within a frame within a frame with General Gabler dead centre."[54] The most significant feature of the overall stage picture, the General's portrait ultimately serves as an immediate backdrop when Hedda's body is revealed after she has committed suicide "beautifully" with a pistol from the matched pair she inherited from her father. As the twin pistols suggest, General Gabler's legacy to his daughter is double, consisting of counterposed aspects that cancel each other out. On the one hand, as the sole parent of a female child, the General instilled in Hedda a taste for such traditionally masculine activities as shooting and riding, as well as a male-associated impulse toward self-determination, understood in the play in sexual and creative terms. On the other hand, as a powerful representative of the patriarchal social order, the General accounts for Hedda's indoctrination into traditional values relating to women, as manifested in her belief that she had "danced [herself] out" and that "[her] time was up" when she reached her late twenties and was still unmarried (725). The title "*Hedda Gabler*" thus underlines the fact that the contradictions inherent in the General's legacy are not resolved over the course of the play (as such titles as "*Hedda*" or "*Hedda Tesman*" might suggest), but instead remain central to Hedda's character. Indeed, as her use of her father's pistol to commit suicide signifies, her patriarchal legacy eventually kills her.

At the start of the play, Hedda has just returned from her honeymoon and is faced with the consequences of having entered into the "everlast-ing" relationship of marriage with George Tesman (724), which include an unwanted pregnancy. Hedda's discomfort with her new roles as wife and prospective mother is evident in her hostility toward her husband's doting Aunt Julie, whose new bonnet she deliberately insults, and, more importantly, in the fact that when she is left alone on stage for a moment, she "moves about the room, raising her arms and clenching her fists as if in a frenzy. Then she flings back the curtains from the glass door and stands there, looking out" (705). Ibsen's stage directions make evident the feelings of claustrophobia and desperation that her marriage and preg-nancy have provoked in Hedda, yet the character herself appears to lack self-awareness as to the motivations that underlie the anti-social behav-ior to which her feelings give rise. Hedda is troubled by her treatment of Aunt Julie and returns to the subject of the bonnet with Judge Brack in Act II, "nervously [. . .] pacing the room" as she tries to account for her conduct: "Well, it's – these things come over me, just like that, suddenly. And I can't hold back. (*Throws herself down in the armchair by the stove.*) Oh, I don't know myself how to explain it" (728). Inga-Stina Ewbank has suggested that Ibsen's female characters share "the sense that experi-ence is constantly outstripping both the vocabulary and the structure of language,"[55] and indeed Hedda experiences her desire for self-determination as an unspeakable impulse. Moments after her loss for words to explain about the bonnet, however, she entertains the notion of getting Tesman to go into politics and thus first acknowledges what she later describes as the desire "to have power over a human being" (745) that is so obviously a displacement of a desire to control her own destiny. In the world of the play, then, which, as Gail Finney has suggested, dramatizes the tragic effects of what Foucault called the "hysterization of women's bodies" – that is, the reduction of women to some version of the maternal function[56] – the possibility of female sexual and creative autonomy is unimaginable and, consequently, unspeakable: "Oh, I don't know myself how to explain it."

In one of the early documents on naturalism in the theatre, Emile Zola wrote, "I am waiting for the surroundings to determine the characters, and for the characters to act according to the logic of facts, combined with the logic of their own temperament."[57] In the case of *Hedda Gabler*, the secondary characters constitute part of the surroundings, for not only does the play posit what Bert States has called "a Ptolomeic universe" which has at its center the Tesmans' drawing room, but, as Elin Diamond has added, "Hedda is the centripetal center" of the centripetal stage world.[58] As determinants of Hedda's character, the men and women that constitute her social surroundings account for the unspeakableness of her desires by representing the ways in which female sexuality and creativity are circumscribed and regulated within the world of the play that is presided over by the image of General Gabler as icon of patriarchal authority. Given a critical tendency to idealize Ibsen's dissolute writer-character Eilert Løvborg – in Joan Templeton's words, "the popular stance that if [Hedda] had sexually yielded to [him], her life would have been happy"[59] – it is worth noting that although Ibsen wrote in his working notes on the play that "[t]he new idea in [Løvborg's] book is that of progress resulting from the comradeship between man and woman,"[60] he chose to leave the subject matter of Løvborg's new work unspecified in the final draft of the play. Indeed, there is nothing particularly progressive about Løvborg's relationship with Thea Elvsted – she of the "unusually abundant and wavy" "white-gold" hair – who has left her husband to serve Løvborg in such conventional feminine roles as babysitter, confessor, muse, and secretary. Thus, Løvborg represents for Hedda no greater prospect of autonomy than her husband, who offers the possibility of motherhood, or the blackmailer Judge Brack, who seeks to subjugate her sexually. Moreover, whereas Freud suggested that double figures often represent "all the unfulfilled but possible futures to which we still like to cling in phantasy,"[61] the doubling of Hedda with an ob/scene counterpart – the off-stage prostitute Mademoiselle Diana, euphemistically described in the play as a "redheaded singer" (715) – functions ironically to underline the unthinkableness of female sexual and creative autonomy within Hedda's determining environment. Unable to conceive of alternatives to the subordinate roles available to women within these social surroundings, Hedda chooses death.

In his 1993 work *Speaking the Unspeakable: A Poetics of Obscenity*, Peter Michelson suggests that

[a]n aesthetics of obscenity implies a perceptual alteration whereby the obscene, a species of the ugly, is reconstituted to a function akin to that of the beautiful. In that sense it is a *contemplation* of the unspeakable and counterpoints traditional

aesthetic assumptions. [. . .] A poetics of obscenity, then, describes *speaking* the unspeakable and is defined by the artistic strategies used to change assumptions and perceptions.[62]

In *Hedda Gabler*, Ibsen exemplified Michelson's "poetics of obscenity," staging the unspeakable ob/scene of patriarchal culture but reconstituting this "obscene" as the beautiful through his sympathetic portrayal of his expressively inarticulate title character as a tragic figure at odds with a "depraving," "corrupting," and therefore obscene world that forecloses the possibility of female subjectivity, exemplified in the interrelated creative and sexual terms with which the play is centrally concerned. For this reason, *Hedda Gabler* is one of the definitive texts of feminist modernism, and it is not surprising that implications of obscenity infused early mainstream critical responses to the play. In an 1891 review of the first London production, for example, the anti-Ibsen critic Clement Scott described Hedda as "a lunatic" and "an unwomanly woman" and noted that "[a] woman more morally repulsive has seldom been seen on the stage,"[63] while another early reviewer complained that Ibsen's play was a "study of a malicious woman of evil instincts, jealous, treacherous, cold-hearted, and, as it seems to us, wholly out of place on the stage."[64] These claims that Ibsen's tragic representation of a female character's refusal to comply with conventional gender ideology was "wholly out of place on the stage" – that is to say, obscene – lend support to Leigh Gilmore's previously cited observation that the charges of obscenity directed at modernist literature were in intent a "form of social control."

Linda Hutcheon has defined parody as "repetition with critical distance that allows ironic signalling of difference at the very heart of similarity."[65] In *The Dove*, Barnes appropriated key motifs from *Hedda Gabler* – the repressed hysteric, the guns, the painting, the off-stage prostitute – but whereas Ibsen used these motifs to construct a tragedy, Barnes reworked them as parody to dramatize other, more emancipatory outcomes in terms of both sexual and representational practice. Barnes's staging of lesbian sexuality in *The Dove* literalizes and makes scenic Ibsen's "obscene" concern with unspeakable female desire, while the Carpaccio painting *Two Venetian Courtesans* makes explicit the gender and sexual politics of representation inherent in the portrait of General Gabler as iconic signifier of the hegemonic values of Hedda's world and her killing inheritance of them. Thus, both Ibsen and Barnes posit a "depraving" and "corrupting" relationship between patriarchal representation and women's lived experience. The General's portrait hangs intact over Hedda's dead body at the end of Ibsen's play, however, thereby arguably reinforcing the values that the play seems to critique. Carpaccio's painting of the courtesans is instead destroyed; and this destruction is essentially analogous to the challenge that Barnes's staging of lesbian desire – as the literalized expression of Hedda's unspeakable desire for sexual autonomy – had in itself already posed to the hegemonic representational tradition encompassing the Carpaccio painting, the portrait of General Gabler, and also, ultimately, as Barnes implies, Ibsen's play itself.

The disruption of the regulatory effect of the patriarchal and heterosexist cultural tradition on female sexuality that is dramatized through the destruction of the painting in *The Dove* corresponds with feminist theatre artist Edith Craig's self-representation through her portrayal of the French painter Rosa Bonheur in the British suffrage drama *A Pageant of Great Women*, which Craig not only performed in, but also conceived, directed, and designed. Unlike that of her lifelong lesbian companion Christopher St. John, Craig's sexuality is not explicitly documented. Biographer Katherine Cockin assumes that she was in fact a lesbian,[66] however, and certainly she was perceived as such by Vita Sackville-West, who was the model for Virginia Woolf's androgynous Orlando and once spent a night with Christopher St. John, and who described Craig, in later years at least, as "the most tearing old Lesbian."[67] In *Out on Stage: Lesbian and Gay Theatre in the Twentieth Century*, Alan Sinfield usefully differentiates the term "sexual dissidence" from "same-sex passion" by suggesting that the former term "invokes a wider range of practices and a degree of purposeful opposition."[68] While it is not possible to know exactly where to position Craig on what Adrienne Rich called "the lesbian continuum,"[69] I would nevertheless argue that through her portrayal of Rosa Bonheur, Craig signaled a sexual dissidence that may as yet have been unrecognizable to most, but that corresponded with the modern emergence of "lesbian" as a category of identity, soon to be exemplified in the figure of the novelist Radclyffe Hall.[70]

The issue of female sexuality was at once central to and problematic for the campaign for votes for women in England in the late-nineteenth and early-twentieth centuries. As Elaine Showalter has argued, *fin de siècle* "[s]exual anarchy began with the odd woman – the woman who could not marry" due to a population disparity of men and women revealed in the 1861 census and who, by her single status, "undermined the comfortable binary system of Victorian sexuality and gender roles."[71] According to

Showalter, at the same time that "unmarried women [. . .] were targeted as the initial beneficiaries of the women's suffrage movement," they were perceived in terms of "new definitions of sexuality" that "[moved] away from a mid-Victorian notion of female 'passionlessness'" toward an acknowledgment of "women's capacity for sexual pleasure" and a view of celibacy as psychologically and biologically harmful.[72] This sense of unmarried women as "a new political and sexual group"[73] informed "[t]he popular image of the odd woman," which, Showalter notes, "conflated elements of the lesbian, the angular spinster, and the hysterical feminist."[74] Prefiguring the so-called "New Woman" of the 1890s, who might remain single by choice,[75] this "odd" or "redundant" woman – exemplified in George Bernard Shaw's character Prossy in *Candida*, played by Edith Craig in the original production in 1897[76] – was, as Yopie Prins has stated, variously "recategorized" between the 1860s and 1890s as "a working woman, a suffragette, a single woman living outside the sphere of the family, a woman living with other women, a celibate woman, a mannish woman, a sexually autonomous woman [. . .]."[77] This late-nineteenth-century emergence of new female sexual identities was initially so closely linked to the suffrage campaign that Gail Cunningham has suggested that "[f]eminist thinkers in the late eighties and nineties appeared to be redirecting their energies from specific political and legal questions towards the formulation of a new morality, a new code of behaviour and sexual ethics."[78] Susan Kingsley Kent has further argued that the suffragists were in fact attempting "to redefine and recreate, by political means, the sexual culture of Britain" and that "[t]he vote became both the symbol of the free, sexually autonomous woman and the means by which the goals of a feminist sexual culture were to be attained."[79] As Lisa Tickner has noted, however, despite the close historical relationship between sexual concerns and the Victorian suffrage campaign, Edwardian suffragists were, for strategic reasons, "at pains to avoid" the association of "women's emancipation with sexual emancipation" and "the hint of promiscuity which hung around the popular image of the advanced woman of the 1890s."[80] *A Pageant of Great Women* shared the tone of righteous high-mindedness that characterized much of the imagery and rhetoric of the Edwardian suffrage campaign, including Elizabeth Robins's groundbreaking 1907 suffrage drama *Votes for Women*. At the same time, however, it tacitly staged some of the concerns with female sexuality associated with nineteenth-century feminism. In doing so, it supported Alan Sinfield's contention that "[t]heatre has been a particular site for the formation of dissident sexual identities" and that, while existing research on gay and lesbian theatre has tended to focus on issues of censorship and thus "produces a story of harassment and repression," there has in fact been "a lot more sexual dissidence in theatre than has been properly registered."[81]

Written by Cicely Hamilton at Edith Craig's request, the pageant was first staged in London in 1909 with a large cast of celebrities and then re-staged with local casts in a number of English cities between 1909 and 1912. Arguably the most important theatrical work of the British suffrage movement, if only for the sheer number of people it involved, the pageant was allegorical in its premise, with the figures of Woman and Prejudice arguing before Justice as to whether or not Woman is fit for and worthy of freedom. To support her claim that her demand is justified and to counter Prejudice's arguments to the contrary, Woman summons a series of "great women" from history, providing an opportunity for between forty and ninety female performers, depending on the particular production, to appear as spectacularly costumed Learned Women, Artists, Saints, Heroes, Rulers, and Warriors. In addition to Rosa Bonheur, this parade of "great women" included such figures as the lesbian poet Sappho, the cross-dressed soldiers Christian Davies and Hannah Snell and drummer-"boy" Mary Ann Talbot, and the then recently beatified Joan of Arc, whom Terry Castle has described as "a peculiarly Sapphic heroine."[82] Rosa Bonheur was played by Edith Craig in the first London production and in all subsequent productions, while the soldiers Hannah Snell and Christian Davies were originally played by Craig's companion Christopher St. John and by Cicely Hamilton, who has been identified as a lesbian by her biographer Lis Whitelaw.[83] The queer dimensions suggested by the involvement of these sexually dissident women in the original production of *A Pageant of Great Women* were further indicated by their conspicuous representation in the illustrations that were selected for publication in the 1910 Suffrage Shop edition of Hamilton's script. Among a total of fifteen illustrations were individual photographic portraits of Craig as Bonheur, St. John as Hannah Snell, and Hamilton as Christian Davies (twice, in both close-up and long-shot), as well as individual photographs of performers whose sexuality is not known in the roles of Sappho and Mary Ann Talbot[84] and a group shot of several of the remaining warriors, among them Joan of Arc, played by Pauline Chase, who, as Katharine Cockin has noted, was known for her portrayal of Peter Pan.[85] A photograph of Craig as Bonheur was featured on the cover of the programme of at least one later production (figure 5). Kerry Powell has noted that "[t]oward the close of the nineteenth century [sexologist] Richard von Krafft-Ebing diagnos[ed] female crossdressing on stage as a manifestation of the 'homosexual instinct.'"[86] The apparent preference on

Figure 5 Edith Craig as Rosa Bonheur (circa 1909–1910).

the part of Craig, Hamilton, and St. John for the cross-dressed characters in *A Pageant of Great Women* might have lent Krafft-Ebing's observation at least some support.

Indeed, the decision of these performers to associate themselves, through performance, with the homosexual and/or cross-dressed historical figures that they chose to portray in the pageant suggests a deliberate use of performance to articulate and make visible a newly emerging lesbian identity within the larger context of a production serving the primary purpose of suffrage propaganda. Notably, the highlight of the pageant in its original London production was the appearance of Edith Craig's mother, the aging but still celebrated actress Ellen Terry, in the role of the eighteenth-century actress Nance Oldfield, who was noteworthy within the pageant as one of the earliest women to perform on the English stage. In a rare moment of levity in a script made weighty by ponderous verse and a high moral tone, Terry as Nance Oldfield interrupted Woman's running commentary on the historical figures parading onto the stage and, in a clever passage connecting character and actress, became the only one of the many great women in the pageant to actually speak:

> By your leave,
> Nance Oldfield does her talking for herself!
> If you, Sir Prejudice, had had your way,
> There would be never an actress on the boards.
> Some lanky, squeaky boy would play my parts:
> And, though I say it, there'd have been a loss!
> The stage would be as dull as now 'tis merry –
> No Oldfield, Woffington, or – Ellen Terry! (31)

The connection between the historical figure and the living performer who was playing her that was made explicit in the case of Nance Oldfield and Ellen Terry pertained more generally to the other performers as well, as is indicated in an account of a 1910 production of the pageant, in which it was reported that

Londoners had opportunities to-day of seeing and hearing two methods of argument for the enfranchisement of women, one the fray or series of frays at Westminster, the other Miss Cicely Hamilton's beautiful pageant of women which filled the Aldwych Theatre to overflowing. Some of the pageant scenes were a curious commentary on the scenes at St Stephen's. For instance, when prejudice [sic] in the handsome form of Mr. Henry Ainley was declaring that women had always shirked warfare, it hardly needed the procession of warrior women to refute him, for many had just seen white-faced women fighting desperately with strong men at Westminster. [. . .] Many who took part in the pageant risked a non-appearance by appearing earlier in the day in the Westminster scenes, but one well-known actress [. . .] seemed none the worse for the spirited argument she conducted outside Palace Yard with some men in the crowd.[87]

Such perceived connections between the historical figures in the pageant and the contemporary women who performed them are of particular significance for a consideration of Edith Craig's ongoing performance of Rosa Bonheur, whose entrance in the pageant was signaled when Woman asked, "A man? No – Rosa Bonheur! / Back from the horse-fair, virile in her garb / As virile in her work!" (29).

Bonheur lived from 1822 to 1899 and achieved distinction as a painter of animals, being particularly acclaimed for her massively scaled 1853 work *The Horse Fair*, to which Woman refers in her commentary in the pageant. In order to gain access to the animal markets, stockyards, and slaughterhouses where she could directly observe the subjects of her paintings, Bonheur attained special permission from the police to wear men's clothing, which was otherwise illegal for women in France at the time. Bonheur preferred to cross-dress in her private life as well, however, and shared a home for forty years with a woman she described as "my wife."[88] Following this first wife's death, Bonheur lived out her own remaining years with another woman and, in 1900, was memorialized in the German sexologist Magnus Hirschfeld's journal of homosexual research with a photograph labeling her as a "mentally and physically pronounced example of a sexual intermediate."[89] As Katharine Cockin has noted, Bonheur was "likely [. . .], at least in some quarters," to have "signified lesbian in Britain" in the early-twentieth century.[90]

Bonheur has typically been seen strictly as a painter of animals and as a woman artist who, in Germaine Greer's words, "eschewed her sexuality altogether and [became] great as a result."[91] James Saslow has recently argued, however, that Bonheur's masterpiece *The Horse Fair* actually includes a covert self-portrait in which the artist represents herself in the guise of one of the horse-handlers and that this masculinized self-portrait necessitates a re-reading of Bonheur's work "as a radical intervention in the visual and cultural construction of nineteenth-century femininity and masculinity," "[presenting] an alternative vision of the modern female body, specifically the lesbian body, as a social and visual identity."[92]

Saslow's queer analysis of Bonheur's covert yet sexually dissident self-portrait invites a similar reading of Edith Craig's deliberate and ongoing association with the role of Bonheur throughout the stage life of *A Pageant of Great Women*. In *Hedda Gabler* and *The Dove*, the possibility of women's sexual and creative autonomy is precluded by the "depraving" and "corrupting" effects of the hegemonic representational tradition exemplified in Carpaccio's *Two Venetian Courtesans* and the portrait of General Gabler. In the pageant, however, Craig framed her own image through the pre-existing figure of a sexually and creatively transgressive woman artist whose life and work posed a challenge to the gender and sexual politics inherent in the paintings in *Hedda Gabler* and *The Dove*. In this way, Craig enacted her own sexual and cultural dissidence as a lesbian–feminist artist on the theatrical and political stage.

In the 1920s, a correspondent for *The Cambridge Daily News* suggested that Craig inspired a considerable female following, remarking on her "undeniable" and "captivating" charm and reporting knowing "quite a number of women who would unhesitatingly lay down their lives" for her and who regarded her not only as "their friend and teacher, but their very goddess."[93] Despite such reported adulation, however, it is unclear to what extent Craig's earlier self-representation through the figure of Bonheur registered with her contemporary spectators: like the painter's covert self-portrait, Craig's making lesbian identity scenic within the larger context of *A Pageant of Great Women* may have gone mostly unnoticed because of the fact that it was, as yet, generally unthinkable.

In her 1993 book *The Apparitional Lesbian*, Terry Castle observes that "[w]hen it comes to lesbians [. . . ,] many people have trouble seeing what's in front of them,"[94] and certainly, the early reviewers of *The Dove* felt that Barnes's play might have been "'over the heads of most of the audience.'"[95] Indeed, at that time, female homosexuality remained largely invisible on the political and cultural stage, perhaps nowhere more ironically so than in England, where it was decided in 1921 that, though acts of "gross indecency" between men had been outlawed since 1885, female homosexuality should not be criminalized because to criminalize it would be to create awareness that it existed, and to create awareness that it existed would in turn be to foster thoughts and desires that would otherwise be unthinkable. According to this logic, the very idea of female homosexuality was obscene in its potential to "deprave" and "corrupt," and therefore the idea had necessarily to be suppressed. Judith Butler has pointed out that

oppression works not merely through acts of overt prohibition, but covertly, through the constitution of viable subjects and through the corollary constitution of a domain of unviable (un)subjects [. . .] who are neither named nor prohibited within the economy of the law. Here oppression works through the production of a

domain of unthinkability and unnameability. Lesbianism is not explicitly prohibited in part because it has not even made its way into the thinkable, the imaginable,
that grid of cultural intelligibility that regulates the real and the nameable. How,
then, to "be" a lesbian in a political context in which the lesbian does not exist?
That is, in a political discourse that wages its violence against lesbianism in part
by excluding lesbianism from discourse itself?[96]

Butler then asks whether this "exclusion [of the lesbian] from ontology" can
"itself become a rallying point for resistance."[97] This appears to have been
the case for the lesbian novelist Radclyffe Hall, whose stated motive for
writing her 1928 work *The Well of Loneliness* was to "[smash] the conspiracy
of silence" in order to "encourage the inverted [. . .] to declare themselves"
and "face up to a hostile world in their true colours . . . with dignity and
courage," and to generate among heterosexuals "a fuller and more tolerant
understanding."[98] Through the highly publicized trial of Hall's novel on
charges of obscenity, "the idea of 'the lesbian' as a specific identity and
image was," as Sonja Ruehl has written, "given wide public currency"[99] –
a currency it did not yet have when Edith Craig took to the stage in the
part of Rosa Bonheur between 1909 and 1912.

In *A Pageant of Great Women*, the potential for "spectacular effect"[100] was
one of the selection criteria for the historical figures, and as an avid theatregoer at the height of her literary career in the 1920s, Radclyffe Hall may
have learned something about the power of costume to articulate identity
from what she saw on the stage. Hall in fact purchased some of her more
striking accessories, including a cape and a sombrero, at a London theatrical costume shop, and her fashionable appearance, together with that
of her equally stylish but more feminine lover Una Troubridge, helped to
establish the early-twentieth-century image of the lesbian as, in Havelock
Ellis's words, "terribly modern & shingled & monocled."[101] Indeed, whereas
Katharine Cockin has suggested that the performers who appeared in *A
Pageant of Great Women* may have been regarded simply as "famous and
beautiful women in fancy dress,"[102] Hall's flamboyance as a public figure
committed to making lesbianism visible in the public sphere appears at
least in part to have precipitated the vicious attack on *The Well of Loneliness*
by James Douglas in *The Sunday Express* that resulted in the prosecution
of the novel on charges of obscenity. Certainly, the increasing visibility
of homosexuals who "flaunt themselves in public places with increasing
effrontery and more insolently provocative bravado" was a recurring com-
plaint in Douglas's editorial.[103] In Douglas's view, homosexuality was an
"unutterable putrefaction," "undiscussable" and "inadmissible,"[104] and
therefore Hall's novel had necessarily to be banned.

The Well of Loneliness is a sympathetic treatment of the development of the lesbian writer Stephen Gordon from painful tomboy childhood through to romantically unhappy adulthood. Toward the end of the novel, in a scene set in a grim Parisian gay bar, a kindly acquaintance, Adolphe Blanc, suggests to Stephen that the tormented and self-loathing frequenters of the homosexual underworld need one of their own to speak out for them, not in specialized medical terms but in plain language that will gain them tolerance and understanding in the world at large.[105] Ed Madden has read this scene as "a self-reflexive justification of [. . .] an autobiographically based novel by an author who sees herself as speaking for her people" and has suggested that the novel is ultimately "about its own inspiration."[106] Thus, Stephen's gradual realization of her role as martyred spokesperson for voiceless gays and lesbians reads as a rationale for Hall's own authorship of the text in which her writer-character figures and which concludes with a cry to God for gays' and lesbians' right to existence.

The metatextual connection between Hall and Stephen Gordon was enhanced by the ensuing obscenity trial, which established Hall in the public imagination as a lesbian martyr in the manner of her suffering protagonist, whose name recalls the first Christian martyr Saint Stephen, stoned to death by non-believers.[107] Over the course of the trial, Hall's own lawyer initially attempted to deny to the court the sexuality of the novel's main characters, and Hall was kept from taking the stand in defense of her own work because her book was on trial rather than she herself. As well, Hall was silenced upon threat of expulsion from the courtroom when she disrupted the proceedings to protest against Judge Chartres Biron's misreading of a passage of her book, and the many defense witnesses assembled to refute the charges of obscenity, among them such prominent literary figures as Virginia Woolf and E. M. Forster, were denied the opportunity to testify on the grounds that it was for the judge, not the witnesses, to determine whether or not the book was obscene. Following these proceedings, Judge Biron concluded that although the novel was artfully written and contained "no gross or filthy words,"[108] it did not "[suggest] that anyone with the horrible tendencies described is in the least degree blameworthy," but, rather, represented homosexuals "with admiration" and as "attractive people" and described "certain acts [. . .] in the most alluring terms."[109] For these reasons, Biron decided, the novel had the potential to "deprave" and "corrupt" and was therefore obscene and unsuitable for public consumption: all seized copies were to be destroyed. The cultural significance of *The Well of Loneliness* was thus perhaps not so much in the novel in and of itself, the literary merits of which many have doubted, but in the real-life enactment in

the obscenity trial proceedings and outcome of the very silencing and efface-
ment that the book was intended to challenge and transform. Paradoxically,
then, in its public staging of the forcible silencing and rendering invisible of
lesbians within patriarchal and homophobic culture through the determination of obscenity, the trial made lesbians more visible in their invisibility
than they had ever been before.

I began this chapter with a consideration of Djuna Barnes's play on the word
"obscene" at the end of *The Dove*, and I want to note now the significance
of her use of the present tense "is" rather than the past tense "was" in the
line "*This* is obscene." Barnes's choice of verb tense in this final line raises
questions about the mode of perception of what is visible on the stage at
the end of the play. While the painting of the Venetian courtesans that was
out of sight off stage is in the end brought on stage and declared obscene,
the sisters Amelia and Vera remain on stage as well, and inasmuch as they
continue to be perceived as obscene for what the 1926 reviewer that I quoted
earlier referred to as their "esoteric sensuality," they are not *truly* seen in the
sense of being regarded from a non-homophobic perspective. Rather, they
remain ob/scene despite their presence on stage, and as long as this misper-
ception of them persists, the obscenity that Barnes ascribes to the canonical
painting that is now in full view is likely to remain unrecognized as well.

In her 1929 work of feminist–modernist literary theory and criticism *A
Room of One's Own*, Virginia Woolf suggested, with a sly reference to the
obscenity trial of *The Well of Loneliness*, that previously unrepresented fictional content relating to the lives of women – say, for example, that a girl
named Chloe liked a girl named Olivia – would require the development
of new fictional forms.[110] More recently, Teresa de Lauretis has linked the
difficulty of "defining an autonomous form of female sexuality and desire"
with the challenge of "devising strategies of representation which will, in
turn, alter the standard of vision, the frame of reference of visibility, of
what can be seen."[111] The modernist theatre theorist and practitioner Bertolt
Brecht would have identified "alienation" as the objective of the representational project that de Lauretis describes. According to Brecht, "alienation
[. . .] is necessary to all understanding,"[112] its intended effect being "to free
socially-conditioned phenomena from that stamp of familiarity which pro-
tects them against our grasp today"[113] and "to allow the spectator to criticize
constructively from a social point of view."[114] This effect of alienation was
to be achieved by taking that which is so familiar as to seem "the most
obvious thing in the world"[115] and representing it in such a way that it
is at once familiar and unfamiliar, denaturalized, or "made strange."[116] In

The Dove, Djuna Barnes set out to alienate, "make strange," or "queer" the hegemonic representational tradition – to free it from its obscuring "stamp of familiarity" and, in de Lauretis's words, "alter the standard of vision, the frame of reference of visibility," so as to enable perception of its naturalized and consequently unseen gender and sexual politics and to gain imaginative space for "defining an autonomous form of female sexuality and desire." By her interlinking of modern sexualities and modernist representation through the question of the obscene, Barnes thus crystallized a central aspect of the development of feminist–modernist theatre and drama ranging from Ibsen's realist classic *Hedda Gabler* to Edith Craig's self-portraiture through the figure of Rosa Bonheur in *A Pageant of Great Women*. The transformative development of previously unscripted gender roles and sexualities in theatre and drama in turn had its off-stage equivalent in the flamboyant performance of lesbian identity through the public persona of the elegantly androgynous Radclyffe Hall, whose "whole aura," remarked one newspaper reporter, was that of "high-brow modernism."[117]

CHAPTER 5

Writing/performing:
Virginia Woolf between the acts

On 10 February 1910, at the invitation of her younger brother Adrian
Stephen and his friend Horace Cole, Virginia Woolf[1] was, as Quentin Bell
reports, "delighted to take part" in the audacious practical joke that became
known as the *Dreadnought* Hoax.[2] Together with five other impostors, she
set off by train for Weymouth, where the Home Fleet was anchored and
the Admiral had received a telegram purporting to be from the head of
the Foreign Office and advising him that the Emperor of Abyssinia and his
entourage would be paying him a visit. The "Abyssinians" – Woolf, Duncan
Grant, Guy Ridley, and Anthony Buxton as the Emperor – had spent the
morning at a theatrical costume shop being done up in dark greasepaint,
false beards and moustaches, turbans, caftans, and jewels (figure 6). Now,
with Stephen and Cole in tow as interpreter and Foreign Office representative, they were met at Weymouth by a naval officer, who escorted
them aboard HMS *Dreadnought*, "the flagship of the Home Fleet, the most
formidable, the most modern and the most secret man o' war then afloat."[3]
The Emperor and princes toured the ship, inspected the Honour Guard,
and conversed with the Admiral through their interpreter Stephen, whose
"Abyssinian" consisted of a few words of Swahili and some mispronounced
Homer and Virgil. Then, declining a twenty-one-gun salute and refresh-
ments that might have disturbed their disguises, they returned undetected
to London, where the story was leaked by Cole to the newspapers and generated concern in the House of Commons that the British Navy had been
made to look ridiculous. When it was rumored that the Admiral and officers of the *Dreadnought* were to be reprimanded for the incident, Stephen
and Grant apologized to the First Lord of the Admiralty and offered to
take the blame upon themselves. The matter only really came to an end,
however, when several officers who had discovered the identities of the
hoaxers visited Cole and Grant privately and subjected each to a caning on
the backside. Whether or not honour was restored by this means, the Navy
reportedly intensified its security measures relating to telegrams as a result

Figure 6 "The Emperor of Abyssinia and his suite" (1910), with Virginia Stephen (later Woolf) seated at the left.

of the hoax, enabling Woolf to remark thirty years later in talks that she gave in 1940 to the Rodmell Women's Institute and the Memoir Club, "I am glad to think that I too have been of help to my country."[4]

The connection between Woolf's involvement in the *Dreadnought* Hoax and her subsequent career as a feminist writer has not gone unnoticed. Quentin Bell, for example, discussing Woolf's incorporation of the hoax and canings into her 1921 short story "A Society," concludes that "the theme of masculine honour, of masculine violence and stupidity, of gold-laced masculine pomposity, remained with her for the rest of her life";[5] Phyllis Rose has described the hoax as "a primal event" in Woolf's life, "emblematic of much of her career" in its enactment of her "rebellion against paternal authority";[6] and Jane Marcus has suggested that the hoax was Woolf's rehearsal for her critique of British imperialism in *The Waves*.[7] But in addition to anticipating the critical perspective that was to emerge in her later work, Woolf's participation in the hoax suggests an interest in performance as a site of subversive potential that is borne out by the fact that when she returned to the subject of the *Dreadnought* in her two 1940 talks, she was also in the process of completing her final novel *Between the Acts* (1941), which incorporates an entire pageant of English literary history and in which performance functions as a central metaphor.[8] This chapter will analyze how Woolf used performance in *Between the Acts* to establish a productive relationship between the creative projects of art and everyday life and to demonstrate how the performative acts of feminist artists like herself might contribute to the transformation of gender norms that she believed were devastating in their personal, social, and political consequences. Woolf's use of performance in her final novel thus ultimately serves to clarify her sense of the emancipatory potential of her own writing, but it also constitutes a theory of the sociopolitical operations of art, and as such, it offers a way to conceptualize the historical impact of feminist–modernist cultural practice more generally.

Woolf's reviews of the Art Theatre production of *The Cherry Orchard* (1920) and the Old Vic production of *Twelfth Night* (1933) provide a useful starting point for this discussion of *Between the Acts*. These reviews are concerned largely with the difference between reading and seeing plays and with the qualities that distinguish the theatre event from other art experiences. They also point toward performance as a way to contest accepted readings of familiar texts and bring alternative readings into the mainstream of cultural discourse. In the reviews, Woolf describes play-readers' initial contact with a stage production as a disturbing confrontation in which a theatre company's "overwhelmingly positive and definite" embodiment of a play[9] crashes up against the highly personalized versions that readers have conceived in the private, insubstantial theatres of their imaginations. During the first act of *The Cherry Orchard*, Woolf recalls, "readers, now transformed into seers, felt themselves shocked and outraged" by what was happening on stage: "The beautiful, mad drama which I had staged often enough in the dim recesses of my mind was now hung within a few feet of me, hard, crude, and over-emphatic, like a cheap coloured print of the real thing."[10] As the production continued, however, and the initial shock dissipated, the actors' version gradually began to influence the "reader's version" until in the end Woolf felt herself completely engaged, "like a piano played upon at last, not in the middle only but all over the keyboard and with the lid left open so that the sound goes on" (447). Having experienced "nothing comparable" when simply reading *The Cherry Orchard*, Woolf can only conclude that "[reading] plays is an occupation for the afflicted only, and one to be viewed with pity, as we pity blind men spelling out their Shakespeare with their fingers upon sheets of cardboard" (447).

The Old Vic's production of *Twelfth Night* was at its outset as appalling for Woolf as the Art Theatre's production of *The Cherry Orchard* had been. So far beyond recognition did the actor-embodied characters "expand [her] visionary characters" that, as she sat "gaping at the ruins of the play, at the travesty of the play," Woolf wanted to say to them, "You are not Malvolio; or Sir Toby either, [. . .] but merely impostors" (46–47). Gradually, however, these disconcerting bodies "remodel[led]" what they had shattered into a play that "[gained] immensely in robustness, in solidity." On the stage, Woolf marvels, "[t]he printed word is changed out of all recognition [because] it is heard by other people." "[T]he flatness of the print is broken up as by crevasses or precipices" into which may be fitted previously unimagined business; moments of silent interaction that "[t]he reader's eye may have slipped over [. . .] entirely" can alter the whole balance of the play (47). But though Woolf was swayed by the actors' version of *Twelfth Night*, she was not completely won over by it. Even so, she concludes that the production "served its purpose"; it challenged readers' expectations and forced them to reconsider Shakespeare's text with different eyes (49–50).

An implication of Woolf's theatre reviews is that every stage production of a familiar text is necessarily, regardless of its degree of conventionality, an alternative interpretation that may impinge on audience members' held beliefs and ideas, which may themselves have been shaped by previous productions as well as by reading. Woolf's sense of the critical potential of the theatre event is at the heart of *Between the Acts*, where she incorporates a complete pageant of English literary history ranging from medieval times to the present day and including scenes that parody the style and subject matter of Elizabethan, eighteenth-century, and Victorian drama. Devised by the lesbian playwright–director Miss La Trobe and performed by a cast of villagers in the grounds of the Oliver family's country estate, the pageant is framed and intersected by narrative passages concerning the Olivers and other spectators before, during, and after the pageant.

Set on the eve of World War II, *Between the Acts* has as its subtextual theme the relationship, explicitly developed in the feminist–pacifist tract *Three Guineas* (1938), between the causes of war and the structure of the English patriarchal family. In *Three Guineas*, Woolf argued that patriarchal domination in English homes and institutions was born of the same seed as Hitler and Mussolini's fascism, and she advocated the formation of a Society of Outsiders whose mandate would be to prevent war by using their newly acquired, if slight, influence as financially independent women to undermine patriarchal authority in all its public and domestic manifestations. In *Between the Acts*, the marginal status of the lesbian artist La Trobe suggests that she was associated in Woolf's mind with the Outsiders of *Three Guineas* and that her pageant is to be regarded as part of an Outsider-like project to undermine patriarchy and put an end to war. If this is the case, then the pageant's persistent playing out in different historical contexts of "[t]he plot of heterosexual romance"[11] may be seen as an intentional thwarting of the expectations of audience members for whom history requires the Army[12] and as an invitation to reflect instead on the relationship of this familiar romance plot to the events that more commonly constitute historical accounts.

The intersection of world affairs and the heterosexual romance as it leads to marriage and the patriarchal family is unambiguously depicted in the Victorian section of the pageant. Here, a truncheon-wielding figure of patriarchal authority asserts his dominion over the home and colonies as a prologue to a short play incorporating a love scene between two aspiring missionaries, a sumptuous picnic, prayers, a chorus about a mother's search for a suitor for her daughter, and ladies' and gentlemen's respective renditions of "I'd Be a Butterfly" and "Rule Britannia." Woolf measures the effectiveness of La Trobe's parody by tracing the response of one of her fictional audience members through roughly the same process of resistance, recognition, and reconsideration outlined in the reviews of *The Cherry Orchard* and *Twelfth Night*. Sensing "that a sneer had been aimed at her father [and] therefore at herself" during the rather brutal opening speech on the reaches of imperialist power, this character, Mrs. Lynn Jones, initially responds by protesting that "[t]here were grand men among" the Victorians (164). Later, however, she is less adamant, acknowledging the truth of the picnic scene's image of Victorian consumption and offering no objection to its parodic prayer of thanks, though her neighbor Mrs. Springett complains that this last irreverence is "too much" (169–171). In the end, after the cast has exited to the tune of "Home, Sweet Home," Mrs. Lynn Jones tries to hold on to her belief in the beauty of Victorian home life but finds that La Trobe's parody has undermined her faith and forced her to reconsider it in a critical light (173–174). In this character's final attitude of reconsideration, Woolf provides an example of the potential impact on individual spectators of the parodic repetition of familiar materials in provocative juxtaposition and of the power of theatre to subvert, through its re-enactment of conventional dramatic plots, some of the long-entrenched ways of seeing and patterns of interaction that help legitimate patriarchal authority.

In the face of World War II, however, parody is not innovative enough for either La Trobe or Woolf, each of whom seeks to realize through a more visionary art "a re-created world" in which the "wandering bodies and floating voices" (153) of the old plots are reconfigured in new relationships. As Linda Hutcheon has pointed out, parody, as "authorized transgression," at once inscribes and subverts that which it repeats[13] and reinscription of the conventional marriage plot in the face of World War II was, for a feminist– pacifist Outsider, unconscionable, given its role in preserving male dominance in English public and private life. Therefore, instead of repeating in a contemporary context the subject matter of her parodies of Elizabethan, eighteenth-century, and Victorian drama, La Trobe experiments by leaving the stage empty during the present-day section of the pageant, implicitly inviting audience members to consider their own actions, words, and silences in relation to those of the Victorians that preceded them.

Later, though, when the pageant has ended and La Trobe is envisioning her next work, she imagines a curtain rising on "two scarcely perceptible figures" speaking unspecified words by a rock at midnight (212). Woolf picks up on this vision in the final passage of *Between the Acts*, collapsing the two central characters of her narrative, a troubled husband and wife, into the unidentified figures of La Trobe's imagined play and concluding her novel with an as yet unwritten drama about to begin:

Left alone together for the first time that day, [Giles and Isa Oliver] were silent. Alone, enmity was bared; also love. Before they slept, they must fight; after they had fought, they would embrace. From that embrace another life might be born. But first they must fight, as the dog fox fights with the vixen, in the heart of darkness, in the fields of night.

Isa let her sewing drop. The great hooded chairs had become enormous. And Giles too. And Isa too against the window. The window was all sky without colour. The house had lost its shelter. It was night before roads were made, or houses. It was the night that dwellers in caves had watched from some high place among rocks.

Then the curtain rose. They spoke. (219)

Though at the very beginning of her career Woolf had considered writing a play in which the hero and heroine lead parallel lives but never actually meet,[14] forty years later, in her final novel, she presented their encounter as being as inevitable and necessary as the instinct-driven meeting of the fox and vixen. Implicated as a cause of war, however, the life-producing relationship between the human male and female seemed to Woolf, paradoxically, to be a threat to the survival of the species and therefore in dire need of transformation. A central question that *Between the Acts* raises is whether such a transformation is possible. Judith Butler has argued that "all signification takes place within the orbit of the compulsion to repeat" and that agency is consequently "to be located within the possibility of a variation on that repetition."[15] *Between the Acts'* final image of the heterosexual romance as theatrical enactment places the determinism of prescription in tension with the agency of performance. Woolf, then, like Butler, asserts not only the force that the conventional structure of the heterosexual relationship exerts on social performers, but also the possibility of its re-plotting and the part that art can play in this vitally important task.

Throughout *Between the Acts*, characters quote poetry and find in literature the terms and structures to contain their emotions, justify their relationships, and explicate their behavior. In the pageant, for example, the eighteenth-century heroine Flavinda interprets her lover Valentine's actions through a filter of fiction: "Lord, how he fingers his sword! He'll run it through his breast like the Duke in the story book!" (138). In the narrative, Isa mitigates her negative feelings for Giles by "slipping into the cliché conveniently provided by fiction" (14): "'He is my husband,' [she] thought, as they nodded across the bunch of many-coloured flowers. 'The father of my children.' It worked, that old cliché; she felt pride; and affection; then pride again in herself, whom he had chosen" (47–48). Isa's dissatisfaction with the pre-scripted emotional possibilities enabled by her marriage is later expressed through the narrative comment that "[s]urely it was time someone invented a new plot, or that the author came out from the bushes . . ." (215). This conflation of life stories and literary plots, together with the pervasive presence of literature in the characters' lives, suggests that in *Between the Acts*, Woolf was using literature to demonstrate how art functions as what Teresa de Lauretis has called a "technology of gender," with "power to control the field of social meaning and thus produce, promote, and 'implant' representations of gender."[16] Not surprisingly, therefore, the subject matter of the pageant – the heterosexual romance – is also the subject matter of the narrative sections of *Between the Acts*, both directly, in the marriage of Giles and Isa, and indirectly, in the socialization to masculinity of their child George, in the sibling relationship of Bart Oliver and Lucy Swithin, and in the treatment of the two homosexual characters, Miss La Trobe and William Dodge.

But if Woolf used literature to represent the totalizing force that the master plot of heterosexual romance exerts on all aspects of social life, she used theatre to make evident the possibility of its disruption and reconfiguration, to disclose what de Lauretis describes as "spaces in the margins of hegemonic discourses, social spaces carved in the interstices of institutions and in the chinks and cracks of the power–knowledge apparati" wherein "the terms of a different construction of gender can be posed."[17] In language that resonates with de Lauretis's, Woolf remarked in her *Twelfth Night* review that live performance reveals, in what had seemed like flat print, "crevasses" or "precipices" that can alter "all the proportions" of the play as the reader knew it (47). Such crevasses continually open up in La Trobe's pageant. During the Victorian section, "the hindquarters of the donkey, represented by Albert the idiot, [become] active" just as the patriarch Mr. Hardcastle is about to ask God's blessing for spreading the Word (171); the bellowing of cows infuses "the primeval voice" of "dumb yearning" into a textual void created when La Trobe's lines about time's erosion of civilizations and individual identities are drowned out by the wind and the rustling leaves (140); her risky experiment with ten minutes of present time is saved from disaster when a sudden rain shower pours down on the audience "like all the people in the world weeping" (180). These chance interpolations of nature and of Albert the village idiot become intrinsic to the meaning of La Trobe's pageant and reveal the seemingly closed and exclusive realm of theatrical representation to be permeable, mutable, and, by inference, deliberately transformable.[18]

Indeed, La Trobe tries repeatedly to implicate her audience in the pageant: her experiment with ten minutes of real time in effect invites spectators to consider themselves in relation to the pageant's representation of history, while a subsequent scene involving mirrors literally pulls them into the stage picture and forces them to see themselves reflected in the on-stage action. Set against the spontaneous interventions of nature, these theatrical experiments point up the audience's passive compliance with the tacitly destructive patriarchal plot that makes them so "damnably unhappy" and that dominates both the pageant and the narrative sections of *Between the Acts* (176). This passivity is one aspect of a more general state of paralysis that has these non-artist characters feeling "caught and caged; prisoners; watching a spectacle," unable to think, see, or move beyond the present moment, to recognize that even in their silence they add an "unmistakable contribution" to discourse, or to situate responsibility anywhere other than outside of themselves (176, 39). Rather than ending with a dialogue of predetermined words, Woolf concludes *Between the Acts* with a declaration of the capacity of enunciation ("They spoke") that differentiates the human being from the fox. In doing so, she suggests, like Michel de Certeau, that the "non-producers of culture" who constitute the common body of society are in fact the "poets of their own acts" whose tactical "procedures of

everyday creativity" can effect "innumerable and infinitesimal transforma-
tions of and within the dominant cultural economy in order to adapt it to
their own interests and their own rules."[19] The paralysis of the spectator
characters, contrasted with the activity of La Trobe, qualifies Woolf's belief
in the possibility of such resistance and transformation, but it also indicates
her sense of the artist's social function.

Woolf believed the creative work of art to be vitally important to human
survival. In a draft of her final essay "Anon," she stated that the "[tough]"
and "deep-rooted" instinct "[t]o enjoy singing [and] to enjoy hearing the
song"

> is indeed the instinct of self preservation. Only when we put two and two together –
> two pencil strokes, two written words, two bricks <notes> do we overcome dis-
> solution and set up some stake against oblivion. The passion with which we seek
> out these creations and attempt endlessly, perpetually, to make them is of a piece
> with the instinct that sets us preserving our bodies, with clothes, food, roofs, from
> destruction.[20]

The philosophy that Woolf sets forth in "A Sketch of the Past," also written
concurrently with *Between the Acts*, further explicates her sense of the importance of art and sheds light on her emphasis, through La Trobe's pageant,
on unity and the essential relationship between the conscious crafting of
cultural artifacts and the less formalized production of lived experience. In
this memoir, Woolf states

> that behind the cotton wool [of everyday life] is hidden a pattern; that we – I mean
> all human beings – are connected with this; that the whole world is a work of art;
> that we are parts of the work of art. *Hamlet* or a Beethoven quartet is the truth
> about this vast mass that we call the world. But there is no Shakespeare, there is
> no Beethoven; certainly and emphatically there is no God; we are the words; we
> are the music; we are the thing itself.[21]

This philosophy, which posits the creative projects of everyday living and
making art as related aspects of a single larger pattern and which therefore
implies that to alter the work of art is to affect lived experience and vice
versa, was both the motivation behind and the subject of Woolf's writing.
"[T]his conception affects me every day," she concludes. "I prove this,
now, by spending the morning writing, when I might be walking, running
a shop, or learning to do something that will be useful if war comes. I
feel that by writing I am doing what is far more necessary than anything
else."[22]

Woolf's philosophy and sense of artistic necessity illuminate her coun-
terpointing, in *Between the Acts*, of Giles and Isa's inability to imagine

themselves beyond the present moment with the constant experimentation and forward-thinking of the visionary artist La Trobe, for whom "another play always lay behind the play she had just written" and who is planning next year's pageant even as she waits for this year's to begin (63). There is a comic dimension to Woolf's portrayal of the intensity of La Trobe's pursuit of her artistic vision, but this comic dimension falls away in the final pages of the novel, where La Trobe is aligned not only with the Outsiders of *Three Guineas* but with the early English minstrel that Woolf described in "Anon." Despised as an outcast, La Trobe, like Anon, is nonetheless an integral member of society in that she fulfills a vitally important social function, one aspect of which is to criticize. But while La Trobe's critical powers are closely related to her social marginality as a lesbian, they also enable her to serve as the "common voice" that can say "out loud what we feel, but are too proud to admit,"[23] and to express through theatrical parody the widespread but inarticulate dissatisfaction with the heterosexual romance plot of *Between the Acts*. Moreover, as Woolf states in "Anon," the "common voice" of the artist goes beyond criticism to articulate the beliefs around which society constructs itself.[24] Thus, when the dialogue of La Trobe's next play comes to her, she is not alone but sits drinking in a pub, surrounded by villagers; the artist in *Between the Acts* is not a romantic genius but the individual whose task it is to plumb the depths of the social as well as the literary imagination in order to find what is present within it but has not yet been brought to the surface.[25] In pushing up against the limits of cultural consciousness, La Trobe seeks the terms for "a re-created world" (153), a re-enactment of history from primordial times onward, with the benefit of hindsight. Whether the words that Giles and Isa speak at the end of *Between the Acts* are such a transformational re-enactment or yet another repetition of the same speeches and relationships that have led up to the deadly impasse of the present moment seems to depend in large measure on whether they have recognized in La Trobe's criticism their common voice and whether they have seen, through the pageant's interaction with the off-stage world and its emphasis on unity, their own "unacted parts" (153) and their instrumentality in determining the design of society.

A recognition such as that required of Giles and Isa seemed to Woolf more likely to occur in the context of a communally attended theatre event than in the less immediate and more fragile one-on-one relationship between reader and writer.[26] In her notes for the book of which "Anon" was to be a part, she wrote that "an actor cuts deeper to the bone" than a character on a page,[27] while in her theatre reviews, she implied that it was the corporeality of staged productions that persuaded initially intractable viewers to compromise their preconceived interpretations. Yet if, in its physical immediacy, theatre exemplified more vividly than literature Woolf's belief in the power of art to engender change, there remains a sense in *Between the Acts*, as in "A Sketch of the Past" and "Anon," that illusion or artistic mediation is necessary for perception. La Trobe sees, for example, during her experiment with ten minutes of present time, that reality can be "too strong" and that it "is death, death, death [. . .] when illusion fails" (179–180). The sudden rain shower that saves her experiment does so because it functions as a simile and, as such, reintroduces illusion to the stage that she has left empty of all but "present-time reality": the rain pours down "*like* all the people in the world weeping"; drops trickle down Isa's "cheeks *as if* they were her own tears" (179–180; my italics).

Part of the fascination of the theatre event for Woolf was its incorporation of elements that retain their reality outside the world of the play and can therefore carry new meanings back into it. Thus, when La Trobe's actors linger on after their final curtain call, they appear still to "[act] the unacted part conferred on them by their clothes" (195), and when swallows fly across the stage seemingly in time to the music playing on the gramophone, the narrative voice marvels, "Real swallows" (182), as if they could possibly be anything else. Bert O. States has written that

theater – unlike fiction, painting, sculpture, and film – is really a language whose words consist to an unusual degree of things that *are* what they seem to be. In theater, image and object, pretense and pretender, sign-vehicle and content, draw unusually close. [. . .] Put bluntly, in theater there is always a possibility that an act of sexual congress between two so-called signs will produce a real pregnancy.[28]

In seeing the physical and temporal conditions of performance as lending validity to staged interpretations, in construing the actor–character relationship as mutually productive, and in concluding *Between the Acts* with an image of her two main spectator-characters as the central figures in La Trobe's play, Woolf suggests that to conceive reconstructed or alternative social realities and to reproduce them on stage is literally to bring them into existence. Her title *Between the Acts*, then, refers not only to the intervals during which are depicted the effects of the pageant on its audience and to the "crevasses" of the pageant into which the forces of nature intrude; it also implies the corporeal reality of performance as a figure for the common ground "between" the inextricably linked and mutually influential "acts" of making art and everyday living, and this common ground as a site on which to stage a collaboration against the gender politics that lead to war.

After seeing a production of *Macbeth* in 1934, Woolf noted in her diary that

the play demands coming to the surface – hence insists upon a reality wh. the novel need not have, but perhaps should have. Contact with the surface. Coming to the top. This is working out my theory of the different levels in writing, & how to combine them: for I begin to think the combination necessary.[29]

In *Between the Acts*, Woolf used the play-within-the-novel and the metaphor of performance to represent how disembodied fiction affects lived experience, but she also made "contact with the surface" through strategic public appearances in the persona of woman writer. Perhaps most notably, though she detested lecturing, she agreed in 1928 to speak on the subject of women and fiction at the women's colleges at Cambridge, writing afterwards in her diary, "I should have liked to deal with real things sometimes. I get such a sense of tingling & vitality from an evenings talk like that; one's angularities & obscurities are smoothed and lit."[30] Appearing in person to deliver the lectures on which *A Room of One's Own* was based, Woolf connected her literary "angularities and obscurities" to "real things," fused the abstract and the concrete, and situated her critical and narrative practices within a continuum of women's history, thereby countering the depoliticization of her work by critics who focused exclusively on its aesthetic qualities. So, whereas, in Woolf's view, the fact of the female body on the historical stage limited actresses such as Ellen Terry to impoverished female roles, her own strategic deployment of her corporeal presence as woman writer made literal the notion of feminist–modernist writing as performative act that is implicit in her writings on actresses, as well as in her final novel. Between the acts of her performative politicization of her literary practice and her fictional usage of performance to represent the transformational possibilities of art, Woolf clarified the role of feminist–modernist artist and suggested the theatrical dimensions of its genealogy.[31]

In *A Room of One's Own*, Judith Shakespeare is a figure for the woman writer in her past and future aspects, yet she tells the actor–manager Nick Greene that she wants to act, not that she wants to write. Woolf's first significant appearance on the public stage as one of the *Dreadnought* hoaxers coincided with her composition of her first novel *The Voyage Out*;[32] and her return to the subject of the *Dreadnought* in the talks that she gave in 1940 as she was completing *Between the Acts* suggests a self-reflexive concern for the effectiveness of her overall performance as a feminist–pacifist writer.

The irony of her comment in these talks that she was glad to have been of help to her country calls attention to the impossibility of quantifying the more substantial contribution of her extraordinary body of literary work, the product of a sustained creative and political act for which her *Dreadnought* performance, as a serio-comic critique of patriarchal gender norms, imperialism, and war, may stand as a metaphor. All the same, when Woolf "put on the body" that the woman writer "has so often laid down,"[33] she was, in effect, bringing into being Judith Shakespeare's "unacted part," for as she remarked to her friend the pioneering woman composer Ethel Smyth on a speech she had given in 1931, "you [. . .] threw in something never yet written by being yourself there in the flesh."[34]

CHAPTER 6

Feminism, tragedy, history: the fate of Isadora Duncan

Perhaps no feminist–modernist artist more vividly epitomized the idea inherent in Woolf's statement to Ethel Smyth about the significance of the fact of her corporeal presence than the American early modern dancer–choreographer Isadora Duncan. Despite Duncan's extraordinary artistic accomplishments, however, references to tragedy figure persistently in accounts of her life. On 15 September 1927, for example, a sub-headline of the *New York Times* report of Duncan's death read, "TRAGEDY MARKED CAREER,"[1] while in the 1986 biography *Isadora: Portrait of the Artist as a Woman*, Fredrika Blair makes reference to "the tragedy of Isadora" and to Duncan's "tragic flaw."[2] The persistence of this rhetoric of tragedy in relation to Duncan suggests that she has acquired "mythical" status as a quintessentially tragic figure, yet as with the various cultural myths that Roland Barthes deconstructs in his 1957 work *Mythologies*, this naturalization of Duncan as a cultural icon of the tragic female artist in fact cloaks "ideological abuse"[3] and effaces her achievements as one of the great artists of the twentieth century. In this chapter, I want to consider elements of tragic discourse in accounts of Duncan's life in order to clarify how, in Duncan's case, tragedy has functioned as a conservative master-narrative, underwritten by a drive to deny female subjectivity. This popular co-optation of Duncan into a narrative that negates what she set out to accomplish as a woman artist ultimately raises questions not only about her unique impact but about the larger possibility of feminist–modernist transformation that has been a current connecting the various artists in this study.

Sarah Pomeroy has noted that "[t]he proper behaviour of women and men is explored in many tragedies,"[4] while in the seminal study of tragedy *The Poetics*, Aristotle raises questions about the suitability of women as heroic tragic subjects.[5] Despite Aristotle's concerns, such characters do exist within the canon of classical Greek tragedy, but the nature of the tragic misstep or error in judgment – the hamartia – that leads to their reversal of fortune may be said to be gender-inflected, relating to their incursions into the male-dominated realm of public life and their violation of accepted decorum for wives, mothers, and daughters: as Nicole Loraux states in *Tragic Ways of Killing a Woman*, "The glory of a woman [in ancient Greece] was to have no glory."[6] This conventional gendering of tragic form was challenged by Ibsen in a number of his "women's plays," so that, as Joan Templeton has pointed out, the power of *Ghosts*, for example, derives not from Mrs. Alving's departure from but, rather, from her "poisonous submission to the ideals of 'woman's place.'"[7] The traditional gender differentiation of hamartia that Ibsen problematized in his modern tragedies is useful in considering the transformation of Isadora Duncan into an icon of the tragic female artist.

Duncan's challenge to dominant cultural prescriptions for women was wide-ranging and included her insistence on the right of women to dress in unconstraining clothing, to refuse the confinement and servitude of traditional marriage, and to take lovers and bear children out of wedlock. Most notably, however, Duncan claimed for women the right to participate actively in cultural production. For this reason, she rejected popular theatrical forms such as musical comedy, which, as noted earlier, she saw as requiring of young female performers rote repetition of "meaningless words and [. . .] meaningless gestures, when they could have been taught to be a force to the nation."[8] Similarly, anticipating Ann Daly's argument that ballet is grounded in an ideology that subjugates women by persistently portraying them "as objects of male desire rather than as agents of their own desire,"[9] Duncan likened ballet dancers to "articulated puppet[s]"[10] and sought instead to "dance the freedom of woman."[11]

Duncan's autobiographical account of her first meeting with the sculptor Rodin graphically illustrates how her determination to reclaim the female body from its objectification in ballet and popular theatrical entertainments and to author the significance of her own artistic image disrupted the traditional gender dynamics of the representational process and transgressed against the male-dominated sociocultural order. As an aspiring artist newly arrived in Paris in 1900, Duncan was so moved by an exhibition of Rodin's sculpture that she made a special pilgrimage to his studio, where he escorted her around to view his work. During this private showing, she was struck by the sensual quality of the master's relationship with his raw materials, his passionate engagement in the process of making art, and his impulse to equate the art object with the female form: "He ran his hands over [his sculptures] and caressed them" and at one point "he took a small quantity of clay and pressed it between his palms. He breathed hard as he did so.

The heat streamed from him like a radiant furnace. In a few moments he had formed a woman's breast, that palpitated beneath his fingers" (*ML* 90). Afterwards, Rodin accompanied Duncan to her studio, where she changed into a dance tunic and performed for him her choreography of an idyll of Theocritus. When she had finished, she began to expound her theories of the dance. Rodin, however, was disinclined to listen. Instead, Duncan recalls,

[h]e gazed at me with lowered lids, his eyes blazing, and then, with the same expression that he had before his works, he came toward me. He ran his hands over my neck, breast, stroked my arms and ran his hands over my hips, my bare legs and feet. He began to knead my whole body as if it were clay, while from him emanated heat that scorched and melted me. My whole desire was to yield to him my entire being and, indeed, I would have done so if it had not been that my absurd up-bringing caused me to become frightened and I withdrew, threw my dress over my tunic and sent him away bewildered. (*ML* 90–91)

Unreceptive to Duncan's discourse on dance and resistant to recognizing her as the fellow artist as which she presented herself, Rodin, as he is characterized in this passage of *My Life*, instead mistakes the dancer for unmediated and feminized nature itself – desirable raw material that he can mold, through a conflated creative and sexual process, into an inanimate object, a sculptor's version of the passive virgin page that awaits male cultural inscription in the patriarchal metaphor so commonly used to denote male literary creativity.[12]

Feminist theorists such as Sherry Ortner and Hélène Cixous have identified the association of women with nature and men with culture in a hierarchically opposed nature/culture dichotomy as one of the primary means by which male dominance has been legitimated and sustained, while Ann Daly has noted that the corporeal medium of dance has caused it to be regarded as "primitive, 'pre-verbal,' idiosyncratic, infantile, female, and uncoded, in opposition to the civilized, social, adult, male[,] reasoned code of language."[13] These cultural assumptions about the relationship of the dancing female body to art were a central concern for Duncan, particularly given the fact that the illusion of spontaneous self-expression and freedom from external mediation was at the heart of her feminist dance project, even though her dances were in actual fact carefully crafted works of art. Therefore, while she claimed that her dance, being fully expressive, was better explained "by dancing than by publishing commentaries and treatises" and argued that "art should be able to do without all that [. . .]; its truth will blaze forth spontaneously if it is really beautiful,"[14] she supplemented her performances with speeches, programme notes, and theoretical treatises throughout her career, stating once, "[. . .] I am a teacher with a mission"; "If I were only a dancer I would not speak."[15] In these supplementary texts, Duncan often inverted the usual hierarchy wherein nature is ranked as inferior to culture and attempted to dislodge ballet from its position of cultural primacy by criticizing it for its unnaturalness.[16] At the same time, however, she also attempted to distinguish between her natural-seeming art and nature itself and to align herself with culture by noting her artful mediation of her body in performance. Consequently, though she claimed to be dancing "in the form of woman in her greatest and purest expression,"[17] she did not simply assume, as Elizabeth Dempster has argued, that her dance was "a pure reflection of the natural, unwritten body of woman."[18] Instead, perhaps casting about for the term "choreographer," which had not yet gained common currency,[19] she stated in an interview, "I use my body as my medium just as the writer uses his words. Do not call me a dancer."[20]

Duncan's autobiography is generally regarded as less authentic than her theoretical essays because it was written late in her life when she had lost her stage popularity and financial necessity forced her to conform to the wishes of publishers, who pressured her to forget her "hifalutin ideas" about art and concentrate instead on "spicy" "love chapters" detailing her relationships with various men.[21] Despite the compromising circumstances of its composition, however, *My Life* still bears traces of Duncan's determination to author the significance of her own performing image by resisting the trivialization and appropriation of her aesthetic of spontaneous- and natural-seeming expressiveness and the attendant relegation to a passive and conventionally feminine position within the representational process. Margaret Thompson Drewal has suggested that "[o]ne of the ways that Duncan constructed her persona was to quote what [. . .] famous men said about her,"[22] but in fact, Duncan was more ambivalent and complex in her autobiographical treatment of the many artists and intellectuals who admired her work but responded to it by transforming her in various ways into the ground of their own professional struggles. In concluding the story of her first meeting with Rodin, for example, Duncan reclaims her status as subject and artist by transforming the sculptor into a sexual object himself and regretting on behalf of civilization the lost fruits of their unconsummated partnership: "What a pity! How often I have regretted this childish miscomprehension which lost to me the divine chance of giving my virginity to the Great God Pan himself, to the mighty Rodin. Surely Art and all Life would have been richer thereby!" (*ML* 91). In describing her initial encounter with set designer Edward Gordon Craig, who became her lover and the father of one of her children, Duncan again represents herself as resistant to a male artist's attempt to reassign her to a traditional female role in the art-making process and subsume her into his own creative work. As Duncan recalls, Craig introduced himself to her by insisting that she had stolen his ideas, that she was "the living realisation" of his dreams, that he had invented her, and that she belonged to his scenery (*ML* 180–181). Later on in their relationship, Duncan adds, Craig continually claimed that his stage designs should have priority over her dances and that she should stop "waving [her] arms about" and stay at home and sharpen his pencils (*ML* 185).[23] Duncan would respond that "the [. . .] human being moving in perfect beauty" would always take precedence over scenery because the soul is the radiant centre of art (*ML* 185),[24] and she concludes her recollection by stating that Craig's professional jealousy "would not allow him to admit that any woman could really be an artist" (*ML* 185–186).

Despite such opposition, Duncan worked to extend the expressive possibilities of dance throughout her career and felt satisfied enough with her achievements in this regard to be able to maintain in her autobiography, "[. . .] I have only danced my life" (*ML* 3). By this claim, Duncan appears to have meant not so much that her work was autobiographical in the usual sense of an account of her life (though some of it indeed had autobiographical resonances),[25] but, rather, that it was the choreographic embodiment of her own responses to particular themes and musical compositions that she chose for herself at different historical moments. She believed that the most expressive and therefore the most beautiful choreography was always relative to the physical and emotional development of the individual dancer, and consequently, she once claimed that even if she were legless she might still create her art.[26] As Deborah Jowitt has noted, Duncan allowed her work to "[evolve] during her lifetime to suit her aging body and battered optimism" so that her later dances were somber and statuesque by comparison with the lighter, fleeter, more lyrical ones of her earlier career.[27] Janet Flanner's description of the programs of new work that Duncan presented in Nice in 1926 bears eloquent witness to the dancer's lifelong evolution in and exploration of her medium. "In all three performances," Flanner wrote,

her art was seen to have changed. She treaded the boards but little, she stood almost immobile or in slow splendid steps with slow splendid arms moved to music, seeking, hunting, finding. Across her face, tilting this way and that, fled the mortal looks of tragedy, knowledge, love, scorn, pain. [. . .] Isadora was still great. By an economy (her first) she had arrived at elimination. As if the movements of dancing had become too redundant for her spirit, she had saved from dancing only its shape.[28]

Duncan died in 1927 at the age of fifty, when, in a freak accident, the scarf that she was wearing became entangled in the wheel of the Bugatti sports car she was riding in, strangled her, and broke her neck; and the fact and manner of her premature death have been key factors in her transformation into a cultural icon of the tragic female artist. Susanne Langer has argued that tragedy is "a cadential form" that is structured according to the "vital rhythm" of "growth, maturity, [and] decline" and that thus reflects the fundamental human life-pattern of "self-consummation" eventuating in the "absolute close" of death.[29] She adds, moreover, that the tragic action "must reveal the limit of the protagonist's powers and mark the end of his self-realization" and that, in the same way that life is an inevitable movement toward death, "the tragic ending must recapitulate the whole action to be a visible fulfillment of a destiny that was implicit in the beginning."[30] With reference to Francis Fergusson's analysis of *Hamlet*, Langer suggests that it is this tragic rhythm of movement toward inevitable self-fulfillment that accounts for the sense of rightness that we feel when the tragic hero meets his end.[31] In *Modern Tragedy*, Raymond Williams observed that "[h]uman death is often the form of the deepest meanings of a culture," pointing out that "in some cultures or in their breakdown, life is regularly read back from the fact of death, which can seem not only the focus but also the source of our values," and that "[w]ithin this emphasis, suffering and disorder of any kind are interpreted by reference to what is seen as the controlling reality. Such an interpretation," Williams states, "is now commonly described as a tragic sense of life."[32] In tragedy, then, the significance of the protagonist's life becomes apparent in and through a death that is fitting.

Duncan's co-optation into the discourse of tragedy depends in large measure on endowing her death with particular significance and representing it as, in Langer's words, the "fulfillment of a destiny that was implicit in the beginning" of her life as a woman artist, a tendency encouraged by the fact that her autobiography was published posthumously in 1927 and was therefore read retrospectively with the knowledge of her death, which consequently seemed to function as its true conclusion. Thus, though *My Life* ends with Duncan's departure for Russia in 1921 and was apparently to be followed by another volume entitled *My Bolshevik Days*,[33] John Martin wrote in his 1928 review that "[f]ollowing so closely on the characteristically tragic death of the great Isadora, her autobiography comes like an epitaph of her own devising,"[34] while Elizabeth Shepley Sergeant asserted in her 1928 review that Duncan's life made it seem that it was "dangerous, perhaps forbidden, for that inhuman creature, the great woman artist, the breaker of laws, to think of human happiness in terms of daily life" and that there was "some tragic rightness in her death, on the shores of the Mediterranean, from the entanglement of her Greek scarf with a modern machine."[35]

As Sergeant's review indicates, the scarf and the sports car both function as key signifiers in the representation of Duncan's death as a fitting end to a tragic life.[36] As a signifier of modernity, the sports car becomes analogous to Duncan's revolutionary dance aesthetics but also to her progressive views about women, the speediness of the car corresponding with her own "fast" living as exemplified in her advocacy of free love, unwed motherhood, and dress reform. According to this signifying logic, Duncan's progressive transgressions against the patriarchal social and cultural order had already betrayed her when a runaway car carried her children by two different lovers to their deaths by drowning. Thus, Mabel Dodge Luhan could suggest that Duncan was somehow culpable in the accidental deaths of her children: "[. . .] I wondered what fatal mistake she had made in her life that had swept that automobile out of control, to go plunging into dark waters. Somewhere the hand had faltered . . . her hand, her beautiful hand dripping essence of life, had lost its magic and turned deathly, dealing herself her own death-blow."[37]

Like the car, the scarf links the progressive aspects of Duncan's personal and professional lives, signifying not only her modernist transformation of dance but also her insistence that the liberation of the female body was a more fundamental requirement than the vote in the movement for women's emancipation.[38] "For Duncan," Elizabeth Dempster has written, "the dancing body was a paradigm of freedom. The loosening of the fetters which bound the body itself [. . .] was part and parcel of her vision of the social and political liberation of women."[39] Similarly, Elizabeth Francis has noted that when Duncan asserted in 1910 that "'[e]verything must be undone,'" she was "playing on the metaphor of loosening the bonds of clothing to express her critique of dominant aesthetics in dance. Unwrapping the garb of culture from her body, Duncan took off shoes, stockings, and corset, all signifiers of constraints on the female body and its expressive potential." In this way, Duncan's costume "became an emblem of women's emancipation, a radical performance of a woman's body freed from the binding and stifling layers of culture."[40] In the representation of Duncan's death as a fitting end to an inevitably tragic life, however, the scarf betrays her just like the car and, in doing so, signals the backfiring of her modernist undertaking to "dance the freedom of woman." As Jean Cocteau wrote of Duncan's end, which he thought was "perfect," "this Jocasta died as she lived, a victim of the complicity of a racing car and a red scarf. A scarf which hated her, threatened her, and warned her; which she braved, and obstinately went on wearing."[41] Max Eastman's remarks on Duncan's death are in a similar vein: he recalls learning that Duncan

was dead – strangled and her neck broken, while driving in the Promenade des Anglais at Nice, by the heavy-painted silk shawl she wore – the same one in which she danced the *Marseillaise*. It had caught and wound up in a wheel of the speeding car, and seized and destroyed her like a living thing. And how living a thing it was! How she had breathed into that frail instrument the bounding pulse of her passion for beauty and freedom! Everyone groped for the symbolism in its turning upon her at the last, but to me it was painfully clear.[42]

He then goes on to describe Duncan's personal and professional decline in her later years and concludes that "[i]f the scarf had really been given life by her dance, it could not have acted more loyally."[43]

As Eastman's recollections indicate, the involvement of Duncan's scarf in her accidental death provoked an odd sense of continuity between the death and Duncan's deliberately choreographed dances that is further apparent in Harriet Monroe's remark in 1928 that "[t]he death of Isadora Duncan – so swift, so beautiful, a mere twist of her dancer's scarf – carried me back to my first sight of her, when she gave me a golden moment, one of those poignant emotions of beauty which shake out the soul like a banner in the wind."[44] The perception of continuity between the death and the dances established by the free-flowing scarf that signified the liberation of women and the dance but that seemed at the last to turn against Duncan in an act of punitive violence may in turn account for the sense that Duncan's accidental death was somehow deliberately performed. Thus, Susan Gubar has stated that Duncan's "costumes and affairs *and death express her creed* as well as her autobiography does,"[45] though Duncan's death – unlike her costumes, affairs, and autobiography – was accidental and intentionally expressive of nothing, despite its seeming "tragic rightness," the sense that it was "poetically appropriate"[46] for the woman dancer who embodied freedom to be strangled by her own scarf.

The manner of Duncan's death bears a striking relation to the conventions of Greek tragedy, in which, as Nicole Loraux has pointed out, the violent deaths of female characters are most often located in the bodily region of the throat, whether death comes through "suicide, murder, or sacrifice."[47] Loraux further notes that in Greek tragedy, suicide is primarily practiced by female characters and that hanging is their method of choice:

Hanging was a woman's death. As practiced by women, it could lead to endless variations, because women and young girls contrived to substitute for the customary rope those adornments with which they decked themselves and which were also the emblems of their sex, as Antigone strangled herself with her knotted veil. Veils, belts, headbands [I might add scarves] – all these instruments of seduction were death traps for those who wore them."[48]

While Duncan's death was not suicide and any correspondence with the deaths of the female characters in Greek tragedy was purely coincidental, the significance that Loraux reads into the conventions relating to the manner of women's deaths in tragedy is worth noting and may illuminate the particular significance that Duncan's death has seemed to hold and the unconscious inclination to interpret her death as deliberately performed. Loraux suggests that "[t]o cast light on the regularity – one might almost say, the monotony – of this pattern [of death by the throat], one should look for a principle outside the universe of tragedy and move toward the gynecological thinking of the Greeks, where woman is caught between two mouths, between two necks, where vagaries of the womb suddenly choke the voice in a woman's throat [. . .]."[49] Sue-Ellen Case has reminded us that the female characters in Greek tragedy were essentially "classic drag" roles[50] created for civic occasions intended to affirm the values of a misogynistic society, while Catherine Belsey has argued that "[t]o be a subject is to be able to speak, to give meaning."[51] In Greek tragedy, the female characters' voluntary containment of their own voices through acts of self-strangulation in a culture where "[s]ilence is the adornment of women"[52] causes women to seem themselves to affirm the values of that culture that seeks to deny female subjectivity, particularly as the female characters often express agreement with this sentiment and suffer greatly for their necessary incursions into the male-associated public domain.[53]

Augusto Boal has argued in *Theatre of the Oppressed* that tragedy, as systematized by Aristotle, serves a repressive sociopolitical function, ensuring passive compliance among subordinated social subjects through the tragic effect of catharsis, which, as Boal sees it, eliminates potentially rebellious impulses from the social body by establishing an empathic relationship between spectators and an "anti-social" hero/heroine who eventually comes to recognize his/her hamartia and to suffer punishment for it, in the process purging similarly anti-social feelings from vicariously transgressive spectators.[54] The gender-differentiation of hamartia in classical Greek

drama and in tragic discourse relating to Isadora Duncan lends support to
Boal's claims, as does the tendency to regard Duncan's death as somehow
deliberate. Margaret Higonnet has stated that "[t]o take one's life is to force
others to read one's death" and that "[t]o embrace death is at the same time
to read one's own life."[55] If one were to expand on Susan Gubar's previously quoted remark that Duncan's death "express[ed] her creed" as well as
her costumes, affairs, and autobiography did and was thus in some sense
deliberately and self-reflexively performed, one might interpret Duncan's
offhand parting words as she rode off in the Bugatti – "*Adieu, mes amis. Je
vais à la gloire!*"[56] – as an expression of hubris that cannot go unpunished,
while her unwitting strangulation by her own scarf might seem an extraordinary performance of an ironic recognition scene, the climactic final act –
like Oedipus' self-blinding or Hedda Gabler's suicide – in a life destined for
catastrophe by the hamartia of her desire to "dance the freedom of woman."
The effect of catharsis would complete the tragedy, and so one might quote
Jean Cocteau, who wrote, "Isadora's end is *perfect* – a kind of horror that
leaves one calm."[57]

   The transformation of Duncan into an icon of the tragic female artist
was perhaps most fully and systematically effected in Karel Reisz's 1968 bio-
pic *Isadora* (also known as *The Loves of Isadora*),[58] which starred Vanessa
Redgrave, who subsequently appeared on the cover of a reissue of Duncan's
autobiography *My Life*, along with the boldly obliterating slogan "Vanessa
is Isadora."[59] In Reisz's film, Duncan's loss of virginity is represented as a
dance, with Redgrave writhing about on the floor beneath a camera posi-
tioned directly above her in the place of the penetrating male lover/artist.
Finding herself pregnant as a result of this intercourse, Duncan as portrayed
by Redgrave admits that she is not so "unnatural" as not to dream about
family life with Edward Gordon Craig, but she refuses to be beguiled by
such dreams, insisting that she is an artist and murmuring to herself immediately after giving birth, "I did it! All by myself! I did it!" Duncan's willfully
independent generation of children parallels her claim to parthenogenesis
in her art, and the impossibility of such a claim is represented through
the haunting images of the accidental drowning of her children that recur
throughout the 1927 scenes of Reisz's film. In one of these scenes, the
middle-aged and dissolute Duncan slurs, "I'm a woman and I'm an artist
and that's hard." Reisz articulates his sense of the irreconcilability of these
terms through the narrative structure of his film, in which scenes leading up to Duncan's fatal automobile ride are intercut with scenes adapted
from *My Life* to suggest that Duncan's catastrophe was ordained from the
moment of her conception when, by her own account, she began dancing

in her mother's womb. The climactic final scene of the film thus features
Duncan performing a tango that is in essence a dance of death with the
handsome Bugatti driver she has pursued since the start of the film. In her
1977 feminist theatre manifesto "Aller à la Mer," Hélène Cixous calls for
an end to "the sadism directed against women" in theatrical representation
and for the creation of a new kind of theatre where "women will be able
to go [. . .] and feel themselves loving and being loved, listening and being
heard, happy as when they go to the sea, the womb of the mother."[60] In
what seems like a perversely prescient thumbing-of-the-nose at Cixous, the
final shot of Reisz's film is of the sea, as if the woman artist who claimed
to have danced in the womb had been returned to the mother's body and
never been born at all.

Roland Barthes has stated "that myth is a system of communication, [. . .]
a message" or "type of social *usage* which is added to pure matter" in a relation of "deformation" or "distortion,"[61] while Walter Benjamin has argued
that "tragedy cannot be understood simply as legend in dramatic form" but
is instead "a tendentious re-shaping of the tradition."[62] I have suggested in
this chapter that the myth of Duncan as a figure of tragedy communicates,
in seemingly innocent, de-politicized speech,[63] the message that the terms
"woman" and "artist" are essentially irreconcilable, tendentiously reshap-
ing her life and death so that she herself appears to have recognized and
accepted this irreconcilability and to have inflicted punishment on herself
for her hamartia in attempting such a reconciliation. In actual fact, while
Duncan recognized the difficulty of being both a woman and an artist
within a male-dominated sociocultural order, she never lost her determination to achieve such a reconciliation, persisting even in her autobiography
despite the compromising conditions of its composition and her sense that
pre-existing conventions of plot and character had already to a great extent
determined how she could represent herself.[64] Indeed, according to Victor
Seroff, though she was nearly destitute around the time she undertook to
write *My Life*, Duncan refused to consider a suggestion by Cecil B. De Mille
that she play herself in a movie written especially for her. She was afraid,
she said, both of what the script-writers, directors, and producers would
do to her and her art in the course of filming her memoirs and that the
jumpiness of the early "flicks," as she called them, would cause her to look
like she had St. Vitus's dance; she preferred not to be remembered in that
way.[65] For Duncan, surrendering her image to the control of Hollywood
movie-makers, who would recast her in their own mediated version of her
and who would in the process empty her work of its significance, was the
equivalent of transforming her choreography – that is, her writing through

the medium of her body in motion – into meaningless movements beyond her power to control, like those of the afflicted with St. Vitus's dance. This denial of her power to be a performing subject – to be a dancer who also speaks – is precisely the effect of her co-optation into narratives of tragedy.

Notably, the appearance of Reisz's film in 1968 coincided with the resurgence or "second wave" of the feminist movement, the "first wave" of which encompassed the years of Duncan's rise to prominence in the early twentieth century. Raymond Williams has questioned the common assertion that a stable belief system is a pre-condition for the appearance of works in the genre of tragedy and has suggested instead that the opposite may in fact be the case, that is, that the condition of tragedy may be the "tension between old and new: between received beliefs, embodied in institutions and responses, and newly and vividly experienced contradictions and possibilities."[66] Williams's claims are supported by the insights of René Girard, who sees the traces of a "sacrificial crisis" in the agons of classical tragedy, where equally matched opponents – for example, Teiresias and Oedipus – exchange verbal blows that threaten to pollute the entire community through the violence that they inflict on the social institutions that the combatants represent.[67] According to Girard, the sacrificial crisis of which such "impure" violence is a sign is the result of a collapse of social distinctions "that gives birth to fierce rivalries and sets members of the same family or social group at one another's throats."[68] The crisis must therefore be "redressed by the destruction of a victim whose removal is required to restore or ensure [the] status quo" through "the redifferentiation of indistinction."[69] The Duncan character in Reisz's 1968 film can be seen as a version of this ritual scapegoat, her victimization as tragic heroine serving to re-assert the hierarchical gender distinctions upon which patriarchal order depends and which were under threat from the equalizing efforts of the second wave of feminism. As Williams has pointed out, while it is common to think of tragedy as "an action in which the hero is destroyed," most tragedies in fact end with the restoration of order so that tragic action is not so much "what happens *to* the hero" as "what happens *through* the hero."[70] "Order," then, "is the *result* of the action, even where it entirely corresponds, in an abstract way, with a pre-existing conventional belief. It is not so much that the order is illustrated as that it is recreated" in relation "to the fact of disorder, through which the action moves."[71] Teresa de Lauretis has further suggested that all narrative – including tragedy – depends at its most fundamental level on an active, morphologically male hero and a passive, morphologically female obstacle, boundary, or space through which the hero must pass. According to de Lauretis, as these two basic "positions [are projected] into the temporal development of plot[,] narrative itself takes over the function of the mythical subject," mapping "sexual difference into each text; and hence, by a sort of accumulation, into the universe of meaning, fiction, and history, represented by the literary–artistic tradition and all the texts of culture."[72] The representation of Duncan as tragic female artist serves as a means by which the patriarchal sociocultural order that is restored through her destruction can recreate and re-assert itself, the "hero of a thousand faces"[73] that is the true subject of this particular tragic vision.

As Raymond Williams makes clear, however, "To read back life from the fact of death is a cultural and sometimes a personal choice,"[74] and so we might choose to read Duncan's life in terms of her accomplishments and the living legacy that exists alongside the popular image. Duncan's favorite poet was Walt Whitman, who wrote in "Song of Myself," "Do I contradict myself? / Very well then I contradict myself, / (I am large, I contain multitudes),"[75] and though the irreducible fact and distinguishing feature of her existence was that, as Gertrude Stein observed, "she was one dancing,"[76] she herself once claimed that she had "never once danced a solo" and thought of her dance "as a chorus or community expression."[77] Joseph Roach has distinguished between "history as it is discursively transmitted and memory as it is publicly enacted by the bodies that bear its consequences."[78] Rather than in the popular image of the doomed woman artist, Duncan may be more properly remembered not only in the continuing practice of the art of the dance, which she unquestionably transformed, but in the common female body that "bears the consequences" of her on-stage art and off-stage life. In "[preaching] freedom of the mind through freedom of the body"[79] and offering herself as an example, she inspired countless girls and women to attempt to emulate her, persuaded by her seemingly simple movement and the identification required of them by her emphasis on self-expression that they themselves could do what she was doing.[80] This exploration of the movement possibilities of the female body through amateur and educational dance was unprecedented and contributed significantly to the outmoding of nineteenth-century standards of beauty, dress, and decorum, so that, as Walter Terry has written,

[m]uch that Isadora stood for during her lifetime is now outmoded, and behavior which once shocked the world is no longer shocking, at least to the same degree. Her freeing of woman's form from the constriction of the corset, her introduction of healthful lightness of dress, her espousal of bobbed hair, have long since been accepted as natural feminine rights.[81]

Through the unconscious re/membering of Duncan in the contemporary female bodies that she helped to shape, the ongoing choreography of daily existence traces an alternate story of the dancer who used her body "just as the writer uses words," thus literalizing Virginia Woolf's claim in *A Room of One's Own* that "great poets do not die" but "are continuing presences."[82] This *incorporation* of Duncan's legacy into what Joseph Roach, citing Pierre Nora, has called "[l]iving memory"[83] may in turn exemplify a way to understand the collective impact of the larger group of feminist–modernist artists that I have discussed here and whose diverse work Duncan complemented through her transformational art.

Conclusion

Rita Felski's proposal of the model of a feminist counter-public sphere, which I outlined in my introduction, arose from her sense of the need for a critical method to encompass both realist and more formally experimental examples of feminist literature, which she defines as "all those texts that reveal a critical awareness of women's subordinate positions and of gender as a problematic category, however this is expressed."[1] Felski's arguments concerning the need for a broad definition of feminist literature resonate with recent debates about how to define modernism. Bonnie Kime Scott, for example, includes "a nonexperimental group of writers, alongside the more traditional experimental canon," in her edited anthology *The Gender of Modernism*,[2] arguing that

[t]he making, the formal experiment, no longer seems to suffice as a definition [of modernism]. Mind, body, sexuality, family, reality, culture, religion, and history were all reconstrued. In settling for a small set of white male modernists and a limited number of texts and genres, we may have paused upon a conservative, anxious, male strain of modernism, however valuable and lasting those texts. The politics and aesthetics of gender may lie at the heart of a comprehensive understanding of early twentieth-century literature and its full array of literary treasures.[3]

Yet while Scott includes both experimental and non-experimental writers in *The Gender of Modernism* in order to address the traditional omission of women from accounts of modernism, the representation of theatre and drama in her anthology is minimal, consisting of Djuna Barnes's one-act play *To the Dogs* and her interview with Provincetown Players director Helen Westley, Zora Neale Hurston's performance-related essay "Characteristics of Negro Expression," and Gertrude Stein's short play *White Wines*. At the opposite extreme, in his contribution to *The Cambridge Companion to Modernism*, Christopher Innes sets out to redress the common neglect of drama in accounts of modernism, but in doing so, he focuses exclusively on formally experimental works by male playwrights, directors, and designers:

Wyndham Lewis, W. B. Yeats, Edward Gordon Craig, August Strindberg, Oskar Kokoschka, Eugene O'Neill, Antonin Artaud, T. S. Eliot, Vsevolod Meyerhold, Erwin Piscator, Bertolt Brecht, and even George Bernard Shaw, who is included for his "infusion of a modernist spirit into standard theatrical forms."[4] Innes makes passing reference to a Living Theatre production of Gertrude Stein's *Ladies' Voices*, and the Japanese performer Sada Yakko is credited with inspiring Yeats.[5] Otherwise, women do not figure in Innes's account, and though he notes that in modernist theatre and drama, "stylistic and social revolution went together,"[6] the "woman question" and gender politics are not mentioned at all.

In his introduction to *The Cambridge Companion to Modernism*, Michael Levenson acknowledges the challenges to traditional accounts of modernism as "the exclusive affair of 'modern masters'"[7] such as T. S. Eliot and Ezra Pound that have been posed by feminist critics, scholars of the Harlem Renaissance, and theatre historians among others, and he suggests that

[a]s we acknowledge the full compass of the work, it will prove better to be minimalist in our definitions of that conveniently flaccid term *Modernist* and maximalist in our accounts of the diverse *modernizing* works and movements, which are sometimes deeply congruent with one another, and just as often opposed or even contradictory.[8]

In my own exploration of women, modernism, and performance in this book, I have adopted a "maximalist" approach – beginning with Ibsen,[9] recognizing the contributions of Ellen Terry, crossing the disciplines of theatre and drama, fiction, and dance, and encompassing realist and nonrealist works – in order to address the omission of women from accounts of modern theatre history and to clarify the relationship of theatrical and dramatic modernism to more recognized modernisms in other fields.

The preceding chapters have followed an approximately but not rigidly chronological order. I began by considering Elizabeth Robins's work as an Ibsen actress in the 1890s and her subsequent feminist critique of Ibsen's work in her 1907 suffrage play *Votes for Women* and 1908 lecture "Some Aspects of Henrik Ibsen." I then looked at Ellen Terry's differently motivated feminist rejection of Ibsen and her alternative proposal of a proto-feminist Shakespeare in the lectures that she gave beginning in 1910. This analysis was followed by a consideration of Virginia Woolf's imaginative engagement with actresses, particularly Terry, in writings dating from 1911 to 1935, and of the relationship of these minor writings to her major feminist–modernist theoretical and fictional works of the 1920s, 30s, and early 40s. The concern with the transformation of limiting gender roles in and through art that was a theme in Woolf's writings on actresses extended into my subsequent discussion of various early-twentieth-century repre- sentations of "ob/scene" new female sexualities both on stage and off by such artists as Edith Craig, Djuna Barnes, and Radclyffe Hall from the first performance of *A Pageant of Great Women* in 1909 through to the publica- tion of *The Dove* in 1923 and the obscenity trial of *The Well of Loneliness* in 1928. A theory of the transformative potential of art for social actors was then extrapolated from Woolf's 1941 novel *Between the Acts*, and finally, this theory was qualified by a consideration of the posthumous reputa- tion of Isadora Duncan, beginning with accounts of her death in 1927 and culminating in the 1968 bio-pic *Isadora*.

This roughly chronological ordering of the chapters and my suggestion in my introduction that the chapters are related to each other in a kind of relay structure might suggest an evolving progress narrative, but as the case of Duncan makes clear, the history of women, modernism, and perfor- mance was not a straightforward linear development. Indeed, the popular co-optation of Duncan into a tragic historiographic narrative that serves to negate what she accomplished as an artist reaffirms the value of Ibsen's earlier interventions into gendered narrative conventions in such modern tragedies as *Ghosts*, *Rosmersholm*, and *Hedda Gabler*. The value of Felski's model of the feminist counter-public sphere is that it can accommodate a range of sometimes seemingly opposite strategies by different artists in and across disciplines and establish resonances that suggest how the work of these artists functioned complementarily and conjunctively to politicize and transform the representation of gender. According to such a model, for example, Ibsen's contribution to feminist discourse through and about theatre would not be negated by, but would instead stand alongside of, sub- sequent feminist critiques of his work by Robins, Terry, and Barnes, even as those critiques generated awareness of the limitations of his work and gave rise to further feminist explorations of the representation of gender. Thus also, while *Votes for Women* in certain respects reinforced conventional gender ideology, it at the same time constituted a valid response to the limitations of Ibsen's dramaturgy for feminism, put forward pro-suffrage arguments, and, in appropriating the stage for the purposes of suffrage propaganda, created a theatrical space for Craig's later sexually dissident self-portraiture through the figure of Rosa Bonheur in *A Pageant of Great Women*. Virginia Woolf's unsettling of fixed gender identities in *A Room of One's Own* and *Orlando* challenged the more unified and essential under- standings of gender of Robins, Terry, and Duncan, but in her own carefully selected public appearances, Woolf herself deployed the essential fact of her female body to insist on the feminist significance of her modernist textual explorations. The effect of combining the different artists considered here into a single study is thus ultimately more kaleidoscopic than progressive, producing a multi-faceted image that shifts continually over the course of its circuitous route before returning in the end to its starting point, which has itself been shifted as a result of the intervening traversal of various shifting perspectives. This kaleidoscopic effect underlines the interrelation and indeed the necessity of the diverse textual and corporeal strategies deployed by the different artists in question.

Michael Levenson has noted that while the "social cataclysms" of the late-nineteenth and early-twentieth centuries "left traces on modernist art, so did that art inform and to an extent *form* the conception of social life within historical crisis,"[10] one aspect of which was the "woman question" and the rise of first-wave feminism. While no single strategy of resistance to women's sociocultural subordination appears to have been fully successful, it seems indisputable that, through the conjunction of these diverse strategies within a feminist–modernist counter-public sphere, the artists that I have considered here collectively contributed to the transformation of the representation of gender in both art and life.

Notes

INTRODUCTION

1 Joan Templeton, *Ibsen's Women* (Cambridge University Press, 1997) 325, 324.

2 Katherine E. Kelly, "Introduction: the Making of Modern Drama," *Modern Drama by Women 1880s–1930s: An International Anthology*, ed. Katherine E. Kelly (London: Routledge, 1996) 3.

3 Templeton, *Ibsen's Women* 325.

4 Virginia Woolf, *The Voyage Out* (San Diego: Harvest–HBJ, 1931) 123–124. In "Out of the Chrysalis: Female Initiation and Female Authority in Virginia Woolf's *The Voyage Out*," *Tulsa Studies in Women's Literature* 5 (Spring 1986), Christine Froula discusses this passage in relation to the resistance of both Rachel and Woolf to the conventional marriage plot (75). Like Louise DeSalvo (*Virginia Woolf's First Voyage: A Novel in the Making* [Totawa, NJ: Rowman and Little-field, 1980] 69–70), Froula suggests that the name of Woolf's character is an allusion to the French actress Rachel ("Out of the Chrysalis" 88–89). Woolf's review of Francis Gribble's biography of Rachel is discussed in chapter 3 of this book.

5 See, for example, Rolf Fjelde, foreword, *Ibsen: Four Major Plays*, vol. 1 (Signet Classic, 1965): "When the troubled applause died away, and the first audience for Ibsen's *A Doll House* rose to their somewhat unsteady feet and filed up the aisles, no one among them could have known that he had participated, four days before Christmas of 1879, in the birth of modern drama. The long view is a privilege reserved for posterity, whereas the shaken spectators in Copenhagen's Royal Theater, still reverberating with the slam of that historic door, had other, more immediate concerns to cope with" (xxiv).

See also Gail Finney, *Women in Modern Drama: Freud, Feminism, and European Theater at the Turn of the Century* (Ithaca, NY: Cornell University Press, 1989) 149–150; John Gassner, introduction, *Four Great Plays by Ibsen* (Bantam Books, 1959) ix; and Michael Meyer, introduction, *Plays: Two*, by Henrik Ibsen (London: Methuen, 1980) 17.

6 For an elaboration of this point, see my essay "Reading, Writing, and Authority in Ibsen's 'Women's Plays,'" *Modern Drama* 45.1 (Spring 2002): 1–8.

7 Isadora Duncan, *My Life* (New York: Liveright, 1927) 41.

8 Isadora Duncan, *Isadora Speaks*, ed. Franklin Rosemont (San Francisco: City Lights Books, 1981) 52–53.

9 Bridget Elliot and Jo-Ann Wallace, *Women Artists and Writers: Modernist (im)positionings* (London: Routledge, 1994) 7.

10 Elin Diamond, introduction, *Performance and Cultural Politics* (London: Routledge, 1996) 1, 4, 6.

11 Ibid. 2.

12 Joseph R. Roach describes cultural studies as an "interdiscipline" and performance studies as a subset of cultural studies in his introduction to the "Cultural Studies" section of *Critical Theory and Performance*, ed. Joseph R. Roach and Janelle Reinelt (Ann Arbor: University of Michigan Press, 1992) 10. Elsewhere, Roach refers to performance studies as an "antidiscipline" (qtd. in Marvin Carlson, *Performance: A Critical Introduction* [London: Routledge, 1996] 189).

13 Rita Felski, *Beyond Feminist Aesthetics: Feminist Literature and Social Change* (Cambridge, MA: Harvard University Press, 1989) 164.

14 Ibid. 166, 171, 168.

15 George Rowell, "Misleading Ladies: Two Biographies of Ellen Terry," rev. of *Ellen Terry: Player in Her Time* by Nina Auerbach and *Ellen and Edy: A Biography of Ellen Terry and Her Daughter, Edith Craig, 1847–1947* by Joy Melville, *Theatre Notebook* 42.3 (1988): 128.

16 Duncan, *My Life* 186–187.

17 Elizabeth Robins, diary, 6 May 1928, Elizabeth Robins Papers, Fales Library, New York University. Robins had apparently never seen Duncan perform, finding it noteworthy enough to record in her diary on 3 June 1928 that an acquaintance she met at the opera, the German dance-writer Dr. Hildebrand, "saw Isadora Duncan dance Parcival and come to the Festspielhaus at Bayreuth barelegged in her tunic."

18 As Jill Edmonds has noted, Bernhardt was herself "aware of the teasing sexual ambiguity of playing the role of a man considered by her contemporaries to be rather feminine" ("Princess Hamlet," *The New Woman and Her Sisters: Feminism and Theatre 1850–1914*, ed. Vivien Gardner and Susan Rutherford [Ann Arbor: University of Michigan Press, 1992] 61). Fielding an interviewer's inquiry as to whether "any man [can] quite grasp the inner nature of Hamlet," she responded, "Perhaps not. There is much that is feminine in it. [. . .] [I]t takes the brains of a man and the intuitive almost psychic power of a woman to give a true rendering of it" (interview, *Daily Chronicle* 17 June 1899, qtd. in Edmonds, "Princess Hamlet" 61). Elsewhere, Bernhardt stated still more bluntly, "I cannot see Hamlet as a man. The things he says, his impulses, his actions entirely indicate to me that he was a woman" (qtd. in Marjorie Garber, *Vested Interests: Cross-Dressing and Cultural Anxiety* [New York: Harper Perennial, 1992] 38).

19 Elizabeth Robins, "On Seeing Madame Bernhardt's Hamlet," *North American Review* 171.6 (December 1900): 910, 908.

20 Sheila Stowell, *A Stage of Their Own: Feminist Playwrights of the Suffrage Era* (Ann Arbor: University of Michigan Press, 1992) 21.

21 Bonnie Kime Scott, introduction, *The Gender of Modernism* (Bloomington, IN: Indiana University Press, 1990) 10; see also Bonnie Kime Scott, *Refiguring Modernism*, vol. 1, *The Women of 1928* (Bloomington, IN: Indiana University Press, 1995) xxiii.

22 See Virginia Stephen [later, Woolf], rev. of *A Dark Lantern* by Elizabeth Robins, *Guardian* 24 May 1905: 899, rpt. in Jane Marcus, *Art and Anger: Reading like a Woman* (Columbus: Ohio State University Press, 1988) 267; and Virginia Woolf, rev. of *The Mills of the Gods* by Elizabeth Robins, *Times Literary Supplement* 17 June 1920, rpt. in Marcus, *Art and Anger* 266–267.

23 See Virginia Woolf, "The Higher Court," *New Statesman* 17 April 1920: 44.

24 See Virginia Woolf, 30 March 1922, *The Diary of Virginia Woolf*, ed. Anne Olivier Bell, assisted by Andrew McNeillie, 5 vols. (London: Hogarth Press, 1977–84) 2: 174.

25 See Jane Marcus, "Some Sources for *Between the Acts*," *Virginia Woolf Miscellany* 6 (Winter 1977): 2; Julie Holledge, *Innocent Flowers: Women in the Edwardian Theatre* (London: Virago, 1981) 161–162; and Nina Auerbach, *Ellen Terry: Player in Her Time* (New York: W. W. Norton, 1987) 427.

26 See Leonard Woolf, "The World of Books: 'I Remember' and Other Motives," rev. of *My Life* by Isadora Duncan, *The Nation & Athenaeum* 19 May 1928: 210.

27 It is unclear whether Woolf actually attended any of Craig's productions at the Barn Theatre. She apparently went to a reading by Vita Sackville-West of her poem *The Land* at the Barn on 18 September 1932 (see Victoria Glendinning, *Vita: The Life of Vita Sackville-West* [Harmondsworth: Penguin Books, 1983] 251), and in letters to Sackville-West dating from 1933 and 1938, she mentioned her intention to subscribe to the Barn Theatre (see *The Letters of Virginia Woolf*, ed. Nigel Nicolson and Joanne Trautmann, 6 vols. [London: Hogarth Press, 1975–80] 5: 225 and 6: 232). In the second of these letters, however, Woolf states, "There's a fate against my joining" (6: 232). In another letter dated 6 March 1941, not long before Woolf's death, Sackville-West offered to take Woolf to visit Ellen Terry's house (*The Letters of Vita Sackville-West to Virginia Woolf*, ed. Louise DeSalvo and Mitchell A. Leaska [New York: William Morrow, 1985] 442), but it does not appear that they actually made this visit.

28 See Djuna Barnes, "How it Feels to be Forcibly Fed," *New York World Magazine* 6 September 1914, rpt. in Djuna Barnes, *New York*, ed. Alyce Barry (London: Virago, 1990) 174–179.

29 Hall was an avid theatregoer, particularly in the 1920s, but I have not come across any mention of her reading or attending Ibsen's plays.

30 The fact that Ibsen's art was itself shaped by his contact with Scandinavian women writers and reformers lends further support to the notion of a feminist counter-public sphere, although this particular extension of the network of connections is beyond the scope of my present study. For details of his relationships with such writers as Magdalene Thoresen (his mother-in-law) and Camilla Collett, as well as of his knowledge of the feminist reformer Asta Hansteen, see Templeton, *Ibsen's Women* 40–44, 68–72, 129–135; see also Katherine Hanson,

"Ibsen's Women Characters and Their Feminist Contemporaries," *Theatre History Studies* 2 (1982): 83–91.

31 Viv Gardner, introduction, *The New Woman and Her Sisters*, ed. Gardner and Rutherford 4.

32 Auerbach, *Ellen Terry: Player in Her Time* 27.

33 See, for example, August Strindberg, "Preface to *Miss Julie*," trans. E. M. Sprinchorn, *Dramatic Theory and Criticism: Greeks to Grotowski*, ed. Bernard F. Dukore (Holt, Rinehart and Winston, 1974) 567; and Georg Lukács, "The Sociology of Modern Drama," trans. Lee Baxandall, *Dramatic Theory and Criticism: Greeks to Grotowski* 934.

34 Virginia Woolf, *Between the Acts* (San Diego: Harvest–HBJ, 1941) 153, 195.

35 Tania Modleski, *Feminism Without Women: Culture and Criticism in a "Postfeminist" Age* (New York: Routledge, 1991) 48.

36 Judith Butler, "Critically Queer," *GLQ: A Journal of Lesbian and Gay Studies* 1.1 (1993): 29.

37 Ibid. 17.

I FROM '*HEDDA GABLER*' TO '*VOTES FOR WOMEN*': ELIZABETH ROBINS'S EARLY FEMINIST CRITIQUE OF IBSEN

1 Elizabeth Robins, "Come and See," *Way Stations* (London: Hodder and Stoughton, 1913) 267. The Princess Bariatinsky, also known as Madame Lydia Yavorska, performed *Hedda Gabler* and *A Doll's House* in London between 1909 and 1911. According to Miriam Alice Franc, she was "the most successful of the foreign interpreters of Ibsen," her "strange, fierce type of acting [making] her a theatrical sensation" (*Ibsen in England*, diss., University of Pennsylvania [Boston: Four Seas, 1919] 97).

2 Claire Hirshfield discusses the reluctance of actresses to identify themselves too closely with the militant suffragists in her article "The Actresses' Franchise League and the Campaign for Women's Suffrage 1908–1914," *Theatre Research International* 10.2 (Summer 1985): 129–153.

3 Elizabeth Robins, "Oscar Wilde: an Appreciation," ts., Elizabeth Robins Papers, Fales Library, New York University, 2.

4 Elizabeth Robins, *Whither and How*, ts. and ms., Elizabeth Robins Papers, Fales Library, New York University, n. pag.; unless otherwise noted, subsequent references will be given parenthetically in the text as *WH*.

5 Elizabeth Robins, *Ibsen and the Actress* (London: Hogarth Press, 1928; rpt. New York: Haskell House, 1973) 55; subsequent references will be given parenthetically in the text as *IA*.

6 George Bernard Shaw, "The Technical Novelty in Ibsen's Plays," *Dramatic Theory and Criticism: Greeks to Grotowski*, ed. Bernard F. Dukore (Fort Worth, TX: Holt, Rinehart and Winston, 1974) 646.

7 Robins, *Whither and How* (chapter 8) 10.

8 Gay Gibson Cima, "Discovering Signs: the Emergence of the Critical Actor in Ibsen," *Theatre Journal* 35.1 (March 1983): 5–22; and Gay Gibson Cima,

Performing Women: Female Characters, Male Playwrights, and the Modern Stage (Ithaca, NY: Cornell University Press, 1993) 20–59.

9 Robins, *Whither and How* ("After Hedda: Offers") n. pag.

10 *Era* 16 March 1889, qtd. in Gay Gibson Cima, "Elizabeth Robins: Ibsen Actress–Manageress," diss., Cornell University, 1978, 47.

11 *Stage* 10 May 1889; *Sporting Life*, 11 May 1889; *Era* 11 May 1889, qtd. in Cima, "Elizabeth Robins: Ibsen Actress–Manageress" 51 (footnote 7).

12 *Pall Mall Gazette*; *Daily Chronicle*; *Daily News*, qtd. in Cima, "Elizabeth Robins: Ibsen Actress–Manageress" 136, 135, 136.

13 Clement Scott, *Illustrated London News* 25 April 1891, *Ibsen: The Critical Heritage*, ed. Michael Egan (London: Routledge and Kegan Paul, 1972) 227.

14 Robins's desire for the "tonic" of the critical spotlight may have motivated her 1893 production of the sensational *Alan's Wife*, which she and Florence Bell anonymously adapted from a story by the Swedish author Elin Ameen and in which a woman murders the deformed baby she gives birth to after her husband is killed in an industrial accident. Robins's reminiscences certainly focus more on the critical controversy that *Alan's Wife* generated than on its actual content (see Elizabeth Robins, *Theatre and Friendship* [New York: G. P. Putnam's Sons, 1932] 117–118; subsequent references will be given parenthetically in the text as *TF*), and her tendency in later, explicitly feminist writings such as *Votes for Women* and "Some Aspects of Henrik Ibsen" was toward the idealization of motherhood, suggesting that her representational standards shifted as her feminist politics evolved.

The original published version of *Votes for Women* has been rpt. in *How the Vote was Won and Other Plays*, ed. Dale Spender and Carole Hayman (London: Methuen, 1985) 35–87; subsequent references will be to this edition of the play and will be given parenthetically in the text. The production version of *Votes for Women* has been rpt. in Katherine E. Kelly, ed., *Modern Drama by Women 1880s–1930s: An International Anthology* (London: Routledge, 1996) and differs slightly from the original published version. The character called Jean Dunbarton in the first published version of the play is called Beatrice (Bee) in the production version, for example, and Vida's speech on motherhood, which comes at the very end of the original published version, is placed a little earlier in the production version.

There are two typescript versions of "Some Aspects of Henrik Ibsen" in the Elizabeth Robins Papers, Fales Library, New York University. The shorter version is entitled simply "Some Aspects of Henrik Ibsen," whereas the longer version, from which I will be quoting in this chapter, is entitled "Some Aspects of Henrik Ibsen: Lecture delivered before The Philosophical Institute, Edinburgh. October 27, 1908." The longer version begins with a biographical sketch of Ibsen and pays somewhat closer attention to his female characters than the shorter version does. Subsequent references to this long version will be cited parenthetically in the text as "SA."

15 Elizabeth Robins, *Both Sides of the Curtain* (London: Heinemann, 1940) 250; subsequent references will be given parenthetically in the text as *BSC*.

16 "Goldsmith and Ibsen: A Dramatic Contrast," *People* 26 April 1891, *Ibsen: The Critical Heritage*, ed. Egan 233.
17 Jiří Veltrusky, "Man and Object in the Theatre," *A Prague School Reader on Esthetics, Literary Structure, and Style*, trans. Paul L. Garvin (Washington, DC: Georgetown University Press, 1964) 86, 85.
18 Jane Marcus, *Art and Anger: Reading Like A Woman* (Columbus: Ohio State University Press, 1988) 58.
19 The prospect of performing Shakespeare may have been the exception for Robins. As late as 1899, she wrote to Henry Irving offering to audition for him in the role of Portia and expressing a fervent and long-standing desire to work with him, even though, by that time, the Lyceum had reached its point of decline as the premier London theatre. Robins's letter to Irving is rpt. in Gail Marshall, *Actresses on the Victorian Stage: Feminine Performance and the Galatea Myth* (Cambridge University Press, 1998) 176.
20 Elizabeth Robins, *Raymond and I* (London: Hogarth Press, 1956) 47.
21 Elizabeth Robins to Florence Bell, 12 December 1899, qtd. in Joanne E. Gates, "'Sometimes Suppressed and Sometimes Embroidered': the Life and Writing of Elizabeth Robins, 1862–1952," diss., University of Massachusetts, Amherst, 1987, 211. Gates's dissertation has been revised and published as *Elizabeth Robins, 1862–1952: Actress, Novelist, Feminist* (Tuscaloosa, AL: University of Alabama Press, 1994).
22 Michael Meyer, introduction, *When We Dead Awaken*, by Henrik Ibsen, *Plays: Four*, trans. Michael Meyer (London: Eyre Methuen, 1980) 205.
23 Adrienne Rich, "*When We Dead Awaken*: Writing as Re-Vision," *On Lies, Secrets, and Silence: Selected Prose 1966–1978* (New York: Norton, 1979) 34.
24 Michael Meyer, introduction, *John Gabriel Borkman*, Ibsen, *Plays: Four* 125.
25 Jane Marcus has argued that "[t]he title, *Ancilla's Share*, was in fact a naming of [Robins's] whole career (or several careers) as a woman artist" and that she went from playing Ancilla to Ibsen to playing Ancilla to the feminist movement ("Elizabeth Robins," diss., Northwestern University, 1973, 3).
26 Elizabeth Robins, *Ancilla's Share: An Indictment of Sex Antagonism* (London: Hutchinson, 1924) 104; subsequent references will be given parenthetically in the text as *AS*.
27 Robins's persistent autobiographical return to the theatre in such works as *Ibsen and the Actress* (1928), *Theatre and Friendship* (1932), and *Both Sides of the Curtain* (1940) suggests that she continued to identify herself primarily in terms of her experience as an actress long after her retirement from the stage.
28 "Some Aspects of Henrik Ibsen" is Robins's only fully developed critique of Ibsen. Addressing a presumably non-theatrical audience at the Edinburgh Philosophical Institute in the heat of the suffrage movement in 1908, she apparently felt obligated or at liberty to look at Ibsen from a theoretical perspective. Perhaps because of her feminist critique of the then well-established playwright, however, her talk was not well received, her diary entry for 27 October 1908 indicating that she had spoken before a "cold audience" (ms., Elizabeth Robins Papers, Fales Library, New York University; subsequent references to Robins's

diaries are from this same source). As noted in the introduction to this chapter, Robins states in *Ibsen and the Actress* that she would not have been as enthusiastic about Ibsen's drama if she had been "thinking politically" about "the emancipation of women" (31), but she does not follow through with a feminist critique, probably because she originally presented the essay as part of a British Drama League lecture series in celebration of the centenary of Ibsen's birth and intended it to compensate for the fact that preceding lectures in the series had made "no mention of the theatre or of acting" (diary, 5 March 1928). In the introductory paragraphs of *Ibsen and the Actress*, therefore, she announces her intention to bring a specifically theatrical perspective to the centenary proceedings and to address "Ibsen's significance to actors" (8), stating that "without the help of the stage the world would not have had an Ibsen to celebrate; and without Ibsen the world would not have had the stage as it became after his plays were acted" (7–8). Her diary entry on 12 March 1928 indicates that, unlike "Some Aspects of Henrik Ibsen," her talk on Ibsen and the actress was warmly received.

29 In locating Ibsen's merit in his poetry more than in his ideas, Robins agreed with her friend William Archer in his debate with George Bernard Shaw.

30 Henrik Ibsen, qtd. in Robins, "Some Aspects of Henrik Ibsen: Lecture delivered before The Philosophical Institute, Edinburgh. October 27, 1908," 14.

31 In the short version of the lecture, the end of this passage reads: "we should be more disposed to quarrel with his limitations as a thinker" (5).

32 In the long version of the lecture, the last sentence of this passage has been crossed out; in the short version, it is retained (5).

33 Henrik Ibsen, qtd. in Robins, "Some Aspects of Henrik Ibsen: Lecture delivered before The Philosophical Institute, Edinburgh. October 27, 1908," 8.

34 Marcus, *Art and Anger* 58.

35 Gates, "'Sometimes Suppressed and Sometimes Embroidered'" 315. In a 1907 essay entitled "The Feministe Movement in England," Robins describes how she was opposed to women's suffrage until she "first heard women talking politics in public" in Trafalgar Square. "[O]n that Sunday afternoon, in front of Nelson's Monument, a new chapter was begun for me in the lesson of faith in the capacities of women" (*Way Stations* 40).

36 Elizabeth Robins to Millicent Fawcett, 1 November 1906, qtd. in Gates, "'Sometimes Suppressed and Sometimes Embroidered'" 316. Gates discusses Robins's fiction at length, as does Angela John in *Elizabeth Robins: Staging a Life, 1862–1952* (London: Routledge, 1995).

37 "Women Writers' Suffrage League," *Way Stations* 112; Elizabeth Robins, "For the Women Writers," *Way Stations* 116.

38 Elizabeth Robins, *The Convert* (London: Women's Press, 1980) 253.

39 Elizabeth Robins, qtd. in Marcus, "Elizabeth Robins" 321 and Sheila Stowell, *A Stage of Their Own: Feminist Playwrights of the Suffrage Era* (Ann Arbor: University of Michigan Press, 1992) 11.

40 William Archer remarked on the rhetorical resemblance between *A Doll's House* and *Votes for Women*: "You remember how, in the last scene of 'A Doll's House,'

the egregious Helmer says to Nora, 'No man sacrifices his honour even for one he loves,' and Nora replies, 'Millions of women have done that!'

"Well, multiply this Helmerism and this Noraism by several hundred, and you have the dialogue of *'Votes for Women!'* And the trouble is that the Helmerisms are quite typical, and the Noraisms exceedingly cogent and crushing" ("Court Theatre. Miss Robins's 'Dramatic Tract,'" *Tribune* 13 May 1907, Elizabeth Robins Papers, Fales Library).

41 Cima remarks on this resemblance between the meeting scene in *An Enemy of the People* and the suffrage rally scene in *Votes for Women* in "Elizabeth Robins: Ibsen Actress–Manageress" 264.

42 Henrik Ibsen, *An Enemy of the People, Plays: Two*, trans. Michael Meyer (London: Methuen, 1980) 194, 195.

43 For a more exhaustive analysis of *Votes for Women* as a feminist response not simply to Ibsen's drama but to a broader range of male-authored nineteenth-century drama, including the "drawing-room plays of the 1890s" and "Drury Lane city spectacle," see Stowell, *A Stage of Their Own* 9–39. Focusing on the play's "[reshaping of] the conventions and traditions of the late Victorian stage" (14) rather than on its relation to Robins's work as an actress, Stowell sees *Votes for Women* as more successful in its subversion of the patriarchal dramatic tradition than I do.

44 Alex M. Thompson, "Stageland. A Masterpiece of Stage Management," *Clarion* 19 April 1907: 3.

45 "Court Theatre: *'Votes for Women!'*" *Times* 10 April 1907: 5.

46 "*Votes for Women!*," *Era* 13 April 1907: 13.

47 See, for example, St. J[ohn]. H[ankins]., rev. of *Votes for Women*, *Academy* 13 April 1907: 370; "Trafalgar Square Dramatised: Suffrage Play at the Court Theatre," *Daily Express* 10 April 1907: 5; and rev. of *Votes for Women*, *Referee* 14 April 1907, qtd. in Jan McDonald, "'The Second Act Was Glorious': the Staging of the Trafalgar Scene from *Votes for Women!* at the Court Theatre," *Theatre History Studies* 15 (June 1995): 159.

48 "A Suffragette Play at the Court," *Pall Mall Gazette* 10 April 1907: 2.

49 "*Votes for Women!*" *Era* 13.

50 Ibid.

51 Michael Meyer, *Ibsen* (Harmondsworth: Penguin, 1967) 480.

52 Cima, "Elizabeth Robins: Ibsen Actress–Manageress" 114.

53 Elizabeth Robins, qtd. in Cima, "Elizabeth Robins: Ibsen Actress–Manageress" 263. Cima herself explains that an actress "had only so many years on the stage, unless she achieved the stature of Bernhardt or Duse, in which case the audience would continue to pay to see her, even in her old age. Many London actor–managers, on the other hand, played youthful roles into their later years, without remonstance [sic] from the audience" ("Elizabeth Robins: Ibsen Actress–Manageress" 49). In *Actresses as Working Women: Their Social Identity in Victorian Culture* (London: Routledge, 1991), Tracy Davis writes: "The termination of an actress's career seemed to have more to do with her age than her family life. Employment was markedly restricted to glamorous

functions demanding young recruits. In other words, the development of a woman's career was largely decided by factors beyond her control and unresponsive to her talents or determination" (52).

54 On a somewhat different note, Max Beerbohm found Robins's characterization of Vida Levering and Geoffrey Stonor so weak as to be improbable, suggesting that such improbability might allow the play to be interpreted as a comic satire of suffragism rather than as a pro-suffrage tract ("Miss Robins' Tract," *Around Theatres*, vol. 2 [New York: Alfred A. Knopf, 1930] 590–595).

55 Ibid. 593.

56 Thompson, "Stageland" 3. On the conventionality of Robins's dramaturgy, see also Hankins, who complained that Robins "knows all the familiar stage characters and all the familiar stage situations," and that in Acts I and III of *Votes for Women* in particular, she drew on "her memories of old St. James's successes and of the heroines of the late Victorian second-rate play and the late Victorian second-rate novel" (370).

57 Suzanne Clark, *Sentimental Modernism: Women Writers and the Revolution of the Word* (Bloomington, IN: Indiana University Press, 1991).

58 Sue Thomas, "Sexual Matter and *Votes for Women*," *Papers on Language and Literature* 33.1 (Winter 1997): 61. Thomas quotes St. John Hankins's statement that "[t]he stalwart propagoose (if that be the correct feminine of propagander) filled every available seat and punctuated all the correct sentiments with frantic applause" (70).

59 Clark, *Sentimental Modernism* 38.

60 For a discussion of the question of whether or not Robins was ever pregnant, see John, *Elizabeth Robins* 79–80.

61 "'Votes for Women!' A Suffragette Tract. Trafalgar Square on the Stage," *Daily News* 10 April 1907: 12.

62 Stowell, *A Stage of Their Own* 5–6, 18–19, 21.

63 Lisa Tickner, *The Spectacle of Women: Imagery of the Suffrage Campaign 1907–14* (London: Chatto and Windus, 1987) 151.

64 Rev. of *Votes for Women*, *Irish News* 15 April 1907, Elizabeth Robins Papers, Fales Library, New York University.

65 "Court Theatre: '*Votes for Women!*'" *Times* 5.

66 Thompson, "Stageland" 3.

67 Archer, "Court Theatre. Miss Robins's 'Dramatic Tract.'"

68 "'Votes for Women!' Extraordinary Play at the Court Theatre," *Daily Mail* 10 April 1907: 5.

69 Jane Marcus, "Transatlantic Sisterhood: Labor and Suffrage Links in the Letters of Elizabeth Robins and Emmeline Pankhurst," *Signs* 3.3 (Spring 1978): 750.

70 Claire Hirshfield, "Suffragettes Onstage: Women's Political Theatre in Edwardian England," *New England Theatre Journal* 2 (1991): 16; Marcus, "Elizabeth Robins" 318.

71 Woolf begins the "peroration" of *A Room of One's Own* (San Diego: Harvest–HBJ, 1929) by reciting for her young female audience a list of what women have failed to achieve: "You have never made a discovery of any sort of importance.

You have never shaken an empire or led an army into battle. The plays of Shakespeare are not by you, and you have never introduced a barbarous race to the blessings of civilization" (112). She concludes by stating that a woman of Shakespeare's genius will only be born when less exceptional women have the opportunity to work to prepare the way for her (113–114).

Citing Woolf's argument that "masterpieces are not single and solitary births" but "the outcome of many years of thinking in common, of thinking by the body of the people, so that the experience of the mass is behind the single voice" (*A Room of One's Own* 65), Jane Marcus has argued that Elizabeth Robins was one of Woolf's literary foremothers and that "[s]he and hundreds of other unknown women writers prepared the literary soil for the eventual creation of the woman of genius, the Shakespeare's sister" (*Art and Anger* 126).

72 Referring to the militant suffragists' first disruption of a parliamentary proceeding, Vida Levering asks an unsympathetic gathering at the house party in Act I of *Votes for Women*, "Isn't it just possible they [the militants] realise they've waked up interest in the Woman Question so that it's advertised in every paper and discussed in every house from Land's End to John O'Groats? Don't you think *they* know there's been more said and written about it in these ten days since the scene, than in the ten years before it?" (57).

2 FEMINIST SHAKESPEARE: ELLEN TERRY'S COMIC IDEAL

1 George Bernard Shaw, "Henry Irving and Ellen Terry," *Pen Portraits and Reviews* (London: Constable, 1932) 166; George Bernard Shaw, "Mr. Grundy's Improvements on Dumas," *Dramatic Opinions and Essays*, vol. 2 (London: Constable, 1912) 309; George Bernard Shaw, *Ellen Terry and Bernard Shaw: A Correspondence*, ed. Christopher St. John (New York: G. P. Putnam's Sons, 1931) 12.

2 Henry James, "On the Occasion of *Hedda Gabler*," *The New Review* 4.25 (1891), *Ibsen: The Critical Heritage*, ed. Michael Egan (London: Routledge and Kegan Paul, 1972) 236, 243.

3 Ellen Terry, "Stray Memories," Part 3, *The New Review* 4.25 (1891): 503–504.

4 Ellen Terry, qtd. in Christopher St. John, *Ellen Terry's Memoirs*, by Ellen Terry, with preface, notes, and additional biographical chapters by Edith Craig and Christopher St. John (New York: Benjamin Blom, 1969) 327.

5 George Bernard Shaw, appendix, *The Quintessence of Ibsenism* (New York: Brentano's, 1910) 148. Shaw and Terry make reference to this passage of *The Quintessence of Ibsenism* in several letters published in *Ellen Terry and Bernard Shaw: A Correspondence* 8–10.

6 George Bernard Shaw, preface, *Ellen Terry and Bernard Shaw* xi.

7 Nina Auerbach, *Ellen Terry: Player in Her Time* (New York: W. W. Norton, 1987) 43.

8 Michael R. Booth, "Ellen Terry," *Bernhardt, Duse, Terry: The Actress in Her Time*, by Michael R. Booth, Susan Bassnett, and John Stokes (Cambridge University Press, 1988) 86.

9 The Lyceum production of *Macbeth* opened on 29 December 1888 and closed in June 1889, after a run of over 150 performances. The Janet Achurch–Charles Charrington production of *A Doll's House* opened on 7 June 1889 and was followed by the Florence Farr production of *Rosmersholm* on 23 February 1891, the Independent Theatre production of *Ghosts* on 13 March 1891, and the Elizabeth Robins–Marion Lea production of *Hedda Gabler* on 20 April 1891.

10 Booth, "Ellen Terry" 69–70.

11 In his listing of the lines of business in the typical nineteenth-century stock company, George Bernard Shaw makes reference to "heavies to whom Lady Macbeth was all in the night's work" (preface, *Ellen Terry and Bernard Shaw* xv).

12 Booth, "Ellen Terry" 106.

13 Frederick Hawkins, "Macbeth on the Stage," part II, *The Theatre*, new series 13 (1 January 1889): 6.

14 Siddons first played Lady Macbeth in London in 1785, though she had played the part earlier in the provinces. See Michael R. Booth, "Sarah Siddons," *Three Tragic Actresses: Siddons, Rachel, Ristori*, by Michael R. Booth, John Stokes, and Susan Bassnett (Cambridge University Press, 1996) 20.

15 G. J. Bell, qtd. in H. C. Fleeming Jenkin, "Mrs. Siddons as Lady Macbeth," *Mrs. Siddons as Lady Macbeth and as Queen Katharine*, by H. C. Fleeming Jenkin, *Papers on Acting*, vol. 3 (New York: Dramatic Museum of Columbia University, 1915) 36.

16 Sarah Siddons, "Remarks on the Character of Lady Macbeth," *Life of Mrs. Siddons*, vol. 2, by Thomas Campbell (London: Effingham Wilson, Royal Exchange, 1834) 11.

17 Ellen Terry, "The Pathetic Women," *Four Lectures on Shakespeare*, ed. Christopher St. John (New York: Benjamin Blom, 1969) 162–163.

18 Austin Brereton, "Ellen Terry, Player-Queen," *The English Illustrated Magazine* (December 1897): 238.

19 Ellen Terry, notes in George Fletcher, "*Macbeth*: Knight's Cabinet Edition of Shakespeare," *Westminster Review* XLI (1843), qtd. in Roger Manvell, *Ellen Terry* (London: Heinemann, 1968) 193.

20 J. Comyns Carr, *Macbeth and Lady Macbeth: An Essay* (London: Bickers & Son, 1889) 6.

21 Ellen Terry, letter to Clement Scott, qtd. in Auerbach, *Ellen Terry* 258.

22 Ellen Terry, letter to William Winter, qtd. in Auerbach, *Ellen Terry* 259.

23 Ellen Terry, qtd. in Joy Melville, *Ellen and Edy: A Biography of Ellen Terry and Her Daughter, Edith Craig, 1847–1947* (London: Pandora, 1987) 131.

24 Nina Auerbach has also noted this correspondence between Terry's Lady Macbeth and Ibsen's Nora Helmer, citing Terry's admission in a letter to Clement Scott that she once committed forgery – Nora's crime – to get money to help her lover: "'Do you think I thought that wicked then? I thought it was right –.'" (*Ellen Terry* 258).

25 Terry, "The Pathetic Women" 162.

26 Clement Scott, rev. of *A Doll's House, Daily Telegraph* 7 June 1889, *Ibsen: The Critical Heritage*, ed. Egan 102.

27 Francis Williams, "Irving and Terry in 'Macbeth,'" *Freund's Music and Drama, The Papers of Henry Irving and Ellen Terry from the Bram Stoker Collection, Shakespeare Centre Library, Stratford-upon-Avon* (Brighton: Harvester Microform, 1987): reel 22, box 56, no. 20.

28 Brereton, "Ellen Terry, Player-Queen" 238.

29 Olive Weston, "Ellen Terry, the Woman," *Philadelphia Press* 12 May 1889.

30 Auerbach, *Ellen Terry* 252.

31 Rev. of *Macbeth, Lock to Lock Times* [?], 5 January 1889, *The Papers of Henry Irving and Ellen Terry*, reel 22, box 56, no. 29.

32 Terry, letter to Clement Scott, qtd. in Auerbach, *Ellen Terry* 258, 259. Auerbach suggests that Terry's notes on Lady Macbeth may have been "unactable, particularly in an opulent Lyceum production" (*Ellen Terry* 255).

33 Ellen Terry, letter to Alfred C. Calmour, qtd. in Manvell, *Ellen Terry* 196.

34 Terry, notes in Fletcher, qtd. in Manvell, *Ellen Terry* 193.

35 Henrik Ibsen, qtd. in Michael Meyer, *Ibsen* (Harmondsworth: Penguin Books, 1985) 467.

36 The production was later taken on tour to North America.

37 An Old Hand [Edward R. Russell], "*Macbeth* at the Lyceum," *Liverpool Daily Post* 31 December 1888, *The Papers of Henry Irving and Ellen Terry*, reel 22, box 55, no. 54.

38 Edward R. Russell, "*Macbeth* Revisited," programme for the 150th performance of *Macbeth* at the Lyceum, 1889, n. pag., *The Papers of Henry Irving and Ellen Terry*, reel 11, box 17, no. 5.

39 Qtd. in Russell, "*Macbeth* Revisited," n. pag.

40 Terry, "Stray Memories," Part 3, 506; Terry, letter to William Winter, qtd. in Auerbach, *Ellen Terry* 259; Terry, notes in Lyceum acting edition, qtd. in Manvell, *Ellen Terry* 194.

41 Manvell, *Ellen Terry* 194.

42 Auerbach, *Ellen Terry* 254.

43 Russell, "*Macbeth* at the Lyceum."

44 Gay Gibson Cima, *Performing Women: Female Characters, Male Playwrights, and the Modern Stage* (Ithaca, NY: Cornell University Press, 1993) 42.

45 Auerbach, *Ellen Terry* 255.

46 Ellen Terry, *The Story of My Life* (New York: Schocken Books, 1982) 111; subsequent references will be given parenthetically in the text as *SML*. Elizabeth Robins, "Oscar Wilde: an Appreciation," ts., Elizabeth Robins Papers, Fales Library, New York University, 2. Gail Marshall has also suggested a correspondence between Terry's experience in playing Lady Macbeth and the experiences of the actresses involved in the early Ibsen productions: "Terry's appearance as Lady Macbeth signalled the commencement of a process of development and mutation in her own career which was echoed in the theatre as a whole with the advent of Ibsen on the English stage [. . .]. Ibsen's plays and the work of a new generation of actresses in them effectively re-wrote Galatea's position in

the English theatre [that is, the position of women as idealized female figures animated by desiring male artists, as exemplified by the mythical Pygmalion]. But this development did not happen in isolation, and it is important to note the complementary changes which came about in the popular Terry's more visible role and activities, and in the new kind of inspiration she was providing for her contemporaries" (*Actresses on the Victorian Stage: Feminine Performance and the Galatea Myth* [Cambridge University Press, 1998] 127).

47 Ellen Terry, letter to William Winter, qtd. in Auerbach, *Ellen Terry* 260.

48 Elizabeth Robins, *Ibsen and the Actress* (London: Hogarth Press, 1928) 33.

49 Ellen Terry, qtd. in Manvell, *Ellen Terry* 210.

50 Ellen Terry, ms. note in Henrik Ibsen, *Hedda Gabler*, trans. Edmund Gosse, 4th edn. (London: William Heinemann, 1891) 37, Ellen Terry Memorial Museum.

51 Ellen Terry, in "Realism and the Actor: an International Symposium," *The Mask* 1.9 (November 1908): 178.

52 Terry's lover Edward Godwin was described by Max Beerbohm as "the greatest aesthete of them all" (qtd. in Auerbach, *Ellen Terry* 144) and, as Michael R. Booth has pointed out, her relationship with him between the years 1868 and 1874 "placed her firmly in the Aesthetic movement" ("Ellen Terry" 77). When Terry returned to the stage following her sojourn in the country with Godwin, her breakthrough performance was as Portia in the Bancrofts' 1875 production of *The Merchant of Venice*, designed by Godwin and acclaimed by an artistic audience that included Oscar Wilde (*SML* 68).

53 Oscar Wilde, "The Decay of Lying," *Dramatic Theory and Criticism: Greeks to Grotowski*, ed. Bernard F. Dukore (Fort Worth, TX: Holt, Rinehart and Winston, 1974) 625.

54 Ibid.

55 Ibid. 628. This rejection of realism by the homosexual writer Oscar Wilde and by Ellen Terry in the service of feminism is an interesting historical precedent to contemporary feminist and queer critiques of realism, which are more often understood as Brechtian in their derivation. For examples of these critiques, see Sue-Ellen Case, "Towards a Butch/Femme Aesthetic," *Making a Spectacle: Feminist Essays on Contemporary Women's Theatre*, ed. Lynda Hart (Ann Arbor: University of Michigan Press, 1989) 297; and Jill Dolan, "'Lesbian' Subjectivity in Realism: Dragging at the Margins of Structure and Ideology," *Performing Feminisms: Feminist Critical Theory and Theatre*, ed. Sue-Ellen Case (Baltimore: Johns Hopkins University Press, 1990) 42. According to this line of argument, realism, with its typical focus on the heterosexual nuclear family unit, reinscribes the patriarchal and homophobic values of the status quo that it represents by making this status quo seem natural, universal, and inevitable, its "'mirror of life' conceit," in Elin Diamond's summary, "[erasing] agency and ideology – the point of view in the angle of the mirror, in the holder of it, and in the life it reflects" (*Unmaking Mimesis* [London: Routledge, 1997] 29). A theatrical exemplification *par excellence* of this line of argument is *Belle Reprieve* by Bette Bourne, Paul Shaw, Peggy Shaw, and Lois Weaver (*Split Britches: Lesbian Practice/Feminist Performance*, ed. Sue-Ellen Case

[London: Routledge, 1996] 149–183). In this adaptation of/critical response to Tennessee Williams's *A Streetcar Named Desire*, the gay and lesbian performers disrupt the rape scene originally scripted by Williams in order to "reprieve" the drag queen playing Blanche Dubois from the violently punitive fate decreed for gay men and sexually transgressive women in the world of Williams's play. The title of the musical number that is the celebratory grand finale of *Belle Reprieve* – "I Love My Art" – perhaps unconsciously but nonetheless uncannily echoes Oscar Wilde's valorization of art over life, aestheticism over realism.

Sheila Stowell has argued that this contemporary critique of realism is insufficiently historicized in that it neglects to address how realism originally functioned "as a means of challenging the ideological assumptions embedded in melodrama and the well-made play" ("Rehabilitating Realism," *Journal of Dramatic Theory and Criticism* 6.2 [Spring 1992]: 84). While Stowell's observation is certainly valid, the career of Elizabeth Robins may be seen to represent a kind of historical middle ground between her position and that of such scholars as Case and Dolan, at least as they might relate to Ibsen. As Gay Gibson Cima has stated, Ibsen's plays initially enabled Robins to "make visible the roles granted to 'woman,' and [to] make perceptible the negative effect of those roles" (*Performing Women* 38), but as I pointed out in the preceding chapter, Robins eventually came to see Ibsen's drama as limited in its feminist value because, with the exception of *A Doll's House*, it did not represent women's recognition and transcendence of their subordination within patriarchal society. Further to Stowell's objections to the categorical rejection of a particular dramatic and theatrical form, however, it is important to note that although Robins was best known for her work on such plays as *Hedda Gabler* and *The Master Builder*, her feminist critique of Ibsen, unlike Ellen Terry's, was not focused on or limited to his realist plays. Moreover, while Terry *was* categorical in her rejection of realism, her understanding of the form was, as I have suggested, superficial, and her comments on it are therefore of interest not so much intrinsically but for their function in enabling her to articulate her alternative feminist vision.

56 Lady Colin Campbell, "The First Ladies of the Day. V. – Miss Ellen Terry," *Madame* 6 December 1902: 605, *The Papers of Henry Irving and Ellen Terry*, reel 17, box 29, no. 61.

57 Auerbach, *Ellen Terry* 300.

58 Christopher St. John, introduction, *Four Lectures on Shakespeare*, by Ellen Terry 7.

59 Christopher St. John, *Ellen Terry: A Short Biography* ([London: Pelican Press], 1947) n. pag.

60 Ellen Terry, qtd. in Auerbach, *Ellen Terry* 423.

61 Terry's only Ibsen role was that of Hiördis in her son Edward Gordon Craig's 1903 production of the comparatively old-fashioned saga drama *The Vikings at Helgeland* (1858). Ironically, though Terry (see Auerbach, *Ellen Terry* 334) and at least one critic of Craig's production compared Hiördis to Lady Macbeth, the "proud, vengeful, bitter-tongued" Lady Macbeth of this comparison (rev. of *The Vikings at Helgeland*, *Daily Telegraph* 16 April 1903, *Ibsen: The Critical*

Heritage, ed. Egan 405) was more along the long-standing interpretive lines that Sarah Siddons had established in the eighteenth century than the more modern dutiful wife that Terry had herself played to such controversy just as Ibsen's realist dramas were beginning to appear on the London stage.

62 See, for example, Ellen Terry, "Some Recollections," *The Tatler* 250, 11 April 1906: 44; and Terry, *Ellen Terry and Bernard Shaw: A Correspondence* 101.

63 Ellen Terry, qtd. in St. John, introduction, *Four Lectures on Shakespeare* 16.

64 Ellen Terry, "The Triumphant Women," *Four Lectures on Shakespeare* 81–82.

65 "Warm Welcome for Miss Ellen Terry," *New York Times* 4 November 1910: 9. In the published text of "The Triumphant Women," the line is "'From a braying mule and a girl who speaks Latin good Lord deliver us!'" (82).

66 Terry, "The Pathetic Women" 151.

67 Ibid. 152.

68 Ibid.

69 Ibid. 117–118.

70 Susan Carlson, *Women and Comedy: Rewriting the British Theatrical Tradition* (Ann Arbor: University of Michigan Press, 1991) 21.

71 Ellen Terry, "More Reminiscences by Ellen Terry: Some Reflections on Shakespeare's Heroines," *McClure's Magazine* 36.1 (November 1910): 101.

72 George Meredith, "An Essay on Comedy," *Dramatic Theory and Criticism*, ed. Dukore 619, 618.

73 Meredith, "An Essay on Comedy" 619.

74 Ibid. 620.

75 Ibid. 619.

76 *Daily Telegraph*, qtd. in St. John, introduction, *Four Lectures on Shakespeare* 13.

77 Rev. of "The Triumphant Women," qtd. in St. John, introduction, *Four Lectures on Shakespeare* 20.

78 St. John, introduction, *Four Lectures on Shakespeare* 12; St. John, in Terry, *Ellen Terry's Memoirs* 293.

79 Shaw, preface, *Ellen Terry and Bernard Shaw* xxii.

80 Terry, "The Triumphant Women" 96.

81 Ibid. 97.

82 St. John, introduction, *Four Lectures on Shakespeare* 16; St. John, in Terry, *Ellen Terry's Memoirs* 293.

83 "Warm Welcome for Miss Ellen Terry" 9.

84 "Ellen Terry Acts Heroines," *New York Times* 11 November 1910: 9.

85 "Shakespeare as Suffragist," *The Vote* 4.92 (29 July 1911): 180.

86 "Warm Welcome for Miss Ellen Terry" 9.

87 William Winter, "Shadows of the Stage: Ellen Terry – Her Personality and Her Lectures," *Harper's Weekly* 17 December 1910: 18. In his attack on Terry's abilities as a lecturer, Winter focuses obsessively on her suggestion that Portia's courtroom quibble is "'not a man's idea' but 'a woman's,'" devoting approximately one third of his quite lengthy review to proving her wrong by arguing that the quibble "is, unmistakably, the technical quibble of a lawyer, and of a shrewd and tricky one" (18). In contrast, his commentary on the Lyceum's

production of *The Merchant of Venice* is full of praise for Terry's femininity in the role of Portia (*"Ellen Terry"* [*"The Merchant of Venice"*], *Shakespeare on the Stage*, first series [New York: Moffat, Yard, 1911] 217–222).

88 Susan Sontag, "Against Interpretation," *Against Interpretation and Other Essays* (New York: Farrar, Straus & Giroux, 1969) 6.
89 Terry, qtd. in St. John, introduction, *Four Lectures on Shakespeare* 15.
90 St. John, introduction, *Four Lectures on Shakespeare* 7.
91 Terry, qtd. in St. John, introduction, *Four Lectures on Shakespeare* 15.
92 Wilde, "The Decay of Lying" 628.
93 August Strindberg, "Preface to *Miss Julie*," trans. E. M. Sprinchorn, *Dramatic Theory and Criticism*, ed. Dukore 567.
94 Georg Lukács, "The Sociology of Modern Drama," trans. Lee Baxandall, *Dramatic Theory and Criticism*, ed. Dukore 934.
95 In fact, a discourse of doubleness pervades commentaries on Terry's life and work. Edward Gordon Craig, for example, entitled his memoir of his mother *Ellen Terry and Her Secret Self* (London: Sampson Low, Marston, 1931); Michael Booth has written of a "darker and more mysterious side" to Terry's image, suggesting that "[s]he was not only the sweet, virginal delicate being of Victorian fancy and Victorian myths of womanhood; paradoxically, she also possessed a sensuality, a seductiveness, a sense of moral and sexual danger [. . .]" (Booth, "Ellen Terry" 71); and Nina Auerbach has suggested that "[t]he comedienne Ellen Terry might have been, instead of the beloved woman she was, hovered over the theater like a poltergeist, hinting to all who entered of identities beyond the acceptable" (*Ellen Terry* 234).
96 Bertolt Brecht, "Short Description of a New Technique of Acting which Produces an Alienation Effect," *Brecht on Theatre*, trans. John Willett (New York: Hill and Wang, 1964) 137.
97 Elizabeth Robins, *Both Sides of the Curtain* (London: William Heineman, 1940) 250.
98 Isadora Duncan, *My Life* (New York: Liveright, 1927) 180.
99 Virginia Woolf, 27 December 1930, *The Diary of Virginia Woolf*, ed. Anne Olivier Bell, assisted by Andrew McNeillie, 5 vols. (London: Hogarth Press, 1977–84) 3: 340.

3 UNIMAGINED PARTS, UNLIVED SELVES:
VIRGINIA WOOLF ON ELLEN TERRY AND THE ART OF ACTING

1 Virginia Woolf, *The Diary of Virginia Woolf*, ed. Anne Olivier Bell, assisted by Andrew McNeillie, 5 vols. (London: Hogarth Press, 1977–84) 4: 273.
2 See, for example, "Bloomsbury Unbuttoned," *The New Yorker* 21 November 1983: 43.
3 Woolf, 30 January 1919, *The Diary of Virginia Woolf* 1: 237.
4 Lucio P. Ruotolo, preface, *Freshwater*, by Virginia Woolf (San Diego: Harvest–HBJ, 1976) vi.

5 Virginia Woolf, letter to Vanessa Bell, *The Letters of Virginia Woolf*, ed. Nigel Nicolson and Joanne Trautmann, 6 vols. (London: Hogarth Press, 1975–80) 3: 75.

6 That Ellen Terry is the central character of *Freshwater* is not generally recognized. In a review of French director Simone Benmussa's 1982–83 production, for example, critic Eva Hoffman writes that Woolf's play "concerns Mr. and Mrs. Cameron's imminent voyage to India, as soon as their coffins arrive" ("Rare Cast from France in a Rare Woolf Play," *New York Times* 22 October 1983: 9), while an article in *The New Yorker* states that "[t]he play [. . .] concerns a day in the life of [. . .] Julia Margaret Cameron, who is a tyrant" ("Bloomsbury Unbuttoned" 43).

7 Virginia Woolf, *Between the Acts* (San Diego: Harvest–HBJ, 1941) 153.

8 Virginia Woolf, "The Memoirs of Sarah Bernhardt," *Books and Portraits: Some Further Selections from the Literary and Biographical Writings of Virginia Woolf*, ed. Mary Lyon (London: Hogarth Press, 1977) 201; subsequent references to this essay will be given parenthetically in the text.

9 Virginia Woolf, "Rachel," *Times Literary Supplement* 20 April 1911: 155; subsequent references to this essay will be given parenthetically in the text.

10 Louise DeSalvo, *Virginia Woolf's First Voyage: A Novel in the Making* (Totawa, NJ: Rowman and Littlefield, 1980) 69–70.

11 Nina Auerbach, *Ellen Terry: Player in Her Time* (New York: Norton, 1987) 85; David Richman, "Directing *Freshwater*," *Virginia Woolf Miscellany* 2 (Spring 1974): 1.

12 In the 1923 version of *Freshwater*, Craig's address is 46 Gordon Square, Bloomsbury, W.C.1; in the 1935 version, the house number is not specified (Virginia Woolf, *Freshwater* [1923 and 1935 versions], ed. Lucio P. Ruotolo [San Diego: Harvest–HBJ, 1976] 83, 47; subsequent references will be given parenthetically in the text and will be to the 1935 version of the play unless otherwise specified).

13 Ellen Terry, *The Story of My Life* (New York: Schocken, 1982) 52.

14 Edward Gordon Craig and Edith Craig apparently chose their surname after seeing the Scottish island Ailsa Craig on a family holiday.

15 Auerbach, *Ellen Terry* 108.

16 Virginia Woolf, "Speech Before the London/National Society for Women's Service, January 21 1931," *The Pargiters: The Novel–Essay Portion of "The Years"*, by Virginia Woolf, ed. Mitchell A. Leaska (New York: New York Public Library, 1977) xxix; subsequent references to this speech will be given parenthetically in the text. Woolf borrowed the phrase "the Angel in the House" from the title of a work by the Victorian poet Coventry Patmore. A shorter version of the "Speech of January 21 1931" was later published as "Professions for Women."

17 The real Terry did in fact pose for Watts and Cameron, and as Nina Auerbach observes, Watts's portraits "concentrate on [her] bust and [her] face, suggesting mobility but banning motion," while "Cameron's photographs [. . .] cut off her legs" (*Ellen Terry* 101). Though Terry was not the subject of an ode by Tennyson, she might have been, since a drowned body discovered at the time

of her disappearance with Godwin was thought by many people to be hers (Terry, *The Story of My Life* 48).

18 Woolf's sense of the conservative relationship of Cameron's art to dominant gender ideology is further suggested by the gender-polarized title of the 1926 Hogarth Press anthology of Cameron's work: *Victorian Photographs of Famous Men and Fair Women*.

19 Woolf, 28 November 1928, *The Diary of Virginia Woolf* 3: 208.

20 Virginia Woolf, *A Room of One's Own* (San Diego: Harvest–HBJ, 1929) 5; subsequent references will be given parenthetically in the text as *AROO*.

21 The porpoise in *Freshwater* may seem to suggest a reference either to Woolf's friend and sometime lover Vita Sackville-West, who is occasionally referred to as a gambolling "dolphin" or "porpoise" in her correspondence with Woolf (see *The Letters of Vita Sackville-West to Virginia Woolf*, ed. Louise DeSalvo and Mitchell A. Leaska [New York: William Morrow, 1985] 213–214, 241, 393, 407, for example), or to Woolf's sister Vanessa Bell, who was nicknamed "Dolphin" because of her "undulating movements" (David Garnett, qtd. in Frances Spalding, *Vanessa Bell* [San Diego: Harvest–HBJ, 1983] 136). Theatrical considerations may have determined Woolf's choice, however: a porpoise is a fish-like animal of a size suitable for portrayal by an actor and of a nature suitable for dramatic interaction with human characters. In any case, in the Bloomsbury production, Vanessa Bell played Julia Margaret Cameron, while Adrian Stephen's daughter Judith played the porpoise.

22 Virginia Woolf, *Orlando* (San Diego: Harvest–HBJ, 1928) 329.

23 Auerbach, *Ellen Terry* 109.

24 Ibid. 109.

25 Virginia Woolf, "Ellen Terry," *Collected Essays*, vol. 4 (London: Hogarth Press, 1967) 68; subsequent references to this essay will be given parenthetically in the text as "ET."

26 Edward Gordon Craig, *Ellen Terry and Her Secret Self* (London: Sampson Low, Marston, 1931) 152.

27 Christine Froula, "Virginia Woolf as Shakespeare's Sister: Chapters in a Woman Writer's Autobiography," *Women's Re-Visions of Shakespeare: On the Responses of Dickinson, Woolf, Rich, H.D., George Eliot, and Others*, ed. Marianne Novy (Urbana, IL: University of Illinois Press, 1990) 137.

28 Ibid.

29 Ibid. 130, 134.

30 Woolf, 20 August 1930, *The Diary of Virginia Woolf* 3: 312.

31 Woolf, *Orlando* 314.

32 Ibid. 309–310.

33 Michael Levenson, introduction, *The Cambridge Companion to Modernism* (Cambridge University Press, 1999) 3.

34 Woolf, 19 January 1935, *The Diary of Virginia Woolf* 4: 275.

35 In April of 1938, when Woolf began work on what was eventually to become *Between the Acts*, she referred again in her diary to a "summers night" and entitled her first draft "Summer Night" (*The Diary of Virginia Woolf* 5: 133).

36 See Jane Marcus, "Some Sources for *Between the Acts*," *Virginia Woolf Miscellany* 6 (Winter 1977): 2; Julie Holledge, *Innocent Flowers: Women in the Edwardian Theatre* (London: Virago, 1981) 161–162; and Auerbach, *Ellen Terry* 427.

4 STAGING THE OB/SCENE

1 Michel Foucault, *The History of Sexuality, Volume 1: An Introduction*, trans. Robert Hurley (New York: Vintage, 1990) 104–105.
2 Leigh Gilmore, "Obscenity, Modernity, Identity: Legalizing *The Well of Loneliness* and *Nightwood*," *Journal of the History of Sexuality* 4.4 (1994): 604.
3 Dianne Chisholm, "Obscene Modernism: *Eros Noir* and the Profane Illumination of Djuna Barnes," *American Literature* 69.1 (March 1997): 167.
4 Ibid. 168.
5 Scrutator, "Ibsen's 'Dolls' in Archer's 'Doll's House,'" *Truth* 13 June 1889: 1127, qtd. in Tracy C. Davis, "Ibsen's Victorian Audience," *Essays in Theatre* 4.1 (November 1985): 24. A reviewer of an 1889 production of *The Pillars of Society* similarly described the audience as consisting of "masculine women and effeminate men" (*Playgoer* [August 1889]: 1, qtd. in Kerry Powell, *Women and Victorian Theatre* [Cambridge University Press, 1997] 71).
6 *Punch*, qtd. in Elin Diamond, *Unmaking Mimesis* (London: Routledge, 1997) 186 and in Gail Cunningham, *The New Woman and the Victorian Novel* (London: Macmillan, 1978) 46.
7 Virginia Woolf, "Speech Before the London/National Society for Women's Service, January 21 1931," *The Pargiters: The Novel–Essay Portion of "The Years"*, by Virginia Woolf, ed. Mitchell A. Leaska (New York: New York Public Library, 1977) xxxviii–xxxix.
8 "Britishers Amuse in Little Theatre: Huddersfield Thespians Heard in Contest – Studio Theatre Presents Freudian Essay," rev. of *The Dove*, *New York Times* 7 May 1926: 12.
9 Djuna Barnes, *The Dove, At the Root of the Stars: The Short Plays*, ed. Douglas Messerli (Los Angeles: Sun & Moon Press, 1995) 149; subsequent references will be given parenthetically in the text.
10 As I will discuss later in this chapter, the title of the Carpaccio painting is controversial. The painting is also known as *Two Venetian Ladies*, but in this analysis, I have followed Barnes's lead in *The Dove*, where it is always assumed to represent Venetian courtesans.
11 Unfortunately, the emphasis on "This" has been omitted from the final line of the play as published in Katherine E. Kelly's anthology *Modern Drama by Women 1880s–1930s: An International Anthology* (London: Routledge, 1996) 307.
12 Anne B. Dalton, "'*This* is obscene': Female Voyeurism, Sexual Abuse, and Maternal Power in *The Dove*," *Review of Contemporary Fiction* 13.3 (Fall 1993): 135.
13 Phillip Herring, *Djuna: The Life and Work of Djuna Barnes* (New York: Viking, 1995) 275.

14 Hank O'Neal, *"Life is painful, nasty & short . . . in my case it has only been painful & nasty." Djuna Barnes 1978–1981: An Informal Memoir* (New York: Paragon House, 1990) 8.

15 Shari Benstock, *Women of the Left Bank: Paris, 1900–1940* (Austin: University of Texas Press, 1986) 25.

16 James B. Scott, *Djuna Barnes* (Boston: Twayne, 1976) n. pag. [preface].

17 Robert Hendrickson, *The Facts on File Encyclopedia of Word and Phrase Origins* (New York: Facts on File, 1997) 490.

18 While Eric Partridge includes this derivation in his *Origins: A Short Etymological Dictionary of Modern English* (New York: Greenwich House, 1983) 446, *The Oxford Dictionary of English Etymology*, ed. C. T. Onions (Oxford: Clarendon Press, 1966) 621 does not.

19 Havelock Ellis, *Impressions and Comments* (London: Constable, 1920) 134.

20 D. H. Lawrence, "Pornography and Obscenity," *Phoenix: The Posthumous Papers of D. H. Lawrence*, ed. Edward D. McDonald (London: Heinemann, 1961) 170.

21 See, for example, Peter Michelson, *Speaking the Unspeakable: A Poetics of Obscenity* (Albany, NY: State University of New York Press, 1993): "I use obscenity in the Greek sense of bringing onstage what is customarily kept offstage in western culture, for example, the Oedipal bedroom or Jocasta's suicide or Oedipus' blinding" (xi).

22 Mary Caputi, *Voluptuous Yearnings: A Feminist Theory of the Obscene* (Lanham, MD: Rowman and Littlefield, 1994) 7.

23 On the subject of theatrical censorship of representations of homosexuality in Europe and North America, and especially in England and the United States, see, for example, Laurence Senelick, general introduction, *Lovesick: Modernist Plays of Same-Sex Love 1894–1925* (London: Routledge, 1999) 2–3; Alan Sinfield, *Out on Stage: Lesbian and Gay Theatre in the Twentieth Century* (New Haven: Yale University Press, 1999) 13; Nicholas de Jongh, *Not in Front of the Audience: Homosexuality on Stage* (London: Routledge, 1992) xi–xii, 12; and Kaier Curtin, *"We Can Always Call Them Bulgarians": The Emergence of Lesbians and Gay Men on the American Stage* (Boston: Alyson Publications, 1987) 11–23. In England, the Lord Chamberlain's Office was responsible for pre-censoring all plays prior to public production. The United States did not have pre-production censorship, but the police had the power to close productions. The reviews of *The Dove* that I have cited are of a New York production that was part of a Little Theatre Tournament of one-act plays; the probably single performance of the play in this context made police intervention unlikely.

24 Christopher Craft, "Alias Bunbury: Desire and Termination in *The Importance of Being Earnest*," *Critical Essays on Oscar Wilde*, ed. Regenia Gagnier (New York: G. K. Hall, 1991) 121.

25 "Pseudo-Freud, Neo-Shaw, Pre-Barrie in the Little Theatres," rev. of *The Dove*, *New York Evening Post* 7 May 1926: 14. Here, the reviewer seems to have conflated a single reference to the picture of a Parisian bathing girl with several references to Carpaccio's *Two Venetian Courtesans*.

26 Ibid.
27 John Ruskin, *The Shrine of the Slaves, St. Mark's Rest: The History of Venice*, first supplement (Orpington, 1877) 38.
28 Jan Lauts, *Carpaccio: Paintings and Drawings: Complete Edition* (London: Phaidon Press, 1962) 252.
29 Vittorio Sgarbi, *Carpaccio*, trans. Jay Hyams (New York: Abbeville Press, 1994) 100.
30 Ibid. 100–102.
31 See, for example, Marlene and Joyce in Caryl Churchill's *Top Girls* (1982) or Procne and Philomele in Timberlake Wertenbaker's *The Love of the Nightingale* (1988).
32 Gilmore, "Obscenity, Modernity, Identity" 606.
33 Qtd. in ibid.
34 Ibid.
35 Ibid. See also Angela Ingram's "'Unutterable Putrefaction' and 'Foul Stuff': Two 'Obscene' Novels of the 1920s," *Women's Studies International Forum* 9.4 (1986), in which Ingram relates Shakespeare's application of the word "obscene" to a perceived transgression against the established political/moral order to early-twentieth-century charges of obscenity directed at feminist works that were perceived to be critical of the patriarchal social order (342).
36 Chisholm, "Obscene Modernism" 170.
37 de Jongh, *Not in Front of the Audience* 10.
38 Senelick, *Lovesick* 8.
39 Andrew Field, *Djuna: The Life and Times of Djuna Barnes* (New York: G. P. Putnam's Sons, 1983) 52; O'Neal, *"Life is painful"* 175.
40 Djuna Barnes, qtd. in Cheryl J. Plumb, introduction to *The Dove, Modern Drama by Women 1880s–1930s*, ed. Kelly 301.
41 Barnes admitted to her friend Emily Coleman that her comments on Ibsen were "merely smarty" (qtd. in Plumb, introduction to *The Dove* 301).
42 In his brief discussion of *The Dove*, Alan Sinfield suggests, but does not develop, a connection between Barnes's play and *Hedda Gabler* (*Out on Stage* 55), as does Susan F. Clark, "Misalliance: Djuna Barnes and the American Theatre," diss., Tufts University, 1989, 156.
43 Elaine Showalter, *The Female Malady: Women, Madness, and English Culture, 1830–1980* (New York: Penguin, 1985) 145.
44 Sigmund Freud, "Fragment of an Analysis of a Case of Hysteria ('Dora')," *The Freud Reader*, ed. Peter Gay (New York: W. W. Norton, 1989) 206.
45 Sigmund Freud, "Hysterical Phantasies and Their Relation to Bisexuality," qtd. in Diamond, *Unmaking Mimesis* 27.
46 Showalter, *The Female Malady* 161.
47 Hélène Cixous, *Portrait of Dora*, trans. Anita Barrows, *Benmussa Directs* (London: John Calder, 1979) 27–67; see also Hélène Cixous and Catherine Clément, *The Newly Born Woman*, trans. Betsy Wing, Theory and History of Literature 24 (Minneapolis: University of Minnesota Press, 1975).

48 Diamond, *Unmaking Mimesis* 3–39; Gail Finney, *Women in Modern Drama: Freud, Feminism, and European Theater at the Turn of the Century* (Ithaca, NY: Cornell University Press, 1989) 149–165.

49 Henrik Ibsen, *Hedda Gabler, Ibsen: The Complete Major Prose Plays*, trans. Rolf Fjelde (New York: New American Library, 1965) 702, 707; subsequent references will be given parenthetically in the text.

50 Diamond, *Unmaking Mimesis* 26; see also Finney, *Women in Modern Drama* 160.

51 Henrik Ibsen, notes on *Hedda Gabler, Playwrights on Playwriting*, ed. Toby Cole (London: MacGibbon and Kee, 1960) 166.

52 Henrik Ibsen, letter to Moritz Prozor, 4 December 1890, *Ibsen: Letters and Speeches*, ed. Evert Sprinchorn (London: MacGibbon and Kee, 1965) 297.

53 Elin Diamond uses this term to describe the inner room that Hedda retreats into and curtains off just prior to her suicide at the end of the play (*Unmaking Mimesis* 28).

54 Kay Unruh Des Roches, "Sight and Insight: Stage Pictures in *Hedda Gabler*," *Journal of Dramatic Theory and Criticism* 5.1 (Fall 1990): 54.

55 Inga-Stina Ewbank, "Ibsen and the Language of Women," *Women Writing and Writing about Women*, ed. Mary Jacobus (London: Croom Helm, 1979) 131.

56 Finney, *Women in Modern Drama* 151.

57 Emile Zola, "Naturalism on the Stage," trans. Belle M. Sherman, *Dramatic Theory and Criticism: Greeks to Grotowski*, ed. Bernard F. Dukore (Fort Worth, TX: Holt, Rinehart and Winston, 1974) 711.

58 Bert O. States, *Great Reckonings in Little Rooms: On the Phenomenology of Theater* (Berkeley, CA: University of California Press, 1985) 62; Diamond, *Unmaking Mimesis* 26.

59 Joan Templeton, *Ibsen's Women* (Cambridge University Press, 1997) 210.

60 Ibsen, notes on *Hedda Gabler* 167.

61 Sigmund Freud, "The 'Uncanny,'" *The Standard Edition of the Complete Psychological Works of Sigmund Freud*, vol. 17, ed. and trans. James Strachey et al. (London: Hogarth Press, 1955) 236.

62 Michelson, *Speaking the Unspeakable* xi–xii.

63 Clement Scott, *Illustrated London News* 25 April 1891, *Ibsen: The Critical Heritage*, ed. Michael Egan (London: Routledge and Kegan Paul, 1972) 227, 226.

64 Rev. of *Hedda Gabler, Saturday Review* 25 April 1891, *Ibsen: The Critical Heritage*, ed. Egan 223.

65 Linda Hutcheon, *A Poetics of Postmodernism: History, Theory, Fiction* (New York: Routledge, 1988) 26.

66 Katharine Cockin, *Edith Craig: Dramatic Lives* (London: Cassell, 1998) 3; as well, see 55–80 for an extended analysis of Craig and St. John's relationship in the context of the history of sexuality and the emergence of "lesbian" as an identity category. See also Joy Melville, *Ellen and Edy: A Biography of Ellen Terry and her Daughter, Edith Craig, 1847–1947* (London: Pandora, 1987) 189–190; and Nina Auerbach, *Ellen Terry: Player in her Time* (New York: W. W. Norton, 1987) 365–436.

67 Vita Sackville-West, qtd. in Victoria Glendinning, *Vita: The Life of Vita Sackville-West* (Penguin, 1983) 250.

68 Sinfield, *Out on Stage* 5.

69 Adrienne Rich, "Compulsory Heterosexuality and Lesbian Existence," *Powers of Desire: The Politics of Sexuality*, ed. Ann Snitow, Christine Stansell, and Sharon Thompson (New York: Monthly Review Press, 1983) 177–205. Rich intends the term "lesbian continuum" to expand the definition of "lesbianism" so that it "include[s] a range [. . .] of woman-identified experience; not simply the fact that a woman has had or consciously desired genital sexual experience with another woman." Among the "many more forms of primary intensity between and among women" that Rich includes on her continuum are "the sharing of a rich inner life, the bonding against male tyranny, [and] the giving and receiving of practical and political support" (192). While this notion of a "lesbian continuum" threatens to elide the specificity of lesbian sexuality, it does seem useful to a discussion of Edith Craig.

70 For discussions of the historical emergence of lesbian identity and of the importance of Radclyffe Hall in this process, see, for example, Jeffrey Weeks, *Coming Out: Homosexual Politics in Britain, from the Nineteenth Century to the Present* (London: Quartet, 1977) 87–111; and Sonja Ruehl, "Inverts and Experts: Radclyffe Hall and the Lesbian Identity," *Feminism, Culture and Politics*, ed. Rosalind Brunt and Caroline Rowan (London: Lawrence and Wishart, 1982) 15–36.

71 Elaine Showalter, *Sexual Anarchy: Gender and Culture at the Fin de Siècle* (New York: Viking, 1990) 19.

72 Ibid. 21.

73 Ibid.

74 Ibid. 23.

75 Ibid. 38.

76 J. Ellen Gainor, *Shaw's Daughters: Dramatic and Narrative Constructions of Gender* (Ann Arbor: University of Michigan Press, 1991) 25–32.

77 Yopie Prins, "Greek Maenads, Victorian Spinsters," *Victorian Sexual Dissidence*, ed. Richard Dellamora (University of Chicago Press, 1999) 47.

78 Cunningham, *The New Woman and the Victorian Novel* 3.

79 Susan Kingsley Kent, *Sex and Suffrage in Britain, 1860–1914* (Princeton University Press, 1987) 3, 13.

80 Lisa Tickner, *The Spectacle of Women: Imagery of the Suffrage Campaign 1907–14* (London: Chatto and Windus, 1987) 183.

81 Sinfield, *Out on Stage* 1, 2.

82 Terry Castle, *The Apparitional Lesbian: Female Homosexuality and Modern Culture* (New York: Columbia University Press, 1993). As Castle notes, "Vita Sackville-West wrote a book about [Joan of Arc]; Radclyffe Hall wanted to. The lesbian actress Eva Le Gallienne played her, in Paris in 1925, in a play written for her by her lover, Mercedes de Acosta. And [Henry] James's Olive Chancellor is an acknowledged, sometimes quivering, member of her cult" (185). Sheila Stowell has accounted for Joan of Arc's status as "an enduring icon

and a popular role (model)" within the suffrage movement by suggesting that "[h]er virginity and gender [rendered] her the ideal symbol of unsexualised womanliness at the same time that her militancy and transvestism precluded containment by conventional domesticity" (*A Stage of Their Own: Feminist Playwrights of the Suffrage Era* [Ann Arbor: University of Michigan Press, 1992] 45).

83 Lis Whitelaw, *The Life and Rebellious Times of Cicely Hamilton: Actress, Writer, Suffragist* (London: The Women's Press, 1990) 107–114. Whitelaw qualifies her claim by acknowledging a lack of explicit documentary evidence.

84 Eva Balfour is shown in the role of Sappho, and Lina Rathbone is shown as Mary Ann Talbot.

85 Cockin, *Edith Craig* 100. Other illustrations include individual portraits of such well-known figures as Ellen Terry in the role of Nance Oldfield, her sister Marion Terry as Florence Nightingale, and the suffragist Charlotte Despard as St. Hilda. Actresses Joy Chatwyn, Suzanne Sheldon, and Vera Coburn are individually featured as Elizabeth Fry, Catherine the Great, and the Maid of Saragossa respectively, and there are group shots of the Rulers and Warriors, played by performers who range from the well-known to the obscure. See Cicely Hamilton, *A Pageant of Great Women* (London: The Suffrage Shop, 1910); hereafter cited parenthetically in the text.

86 Powell, *Women and Victorian Theatre* 35.

87 *Aberdeen Free Press* 19 November 1910, Edy Craig Papers, Ellen Terry Memorial Museum.

88 James M. Saslow, "'Disagreeably Hidden': Construction and Constriction of the Lesbian Body in Rosa Bonheur's *Horse Fair*," *Queer Representations: Reading Lives, Reading Cultures*, ed. Martin Duberman (New York University Press, 1997) 70.

89 *Jahrbuch für sexuelle Zwischenstufen*, qtd. in James M. Saslow, "'Disagreeably Hidden'" 80.

90 Cockin, *Edith Craig* 106.

91 Germaine Greer, *The Obstacle Race* (New York: Farrar, Straus & Giroux, 1979) 320.

92 Saslow, "'Disagreeably Hidden'" 69. More specifically, in his re-reading of Bonheur's covert self-portraiture in the context of a painting that has traditionally been understood as belonging to the genre of animal art, Saslow proposes that the artist's "masculine attire was an attempt to claim male prerogatives and create an androgynous and proto-lesbian visual identity that would embody, literally and figuratively, her social and sexual views"; that "her coded representation of this identity reveals her work as more socially engaged and subversive than had been thought"; and "that the relative absence of human subjects from her work can be read as a displacement of interest from what could not be publicly 'image-ined' onto an alternative subject matter that, while socially acceptable and even popular, provided some scope for symbolizing nonconformist ideas about nature that justified Bonheur's own sexual and gender identity" ("'Disagreeably Hidden'" 73).

93 "London Letter," *Cambridge Daily News* 30 January 192[?], Edy Craig Papers, Ellen Terry Memorial Museum.

94 Castle, *The Apparitional Lesbian* 2.

95 "Pseudo-Freud, Neo-Shaw, Pre-Barrie in the Little Theatres" 14; see also "Britishers Amuse in Little Theatre" 12.

96 Judith Butler, "Imitation and Gender Insubordination," *Inside/Out: Lesbian Theories, Gay Theories*, ed. Diana Fuss (New York: Routledge, 1991) 20.

97 Ibid.

98 Radclyffe Hall, qtd. in Sally Cline, *Radclyffe Hall: A Woman Called John* (Woodstock, NY: Overlook Press, 1997) 248, 263, 264; the first ellipsis is mine; the second is in Cline.

99 Ruehl, "Inverts and Experts" 15. See also Jeffrey Weeks, who states, "The publication in 1928 of [Hall's] novel *The Well of Loneliness*, along with the controversy that surrounded it and her, was a crucial stage in the evolution of a public image of lesbianism; in many ways it had for women an equivalent social impact to the one the Wilde trial had for men" (*Coming Out* 101).

100 Cicely Hamilton, qtd. in Cockin, *Edith Craig* 102.

101 Havelock Ellis, qtd. in Michael Baker, *Our Three Selves: The Life of Radclyffe Hall* (London: Hamish Hamilton, 1985) 203.

102 Cockin, *Edith Craig* 94.

103 James Douglas, qtd. in Vera Brittain, *Radclyffe Hall: A Case of Obscenity?* (New York: A. S. Barnes, 1969) 54. As Katrina Rolley has pointed out, Douglas's editorial was illustrated with a particularly masculine-looking photograph of Hall ("Cutting a Dash: the Dress of Radclyffe Hall and Una Troubridge," *Feminist Review* [Summer 1990]: 65).

104 Douglas, qtd. in Brittain, *Radclyffe Hall* 54–55.

105 Radclyffe Hall, *The Well of Loneliness* (New York: Anchor–Doubleday, 1990) 389–390.

106 Ed Madden, "*The Well of Loneliness*: the Gospel According to Radclyffe Hall," *Journal of Homosexuality* 33.3 (June–July 1997): 172.

107 Beresford Egan's 1928 cartoon "St. Stephen," for example, depicted Radclyffe Hall crucified (rpt. in Cline, *Radclyffe Hall* 279), while Rebecca West observed in her article "Concerning the Censorship," "The imprisonment of Oscar Wilde was the best propaganda that was ever put in for male homosexuality, and now that the government has supplied female homosexuality with a handsome, noble, and intrepid martyr the word Lesbian will in no time suggest to the young girl something other than the friend of Catullus who had bad luck with a sparrow" (*Ending in Earnest: A Literary Log* [Garden City, NY: Doubleday, Doran, 1931] 11).

108 Chartres Biron, qtd. in Brittain, *Radclyffe Hall* 99.

109 Biron, qtd. in ibid. 100.

110 Virginia Woolf, *A Room of One's Own* (San Diego: Harvest–HBJ, 1981) 80–85.

111 Teresa de Lauretis, "Sexual Indifference and Lesbian Representation," *Performing Feminisms: Feminist Critical Theory and Theatre*, ed. Sue-Ellen Case (Baltimore: Johns Hopkins University Press, 1990) 32–33.

112 Bertolt Brecht, "Theatre for Pleasure or Theatre for Instruction," *Brecht on Theatre*, trans. John Willett (New York: Hill and Wang, 1964) 71.
113 Bertolt Brecht, "A Short Organum for the Theatre," *Brecht on Theatre* 192.
114 Bertolt Brecht, "The Street Scene: a Basic Model for an Epic Theatre," *Brecht on Theatre* 125.
115 Brecht, "Theatre for Pleasure or Theatre for Instruction" 71.
116 See, for example, Brecht, "Theatre for Pleasure or Theatre for Instruction" 71; and "A Short Organum for the Theatre" 192.
117 *Newcastle Daily Journal*, qtd. in Rolley, "Cutting a Dash" 57.

5 WRITING/PERFORMING: VIRGINIA WOOLF BETWEEN THE ACTS

1 I have used Woolf's married name here for the sake of clarity, convenience, and consistency, but she was still Virginia Stephen at the time of the *Dreadnought* Hoax.
2 Quentin Bell, *Virginia Woolf: A Biography*, 2 vols. (San Diego: Harvest–HBJ, 1972) 1: 158.
3 Bell, *Virginia Woolf* 1: 157.
4 Virginia Woolf, "The *Dreadnought* Hoax," appendix E, Quentin Bell, *Virginia Woolf: A Biography* 1: 215.
5 Bell, *Virginia Woolf* 1: 160–161.
6 Phyllis Rose, *A Woman of Letters: A Life of Virginia Woolf* (New York: Harvest–HBJ, 1978) 102–103.
7 Jane Marcus, "Britannia Rules *The Waves*," *Decolonizing Tradition: New Views of Twentieth-Century "British" Literary Canons*, ed. Karen R. Lawrence (Urbana, IL: University of Illinois Press, 1992) 142.
8 Woolf's essay on Ellen Terry was also researched and written around this time and published in 1941. See "Ellen Terry," *Collected Essays*, vol. 4 (London: Hogarth Press, 1967) 67–72.
9 Virginia Woolf, "*Twelfth Night* at the Old Vic," *The Death of the Moth and Other Essays* (New York: Harcourt, Brace, 1942) 46; subsequent references will be given parenthetically in the text.
10 Virginia Woolf, "*The Cherry Orchard*," *The New Statesman* 24 July 1920: 446; subsequent references will be given parenthetically in the text.
11 Karen Schneider, "Of Two Minds: Woolf, the War and *Between the Acts*," *Journal of Modern Literature* 16.1 (1989): 103. Schneider writes of the three parodic plays contained in the pageant: "All enact narratives of lovers united, each foregrounding and satirizing various roles codified in this apparently timeless story: the Prince, lover as lord, and his beautiful, adoring princess; lovers who play foolish courtship games of faithless love modeled on fictional romances; conniving materialists who trade women – or, if they are women, sell themselves – for capital in the form of dowry; mothers who scheme to marry off their daughters; sheltered wives who live their impoverished lives through their husbands; women who internalize patriarchal values and regard marriage

as the acme of bliss" (104). My analysis of *Between the Acts* shares points of convergence with Schneider's but differs in its emphasis on performance.

12 Virginia Woolf, *Between the Acts* (San Diego: Harvest–HBJ, 1941) 157; subsequent references will be given parenthetically in the text.

13 Linda Hutcheon, *The Politics of Postmodernism* (London: Routledge, 1989) 101.

14 Woolf wrote in a 1902 letter to Violet Dickinson, "I[']m going to have a man and a woman – show them growing up – never meeting – not knowing each other – but all the time you'll feel them come nearer and nearer. This will be the real exciting part (as you see) – but when they almost meet – only a door between – you see how they just miss – and go off at a tangent, and never come anywhere near again" (*The Letters of Virginia Woolf*, ed. Nigel Nicolson and Joanne Trautmann, 6 vols. [London: Hogarth Press, 1975–80] 1: 60).

15 Judith Butler, *Gender Trouble: Feminism and the Subversion of Identity* (New York: Routledge, 1990) 145.

16 Teresa de Lauretis, "The Technology of Gender," *Technologies of Gender: Essays on Theory, Film, and Fiction* (Bloomington, IN: Indiana University Press, 1987) 18.

17 Ibid. 25.

18 Barbara A. Babcock has similarly argued that the "interstitial aesthetic" of *Between the Acts* signals Woolf's opposition "to formal closure and a radical separation of art and life" and her insistence "on the audience's share in the performance" ("Mud, Mirrors, and Making Up: Liminality and Reflexivity in *Between the Acts*," *Victor Turner and the Construction of Cultural Criticism*, ed. Kathleen M. Ashley [Bloomington, IN: Indiana University Press, 1990] 105).

19 Michel de Certeau, *The Practice of Everyday Life*, trans. Steven Rendall (Berkeley, CA: University of California Press, 1984) xvii, xviii, xiv.

20 Virginia Woolf, "'Anon' and 'The Reader,'" ed. Brenda R. Silver, *Twentieth-Century Literature* 25.3–4 (1979): 403.

21 Virginia Woolf, "A Sketch of the Past," *Moments of Being*, ed. Jeanne Schulkind (San Diego: Harvest–HBJ, 1985) 72.

22 Ibid. 73.

23 Woolf, "'Anon' and 'The Reader'" 382–383.

24 Woolf wrote: "It was Anon who gave voice to the old stories, who incited the peasants when he came to the back door to put off their working clothes and deck themselves in green leaves. He it was who found words for them to sing, when they went at the great seasons to do homage to the old pagan Gods. He taught them the songs they sang at Christmas and at midsummer. He led them to the haunted tree; to the well; to the old burial place where they did homage to the pagan gods" ("'Anon' and 'The Reader'" 383).

25 See Brenda R. Silver's introduction to "Anon" ("'Anon' and 'The Reader'" 380) for a similar discussion of the relationship between Anon and La Trobe and of Woolf's sense of the artist's social function.

26 In a draft of her unfinished late essay "The Reader," Woolf states that when readers are "distracted, in times of public crisis, the writer exclaims: 'I can write no more'" ("'Anon' and 'The Reader'" 428). Lamenting her own loss of a sense

of a public, she observed in her diary in 1940, "It struck me that one curious feeling is, that the writing 'I', has vanished. No audience. No echo. That's part of one's death. Not altogether serious [. . .]. But it is a fact – this disparition of an echo" (9 June 1940, *The Diary of Virginia Woolf*, ed. Anne Olivier Bell, assisted by Andrew McNeillie, 5 vols. [London: Hogarth Press, 1977–84] 5: 293; see also 5: 299 and 5: 304). In "Anon," she argues that the invention of the printing press separated the artist from the audience so that "[it] no longer joined in the song and added [its] own verses to the poem" ("'Anon' and 'The Reader'" 389).

27 Woolf, "'Anon' and 'The Reader'" 377.
28 Bert O. States, *Great Reckonings in Little Rooms: On the Phenomenology of Theatre* (Berkeley: University of California Press, 1985) 20.
29 Virginia Woolf, 17 April 1934, *The Diary of Virginia Woolf* 4: 207.
30 Ibid. 27 October 1928, 3: 201.
31 My use of this term derives from Joseph Roach, who writes in *Cities of the Dead: Circum-Atlantic Performance* (New York: Columbia University Press, 1996): "Performance genealogies draw on the idea of expressive movements as mnemonic reserves, including patterned movements made and remembered by bodies, residual movements retained implicitly in images and words (or in the silences between them), and imaginary movements dreamed in minds, not prior to language but constitutive of it, a psychic rehearsal for physical actions drawn from a repertoire that culture provides" (26).
32 Woolf began writing *The Voyage Out* in 1908 and published it in 1915.
33 Virginia Woolf, *A Room of One's Own* (San Diego: Harvest–HBJ, 1981) 114.
34 Virginia Woolf, qtd. in Jane Marcus, *Art and Anger: Reading Like a Woman* (Columbus, OH: Ohio State University Press, 1988) 94.

6 FEMINISM, TRAGEDY, HISTORY: THE FATE OF ISADORA DUNCAN

1 "Isadora Duncan, Dragged By Scarf From Auto, Killed," *New York Times* 15 September 1927: 1.
2 Fredrika Blair, *Isadora: Portrait of the Artist As A Woman* (New York: McGraw Hill, 1986) xii, 407.
3 Roland Barthes, *Mythologies*, trans. Annette Lavers (London: Paladin, 1973) 11.
4 Sarah B. Pomeroy, "Images of Women in the Literature of Classical Athens," *Tragedy*, ed. John Drakakis and Naomi Conn Liebler (London: Longman, 1998) 218.
5 Aristotle, *Poetics*, trans. S. H. Butcher, *Dramatic Theory and Criticism: Greeks to Grotowski*, ed. Bernard F. Dukore (Forth Worth, TX: Holt, Rinehart and Winston, 1974) 44.
6 Nicole Loraux, *Tragic Ways of Killing a Woman*, trans. Anthony Forster (Cambridge, MA: Harvard University Press, 1987) 2.
7 Joan Templeton, "Fallen Women and Upright Wives: 'Woman's Place' in Early Modern Tragedy," *Reconfigured Spheres: Feminist Explorations of Literary Space*, ed. Margaret R. Higgonet and Joan Templeton (Amherst, MA: University of

Massachusetts Press, 1994) 60; see also Templeton's discussion of *Ghosts* in *Ibsen's Women* (Cambridge University Press, 1997) 146–162.

8 Isadora Duncan, *Isadora Speaks*, ed. Franklin Rosemont (San Francisco: City Lights Books, 1981) 52–53.

9 Ann Daly, "The Balanchine Woman: of Hummingbirds and Channel Swimmers," *TDR* 31.1 (T113) (Spring 1987): 17. See also Susan Leigh Foster, "The Ballerina's Phallic Pointe," *Corporealities: Dancing Knowledge, Culture and Power* (London: Routledge, 1996) 1–24.

10 Isadora Duncan, *My Life* (New York: Liveright, 1927) 75. Subsequent references will be given parenthetically in the text as *ML*; all quotations will be from this edition.

11 Isadora Duncan, "The Dance of the Future," *The Art of the Dance*, ed. Sheldon Cheney (New York: Theatre Arts, 1928) 63.

12 Susan Gubar, "'The Blank Page' and the Issues of Female Creativity," *The New Feminist Criticism: Essays on Women, Literature, and Theory*, ed. Elaine Showalter (New York: Pantheon, 1985) 292–313.

13 Sherry Ortner, "Is Female to Male as Nature is to Culture?" *Women, Culture and Society*, ed. Michelle Z. Rosaldo and Louise Lamphere (Stanford University Press, 1974) 67–87; Hélène Cixous, "Sorties: Out and Out: Attacks/Ways Out/Forays," *The Newly Born Woman*, by Hélène Cixous and Catherine Clément, trans. Betsy Wing (Minneapolis: University of Minnesota Press, 1986) 61–132; Ann Daly, "Dance History and Feminist Theory: Reconsidering Isadora Duncan and the Male Gaze," *Gender in Performance: The Presentation of Difference in the Performing Arts*, ed. Laurence Senelick (Hanover, NH: University Press of New England, 1992) 246.

14 Isadora Duncan, "The Great Source," *The Art of the Dance* 101.

15 Isadora Duncan, *Isadora Speaks* 55.

16 In her essay "The Dancer and Nature," for example, Duncan disdained those who held that ballet was an "evolution in form to something higher" and that dance which was "appropriate to women's natural form" was "primitive and uncultivated" (*The Art of the Dance* 70), while in her manifesto "The Dance of the Future," she described ballet dancers as "deformed skeletons" and argued that ballet was degenerate because, "striving against the natural laws of gravitation or the natural will of the individual, and working in discord in its form and movement with the form and movement of nature, [it] produces a sterile movement which gives no birth to future movements, but dies as it is made" (55–56).

17 Duncan, "The Dance of the Future" 63.

18 Elizabeth Dempster, "Women Writing the Body: Let's Watch a Little How She Dances," *Grafts: Feminist Cultural Criticism*, ed. Susan Sheridan (London: Verso, 1988) 50–51; see also Janet Wolff, "Reinstating Corporeality: Feminism and Body Politics," *Feminine Sentences: Essays on Women and Culture* (Cambridge: Polity Press, 1990) 136–137.

19 Daly, "Dance History and Feminist Theory" 256.

20 Isadora Duncan, qtd. in Deborah Jowitt, *Time and the Dancing Image* (Berkeley, CA: University of California Press, 1988) 81.

21 Qtd. in Victor Seroff, *The Real Isadora* (New York: Dial, 1971) 50. Seroff, Blair (*Isadora: Portrait of the Artist*), and Walter Terry (*Isadora Duncan: Her Life, Her Art, Her Legacy* [New York: Dodd, Mead, 1963]) have all pointed out omissions, inconsistencies, errors, and possibly spurious passages in *My Life* while at the same time drawing heavily on it as a historical record; Elizabeth Kendall has categorized *My Life* as a "fake" ("Victim of History," *Ballet News* [February 1982]: 19); and Ann Daly has described it as "a strictly commercial venture" that "clearly belongs more on the side of fiction than history." Daly adds, however, that she does not mean "that the book is an untruth or useless," but, rather, that "[t]he work of Duncan's autobiography as historical evidence is not so much in the 'truths' it imparts as in how Duncan constructs her vision of those 'truths'" ("Dance History and Feminist Theory" 241, 256).

22 Margaret Thompson Drewal, "Isis and Isadora," *Proceedings of the Tenth Annual Conference, Society of Dance History Scholars, University of California, Irvine, February 13–15, 1987* (Riverside: Dance History Scholars, 1987) 188.

23 Craig denied saying such things to Duncan, suggesting that someone else authored this section of *My Life* (see Seroff, *The Real Isadora* 74), but Nina Auerbach has argued that Duncan's representation of Craig rings true, citing as evidence "Book Topsy," his notebook-memoir of his relationship with Duncan, in which he "dwells less on Isadora's dancing than on the haunting familiarity of her presence" (*Ellen Terry: Player in Her Time* [New York: Norton, 1987] 353).

24 Duncan's argument was especially pertinent given Craig's dream of replacing live performers with more manageable *Uebermarionetten* and her own aversion to the "articulated puppet" movements of ballet.

25 *Mother*, for example, suggested her anguish at the loss of her children.

26 Isadora Duncan, "Lies: Letter to the Journal *L'Eclair*," *Isadora Speaks* 100.

27 Jowitt, *Time and the Dancing Image* 92.

28 Janet Flanner, "Isadora (1878–1927)," *Paris Was Yesterday: 1925–1939*, ed. Irving Drutman (San Diego: Harvest–HBJ, 1972) 32.

29 Susanne K. Langer, "The Great Dramatic Forms: the Tragic Rhythm," *Tragedy*, ed. Drakakis and Conn Liebler 323.

30 Ibid. 328.

31 Ibid. 327.

32 Raymond Williams, "From *Modern Tragedy*," *Tragedy*, ed. Drakakis and Conn Liebler 156.

33 Irma Duncan and Allan Ross Macdougall, *Isadora Duncan's Russian Days and Her Last Years in France* (London: Victor Gollancz, 1929) 9.

34 John Martin, "Isadora Duncan Danced Like a 'Puritanical Pagan,'" rev. of *My Life*, *The New York Times Book Review* 8 January 1928: 3.

35 Elizabeth Shepley Sergeant, "Heroic Isadora," rev. of *My Life*, *The New Republic* 21 March 1928: 165.

36 Lillian Loewenthal notes but does not fully analyze the seeming significance of the manner of Duncan's death, writing only that "[w]hat did strike many of those reflecting on the highly publicized and bizarre event was how glaringly the symbols of both the life and the dance were coupled in their macabre finality: the shawl she wore on that fateful day – an endearing image of her colorful scarves, so lively and harmonious an accompaniment to the consummate beauty and order of her dance – and a sports car of *grande vitesse* – the great speed she so loved, driving her faster out of paradise lost" (*The Search for Isadora: The Legend and Legacy of Isadora Duncan* [Pennington, NJ: Dance Horizons/Princeton Book Company, 1993] 179).

37 Mabel Dodge Luhan, *Movers and Shakers* (Albuquerque: University of New Mexico Press, 1985) 320.

38 Ann Daly, *Done into Dance: Isadora Duncan in America* (Bloomington, IN: Indiana University Press, 1995) 163.

39 Dempster, "Women Writing the Body" 50.

40 Elizabeth Francis, "From Event to Monument: Modernism, Feminism and Isadora Duncan," *American Studies* 35.1 (Spring 1994): 26.

41 Jean Cocteau, letter to Glenway Wescott, qtd. in Francis Steegmuller, ed., *"Your Isadora": The Love Story of Isadora Duncan and Gordon Craig Told Through Letters and Diaries* (New York: Vintage, 1976) 340; Jean Cocteau, "Isadora, Sarah and De Max," *Paris Album 1900–1914*, trans. Margaret Crosland (London: W. H. Allen, 1956) 109–111.

42 Max Eastman, *Heroes I Have Known: Twelve Who Lived Great Lives* (New York: Simon and Schuster, 1942) 69–70.

43 Ibid. 71.

44 Harriet Monroe, "Golden Moments," *Poetry: A Magazine of Verse* 31.4 (January 1928): 206.

45 Gubar, "'The Blank Page' and the Issues of Female Creativity" 299; my emphasis.

46 Sergeant, "Heroic Isadora" 165; Andrew Sarris, "Films: the Loves of Isadora," *The Village Voice* 10 July 1969: 43.

47 Loraux, *Tragic Ways of Killing a Woman* 52.

48 Ibid. 10.

49 Ibid. 61.

50 Sue-Ellen Case, *Feminism and Theatre* (New York: Methuen, 1988) 5–27.

51 Catherine Belsey, *The Subject of Tragedy: Identity and Difference in Renaissance Drama* (London: Routledge, 1985) x.

52 Loraux, *Tragic Ways of Killing a Woman* 21.

53 By way of example, Loraux cites Euripides' character Macaria, who, "as she prepares to take an active role, makes a point of showing her awareness of this sentiment, remarking that the best thing for a woman is not to leave the closed interior of her house. But women in tragedy have become involved in men's world of action and have suffered for it. So, silently, the heroines of Sophocles return to die in the home that they had left behind" (*Tragic Ways of Killing a Woman* 21).

54 Augusto Boal, *Theatre of the Oppressed*, trans. Charles A. and Maria-Odilia Leal McBride (New York: Theatre Communications Group, 1985) 1–50.
55 Margaret Higgonet, "Suicide: Representations of the Feminine in the Nineteenth Century," *Poetics Today* 6.1–2 (1985): 103–104.
56 Isadora Duncan, qtd. in Seroff, *The Real Isadora* 432.
57 Jean Cocteau, qtd. in Steegmuller, *"Your Isadora"* 340.
58 *Isadora* [*The Loves of Isadora*], dir. Karel Reisz, Universal Pictures, 1968.
59 See the Sphere Books edition of *My Life*, published in London in 1968 and rpt. in 1969.
60 Hélène Cixous, "Aller à la Mer," trans. Barbara Kerslake, *Modern Drama* 27.4 (December 1984): 546, 548.
61 Barthes, *Mythologies* 109, 122.
62 Walter Benjamin, "Trauerspiel and Tragedy," trans. John Osborne, *Tragedy*, ed. Drakakis and Conn Liebler 109.
63 Barthes, *Mythologies* 143.
64 Duncan wrote in the introductory chapter of *My Life*, "How can we write the truth about ourselves? Do we even know it? There is the vision our friends have of us; the vision we have of ourselves, and the vision our lover has of us. Also the vision our enemies have of us – and all these visions are different. [. . .]
    "So, if at each point of view others see in us a different person how are we to find in ourselves yet another personality of whom to write in this book? Is it to be the Chaste Madonna, or the Messalina, or the Magdalen, or the Blue Stocking? Where can I find the woman of all these adventures? It seems to me that there was not one, but hundreds – and my soul soaring aloft, not really affected by any of them" (1–2).
65 Seroff, *The Real Isadora* 47, 239.
66 Williams, "From *Modern Tragedy*" 154.
67 René Girard, "The Sacrificial Crisis," trans. Patrick Gregory, *Tragedy*, ed. Drakakis and Conn Liebler 283–287.
68 Ibid. 288.
69 John Drakakis and Naomi Conn Liebler, "Ritual and Tragedy," *Tragedy*, ed. Drakakis and Conn Liebler 255.
70 Williams, "From *Modern Tragedy*" 155; my italics.
71 Ibid. 153.
72 Teresa de Lauretis, "Desire in Narrative," *Alice Doesn't: Feminism, Semiotics, Cinema* (Bloomington, IN: Indiana University Press, 1984) 120–122.
73 This phrase is borrowed from Joseph Campbell, *The Hero with a Thousand Faces* (New York: Pantheon, 1949).
74 Williams, "From *Modern Tragedy*" 156.
75 Walt Whitman, "Song of Myself," *The Norton Anthology of Modern Poetry*, ed. Richard Ellmann and Robert O'Clair, 2nd edn. (New York: Norton, 1973) 34. Irma Duncan and Allan Ross Macdougall cited the first part of this quotation in the foreword to *Isadora Duncan's Russian Days and Her Last Years in France* 12.

76 Gertrude Stein, "Orta or One Dancing," *Two: Gertrude Stein and her Brother and Other Early Portraits [1908–12], The Unpublished Writings of Gertrude Stein*, vol. 1 (New Haven: Yale University Press, 1951) 286–304.

77 Isadora Duncan, "The Dance of the Greeks," *The Art of the Dance* 96; Duncan, *My Life* 140. The similarities between Duncan and Walt Whitman are discussed in Ellen Graff, "Walt Whitman and Isadora Duncan: the Construction of a Personal Mythology," *Proceedings of the Tenth Annual Conference, Society of Dance History Scholars, University of California, Irvine, February 13–15, 1987* (Riverside: Dance History Scholars, 1987) 65.

78 Joseph Roach, *Cities of the Dead: Circum-Atlantic Performance* (New York: Columbia University Press, 1996) 26.

79 Duncan, *Isadora Speaks* 53.

80 Susan Foster has suggested that with the work of Duncan, "audiences, for the first time, were asked to identify with dancer and dance and to feel rather than see their own life experiences on the stage" (*Reading Dancing: Bodies and Subjects in Contemporary American Dance* [Berkeley, CA: University of California Press, 1986] 145). Susan Manning has noted that "[w]atching Duncan dancing, spectators could imagine themselves doing the same moves, and indeed, many of her female spectators did try to do the same moves. Imitators of Duncan taught and performed across the United States and Europe" (*Ecstasy and the Demon: Feminism and Nationalism in the Dances of Mary Wigman* [Berkeley, CA: University of California Press, 1993] 35).

81 Walter Terry, *Isadora Duncan* 137.

82 Virginia Woolf, *A Room of One's Own* (San Diego: Harvest/HBJ, 1981) 113.

83 Roach, *Cities of the Dead* 26.

CONCLUSION

1 Rita Felski, *Beyond Feminist Aesthetics: Feminist Literature and Social Change* (Cambridge, MA: Harvard University Press, 1989) 14.

2 Bonnie Kime Scott, introduction, *The Gender of Modernism* (Bloomington, IN: Indiana University Press, 1990) 5.

3 Ibid. 16.

4 Christopher Innes, "Modernism in Drama," *The Cambridge Companion to Modernism*, ed. Michael Levenson (Cambridge University Press, 1999) 147.

5 Ibid. 146, 135.

6 Ibid. 153.

7 Michael Levenson, introduction, *The Cambridge Companion to Modernism* 2.

8 Levenson, introduction, *The Cambridge Companion to Modernism* 3.

9 The consideration of Ibsen within the context of modernism is not uncontroversial. Christopher Innes, for example, does not include him in his essay "Modernism in Drama." However, in terms of the representation of gender at least, Ibsen's modernism seems to me to be less ambiguous than, say, Strindberg's or Shaw's. In any case, in *Modernism: A Guide to European Literature 1890–1930* (New York: Penguin, 1991), Malcolm Bradbury and James McFarlane note the

centrality of Ibsen in accounts of Scandinavian modernism ("The Name and Nature of Modernism" 19–55), while McFarlane and James Fletcher focus on Ibsen's innovations in terms of both form and content in their essay in the same volume, "Modernist Drama: Origins and Patterns" (499–513). Finally, Raymond Williams has pointed out that while later modernist forms such as expressionism and epic theatre rejected the external staging and dramaturgical conventions of what he called "serious naturalism," these later forms were in fact a refinement of the basic structure of feeling that gave rise to realism and naturalism and that Williams identified as the tension between what individual subjects "feel themselves capable of becoming, and a thwarting, directly present environment" ("Conclusion from *Drama from Ibsen to Brecht*," *Modern Drama: Plays/Criticism/Theory*, ed. W. B. Worthen [Fort Worth: Harcourt Brace, 1995] 1174, 1172). Like Joan Templeton, then, whose book *Ibsen's Women* I quoted in the opening paragraph of my introduction, I consider Ibsen to be a central figure in the development of feminist modernism.

10 Levenson, introduction, *The Cambridge Companion to Modernism* 4.

Bibliography

Aberdeen Free Press 19 November 1910. Edy Craig Papers, Ellen Terry Memorial Museum.

A[rcher], W[illiam]. "Court Theatre. Miss Robins's 'Dramatic Tract.'" *Tribune* 13 May 1907. Elizabeth Robins Paper, Fales Library, New York University.

Aristotle. *Poetics*. Trans. S. H. Butcher. Dukore, *Dramatic Theory and Criticism*. 31–55.

Auerbach, Nina. *Ellen Terry: Player in Her Time*. New York: W. W. Norton, 1987.

Babcock, Barbara A. "Mud, Mirrors, and Making Up: Liminality and Reflexivity in *Between the Acts*." *Victor Turner and the Construction of Cultural Criticism*. Ed. Kathleen M. Ashley. Bloomington, IN: Indiana University Press, 1990. 86–116.

Baker, Michael. *Our Three Selves: The Life of Radclyffe Hall*. London: Hamish Hamilton, 1985.

Barnes, Djuna. "How it Feels to be Forcibly Fed." *New York World Magazine* 6 September 1914. Rpt. in *New York*, by Djuna Barnes. Ed. Alyce Barry. London: Virago, 1990. 174–179.

   The Dove. At the Root of the Stars: The Short Plays. Ed. Douglas Messerli. Los Angeles: Sun & Moon Press, 1995. 147–161.

Barthes, Roland. *Mythologies*. Trans. Annette Lavers. London: Paladin, 1973.

Beerbohm, Max. "Miss Robins' Tract." *Around Theatres*. Vol. 2. New York: Alfred A. Knopf, 1930. 590–595.

Bell, Quentin. *Virginia Woolf: A Biography*. 2 vols. San Diego: Harvest–HBJ, 1972.

Belsey, Catherine. *The Subject of Tragedy: Identity and Difference in Renaissance Drama*. London: Routledge, 1985.

Benjamin, Walter. "Trauerspiel and Tragedy." Trans. John Osborne. Drakakis and Conn Liebler, *Tragedy* 106–122.

Benstock, Shari. *Women of the Left Bank, Paris 1900–1940*. Austin: University of Texas Press, 1986.

Blair, Fredrika. *Isadora: Portrait of the Artist as a Woman*. New York: McGraw Hill, 1986.

"Bloomsbury Unbuttoned." *The New Yorker* 21 November 1983: 42–44.

Boal, Augusto. *Theatre of the Oppressed*. Trans. Charles A. and Maria-Odilia Leal McBride. New York: Theatre Communications Group, 1985.

Booth, Michael R. "Ellen Terry." *Bernhardt, Duse, Terry: The Actress in Her Time*, by Michael R. Booth, Susan Bassnett, and John Stokes. Cambridge University Press, 1988. 65–117, 176–180.

"Sarah Siddons." *Three Tragic Actresses: Siddons, Rachel, Ristori*, by Michael R. Booth, John Stokes, and Susan Bassnett. Cambridge University Press, 1996. 10–65, 171–177.

Bourne, Bette, Paul Shaw, Peggy Shaw, and Lois Weaver. *Belle Reprieve. Split Britches: Lesbian Practice/Feminist Performance*. Ed. Sue-Ellen Case. London: Routledge, 1996. 149–183.

Bradbury, Malcolm, and James McFarlane, eds. *Modernism: A Guide to European Literature 1890–1930*. New York: Penguin, 1991.

Brecht, Bertolt. *Brecht on Theatre*. Trans. John Willett. New York: Hill and Wang, 1964.

Brereton, Austin. "Ellen Terry, Player-Queen." *The English Illustrated Magazine* (December 1897): 229–240.

"Britishers Amuse in Little Theatre: Huddersfield Thespians Heard in Contest – Studio Theatre Presents Freudian Essay." Rev. of *The Dove*. *New York Times* 7 May 1926: 12.

Brittain, Vera. *Radclyffe Hall: A Case of Obscenity?* New York: A. S. Barnes, 1969.

Butler, Judith. "Critically Queer." *GLQ: A Journal of Lesbian and Gay Studies* 1.1 (1993): 17–32.

Gender Trouble: Feminism and the Subversion of Identity. New York: Routledge, 1990.

"Imitation and Gender Insubordination." *Inside/Out: Lesbian Theories, Gay Theories*. Ed. Diana Fuss. New York: Routledge, 1991. 13–31.

Cameron, Julia Margaret. *Victorian Photographs of Famous Men and Fair Women*. With introductions by Virginia Woolf and Roger Fry. London: Hogarth Press, 1926.

Campbell, Lady Colin. "The First Ladies of the Day. V. – Miss Ellen Terry." *Madame* 6 December 1902: 603–605. *The Papers of Henry Irving and Ellen Terry*. Reel 17, box 29, no. 61.

Campbell, Joseph. *The Hero with a Thousand Faces*. New York: Pantheon, 1949.

Caputi, Mary. *Voluptuous Yearnings: A Feminist Theory of the Obscene*. Lanham, MD: Rowman and Littlefield, 1994.

Carlson, Marvin. *Performance: A Critical Introduction*. London: Routledge, 1996.

Carlson, Susan. *Women and Comedy: Rewriting the British Theatrical Tradition*. Ann Arbor: University of Michigan Press, 1991.

Carr, J. Comyns. *Macbeth and Lady Macbeth: An Essay*. London: Bickers & Son, 1889.

Case, Sue-Ellen. "Towards a Butch/Femme Aesthetic." *Making a Spectacle: Feminist Essays on Contemporary Women's Theatre*. Ed. Lynda Hart. Ann Arbor: University of Michigan Press, 1989. 282–299.

Feminism and Theatre. New York: Methuen, 1988.

Castle, Terry. *The Apparitional Lesbian: Female Homosexuality and Modern Culture*. New York: Columbia University Press, 1993.

Chisholm, Dianne. "Obscene Modernism: *Eros Noir* and the Profane Illumination of Djuna Barnes." *American Literature* 69.1 (March 1997): 167–206.

Cima, Gay Gibson. "Discovering Signs: the Emergence of the Critical Actor in Ibsen." *Theatre Journal* 35.1 (March 1983): 5–22.

"Elizabeth Robins: Ibsen Actress–Manageress." Diss. Cornell University, 1978.

Performing Women: Female Characters, Male Playwrights, and the Modern Stage. Ithaca, NY: Cornell University Press, 1993.

Cixous, Hélène. "Aller à la Mer." Trans. Barbara Kerslake. *Modern Drama* 27.4 (December 1984): 546–548.

Portrait of Dora. Trans. Anita Barrows. *Benmussa Directs.* London: John Calder, 1979. 27–67.

Cixous, Hélène, and Catherine Clément. *The Newly Born Woman.* Trans. Betsy Wing. Theory and History of Literature 24. Minneapolis: University of Minnesota Press, 1986.

Clark, Susan F. "Misalliance: Djuna Barnes and the American Theatre." Diss. Tufts University, 1989.

Clark, Suzanne. *Sentimental Modernism: Women Writers and the Revolution of the Word.* Bloomington, IN: Indiana University Press, 1991.

Cline, Sally. *Radclyffe Hall: A Woman Called John.* Woodstock, NY: Overlook Press, 1997.

Cockin, Katharine. *Edith Craig: Dramatic Lives.* London: Cassell, 1998.

Cocteau, Jean. "Isadora, Sarah and De Max." *Paris Album 1900–1914.* Trans. Margaret Crosland. London: W. H. Allen, 1956. 107–119.

"Court Theatre: '*Votes for Women!*'" *The Times* 10 April 1907: 5.

Craft, Christopher. "Alias Bunbury: Desire and Termination in *The Importance of Being Earnest.*" *Critical Essays on Oscar Wilde.* Ed. Regenia Gagnier. New York: G. K. Hall, 1991. 119–137.

Craig, Edward Gordon. *Ellen Terry and Her Secret Self.* London: Sampson Low, Marston, 1931.

Cunningham, Gail. *The New Woman and the Victorian Novel.* London: Macmillan, 1978.

Curtin, Kaier. *"We Can Always Call Them Bulgarians": The Emergence of Lesbians and Gay Men on the American Stage.* Boston: Alyson Publications, 1987.

Dalton, Anne B. "'*This* is obscene': Female Voyeurism, Sexual Abuse, and Maternal Power in *The Dove.*" *Review of Contemporary Fiction* 13.3 (Fall 1993): 117–139.

Daly, Ann. "The Balanchine Woman: of Hummingbirds and Channel Swimmers." *TDR* 31.1 (T113) (Spring 1987): 8–21.

"Dance History and Feminist Theory: Reconsidering Isadora Duncan and the Male Gaze." *Gender in Performance: The Presentation of Difference in the Performing Arts.* Ed. Laurence Senelick. Hanover, NH: University Press of New England, 1992. 239–259.

Done into Dance: Isadora Duncan in America. Bloomington, IN: Indiana University Press, 1995.

Davis, Tracy C. *Actresses as Working Women: Their Social Identity in Victorian Culture.* London: Routledge, 1991.

"Ibsen's Victorian Audience." *Essays in Theatre* 4.1 (November 1985): 21–38.

de Certeau, Michel. *The Practice of Everyday Life*. Trans. Steven Rendall. Berkeley, CA: University of California Press, 1984.

de Jongh, Nicholas. *Not in Front of the Audience: Homosexuality on Stage*. London: Routledge, 1992.

de Lauretis, Teresa. "Desire in Narrative." *Alice Doesn't: Feminism, Semiotics, Cinema*. Bloomington, IN: Indiana University Press, 1984. 103–157.

———. "Sexual Indifference and Lesbian Representation." *Performing Feminisms: Feminist Critical Theory and Theatre*. Ed. Sue-Ellen Case. Baltimore: Johns Hopkins University Press, 1990. 17–39.

———. "The Technology of Gender." *Technologies of Gender: Essays on Theory, Film, and Fiction*. Bloomington, IN: Indiana University Press, 1987. 1–30.

Dempster, Elizabeth. "Women Writing the Body: Let's Watch a Little How She Dances." *Grafts: Feminist Cultural Criticism*. Ed. Susan Sheridan. London: Verso, 1988. 35–54.

DeSalvo, Louise. *Virginia Woolf's First Voyage: A Novel in the Making*. Totawa, NJ: Rowman and Littlefield, 1980.

DeSalvo, Louise, and Mitchell A. Leaska, eds. *The Letters of Vita Sackville-West to Virginia Woolf*. New York: William Morrow, 1985.

Des Roches, Kay Unruh. "Sight and Insight: Stage Pictures in *Hedda Gabler*." *Journal of Dramatic Theory and Criticism* 5.1 (Fall 1990): 49–68.

Diamond, Elin. Introduction. *Performance and Cultural Politics*. London: Routledge, 1996. 1–12.

———. Introduction. *Unmaking Mimesis*. London: Routledge, 1997.

Dolan, Jill. "'Lesbian' Subjectivity in Realism: Dragging at the Margins of Structure and Ideology." *Performing Feminisms: Feminist Critical Theory and Theatre*. Ed. Sue-Ellen Case. Baltimore: Johns Hopkins University Press, 1990. 40–53.

Drakakis, John, and Naomi Conn Liebler, eds. *Tragedy*. London: Longman, 1998.

Drewal, Margaret Thompson. "Isis and Isadora." *Proceedings of the Tenth Annual Conference, Society of Dance History Scholars, University of California, Irvine, February 13–15, 1987*. Riverside: Dance History Scholars, 1987. 185–194.

Dukore, Bernard F., ed. *Dramatic Theory and Criticism: Greeks to Grotowski*. Fort Worth, TX: Holt, Rinehart and Winston, 1974.

Duncan, Irma, and Allan Ross Macdougall. *Isadora Duncan's Russian Days and Her Last Years in France*. London: Victor Gollancz, 1929.

Duncan, Isadora. *The Art of the Dance*. Ed. Sheldon Cheney. New York: Theatre Arts, 1928.

———. *Isadora Speaks*. Ed. Franklin Rosemont. San Francisco: City Lights Books, 1981.

———. *My Life*. New York: Liveright, 1927.

———. *My Life*. London: Sphere Books, 1969.

Eastman, Max. *Heroes I Have Known: Twelve Who Lived Great Lives*. New York: Simon and Schuster, 1942.

Edmonds, Jill. "Princess Hamlet." *The New Woman and Her Sisters: Feminism and Theatre 1850–1914*. Ed. Vivien Gardner and Susan Rutherford. Ann Arbor: University of Michigan Press, 1992. 59–76.

Egan, Michael, ed. *Ibsen: The Critical Heritage*. London: Routledge and Kegan Paul, 1972.

"Ellen Terry Acts Heroines." *New York Times* 11 November 1910: 9.

Elliot, Bridget, and Jo-Ann Wallace. *Women Artists and Writers: Modernist (im)positionings*. London: Routledge, 1994.

Ellis, Havelock. *Impressions and Comments*. London: Constable, 1920.

Ewbank, Inga-Stina. "Ibsen and the Language of Women." *Women Writing and Writing about Women*. Ed. Mary Jacobus. London: Croom Helm, 1979. 114–132.

Farfan, Penny. "Reading, Writing, and Authority in Ibsen's 'Women's Plays.'" *Modern Drama* 45.1 (Spring 2002): 1–8.

Felski, Rita. *Beyond Feminist Aesthetics: Feminist Literature and Social Change*. Cambridge, MA: Harvard University Press, 1989.

Field, Andrew. *Djuna: The Life and Times of Djuna Barnes*. New York: G. P. Putnam's Sons, 1983.

Finney, Gail. *Women in Modern Drama: Freud, Feminism, and European Theater at the Turn of the Century*. Ithaca, NY: Cornell University Press, 1989.

Fjelde, Rolf. Foreword. *Ibsen: Four Major Plays*. Trans. Rolf Fjelde. Vol. 1. New York: Signet Classic, 1965. ix–xxxv.

Flanner, Janet. "Isadora (1878–1927)." *Paris Was Yesterday: 1925–1939*. Ed. Irving Drutman. San Diego: Harvest–HBJ, 1972. 28–35.

Foster, Susan Leigh. "The Ballerina's Phallic Pointe." *Corporealities: Dancing Knowledge, Culture and Power*. London: Routledge, 1996. 1–24.

Reading Dancing: Bodies and Subjects in Contemporary American Dance. Berkeley, CA: University of California Press, 1986.

Foucault, Michel. *The History of Sexuality, Volume 1: An Introduction*. Trans. Robert Hurley. New York: Vintage, 1990.

Franc, Miriam Alice. *Ibsen in England*. Diss. University of Pennsylvania. Boston: Four Seas, 1919.

Francis, Elizabeth. "From Event to Monument: Modernism, Feminism and Isadora Duncan." *American Studies* 35.1 (Spring 1994): 25–45.

Freud, Sigmund. "Fragment of an Analysis of a Case of Hysteria ('Dora')." *The Freud Reader*. Ed. Peter Gay. New York: W. W. Norton, 1989. 172–239.

"The 'Uncanny.'" *The Standard Edition of the Complete Psychological Works of Sigmund Freud*. Ed. James Strachey. Vol. 17. London: Hogarth Press, 1955. 217–256.

Froula, Christine. "Out of the Chrysalis: Female Initiation and Female Authority in Virginia Woolf's *The Voyage Out*." *Tulsa Studies in Women's Literature* 5 (Spring 1986): 63–90.

"Virginia Woolf as Shakespeare's Sister: Chapters in a Woman Writer's Autobiography." *Women's Re-Visions of Shakespeare: On Responses of Dickinson, Woolf, Rich, H.D., George Eliot, and Others*. Ed. Marianne Novy. Urbana, IL: University of Illinois Press, 1990. 123–142.

Gainor, J. Ellen. *Shaw's Daughters: Dramatic and Narrative Constructions of Gender*. Ann Arbor: University of Michigan Press, 1991.

Garber, Marjorie. *Vested Interests: Cross-Dressing and Cultural Anxiety.* New York: HarperPerennial, 1992.

Gardner, Viv. Introduction. *The New Woman and Her Sisters: Feminism and Theatre 1850–1914.* Ed. Vivien Gardner and Susan Rutherford. Ann Arbor: University of Michigan Press, 1992. 1–14.

Gassner, John. Introduction. *Four Great Plays by Ibsen.* Trans. R. Farquharson Sharp. New York: Bantam Books, 1959. vii–xiii.

Gates, Joanne E. *Elizabeth Robins, 1862–1952: Actress, Novelist, Feminist.* Tuscaloosa, AL: University of Alabama Press, 1994.

"'Sometimes Suppressed and Sometimes Embroidered': the Life and Writing of Elizabeth Robins, 1862–1952." Diss. University of Massachusetts, Amherst, 1987.

Gilmore, Leigh. "Obscenity, Modernity, Identity: Legalizing *The Well of Loneliness* and *Nightwood.*" *Journal of the History of Sexuality* 4.4 (1994): 603–624.

Girard, René. "The Sacrificial Crisis." Trans. Patrick Gregory. Drakakis and Conn Liebler, *Tragedy.* 278–297.

Glendinning, Victoria. *Vita: The Life of Vita Sackville-West.* Harmondsworth: Penguin Books, 1983.

Graff, Ellen. "Walt Whitman and Isadora Duncan: the Construction of a Personal Mythology." *Proceedings of the Tenth Annual Conference, Society of Dance History Scholars, University of California, Irvine, February 13–15, 1987.* Riverside: Dance History Scholars, 1987. 177–184.

Greer, Germaine. *The Obstacle Race.* New York: Farrar, Straus & Giroux, 1979.

Gubar, Susan. "'The Blank Page' and the Issues of Female Creativity." *The New Feminist Criticism: Essays on Women, Literature, and Theory.* Ed. Elaine Showalter. New York: Pantheon, 1985. 292–313.

Hall, Radclyffe. *The Well of Loneliness.* New York: Anchor–Doubleday, 1990.

Hamilton, Cicely. *A Pageant of Great Women.* London: The Suffrage Shop, 1910.

H[ankins] St. J[ohn]. Rev. of *Votes for Women. The Academy* 13 April 1907: 370.

Hanson, Katherine. "Ibsen's Women Characters and Their Feminist Contemporaries." *Theatre History Studies* 2 (1982): 83–91.

Hawkins, Frederick. "Macbeth on the Stage." Part II. *The Theatre,* new series 13 (1 January 1889): 6.

Hendrickson, Robert. *The Facts on File Encyclopedia of Word and Phrase Origins.* New York: Facts on File, 1997.

Herring, Phillip. *Djuna: The Life and Work of Djuna Barnes.* New York: Viking, 1995.

Higgonet, Margaret. "Suicide: Representations of the Feminine in the Nineteenth Century." *Poetics Today* 6.1–2 (1985): 103–118.

Hirshfield, Claire. "The Actresses' Franchise League and the Campaign for Women's Suffrage 1908–1914." *Theatre Research International* 10.2 (Summer 1985): 129–153.

"Suffragettes Onstage: Women's Political Theatre in Edwardian England." *New England Theatre Journal* 2 (1991): 13–26.

Hoffman, Eva. "Rare Cast from France in a Rare Woolf Play." *New York Times* 22 October 1983: 9.

Holledge, Julie. *Innocent Flowers: Women in the Edwardian Theatre.* London: Virago, 1981.

Hutcheon, Linda. *A Poetics of Postmodernism: History, Theory, Fiction.* New York: Routledge, 1988.

The Politics of Postmodernism. London: Routledge, 1989.

Ibsen, Henrik. *An Enemy of the People. Plays: Two.* Ed. and trans. Michael Meyer. London. Methuen, 1980. 107–223.

Hedda Gabler. Ibsen: The Complete Major Prose Plays. Trans. Rolf Fjelde. New York: New American Library, 1965. 689–778.

"*Hedda Gabler.*" *Playwrights on Playwriting.* Ed. Toby Cole. London: Mac-Gibbon and Kee, 1960. 156–170.

Ibsen: Letters and Speeches. Ed. Evert Sprinchorn. London: MacGibbon and Kee, 1965.

Ingram, Angela. "'Unutterable Putrefaction' and 'Foul Stuff': Two 'Obscene' Novels of the 1920s." *Women's Studies International Forum* 9.4 (1986): 341–354.

Innes, Christopher. "Modernism in Drama." *The Cambridge Companion to Modernism.* Ed. Michael Levenson. Cambridge University Press, 1999. 130–156.

Isadora [*The Loves of Isadora*]. Dir. Karel Reisz. Universal Pictures, 1968.

"Isadora Duncan, Dragged By Scarf From Auto, Killed." *New York Times* 15 September 1927: 1, 4.

Jenkin, H. C. Fleeming. "Mrs. Siddons as Lady Macbeth." *Mrs. Siddons as Lady Macbeth and as Queen Katharine. Papers on Acting.* Vol. 3. New York: Dramatic Museum of Columbia University, 1915. 25–68.

John, Angela. *Elizabeth Robins: Staging a Life, 1862–1952.* London: Routledge, 1995.

Jowitt, Deborah. *Time and the Dancing Image.* Berkeley, CA: University of California Press, 1988.

Kelly, Katherine E., ed. *Modern Drama by Women 1880s–1930s: An International Anthology.* London: Routledge, 1996.

Kendall, Elizabeth. "Victim of History." *Ballet News* (February 1982): 19–20, 42.

Where She Danced: The Birth of American Art-Dance. Berkeley, CA: University of California Press, 1979.

Kent, Susan Kingsley. *Sex and Suffrage in Britain, 1860–1914.* Princeton University Press, 1987.

Langer, Susanne K. "The Great Dramatic Forms: the Tragic Rhythm." Drakakis and Conn Liebler, *Tragedy.* 323–336.

Lauts, Jan. *Carpaccio: Paintings and Drawings: Complete Edition.* London: Phaidon Press, 1962.

Lawrence, D. H. "Pornography and Obscenity." *Phoenix: The Posthumous Papers of D. H. Lawrence.* Ed. Edward D. McDonald. London: Heinemann, 1961. 170–187.

Levenson, Michael. Introduction. *The Cambridge Companion to Modernism.* Cambridge University Press, 1999. 1–8.

Loewenthal, Lillian. *The Search for Isadora: The Legend and Legacy of Isadora Duncan.* Pennington, NJ: Dance Horizons/Princeton Book Company, 1993.

"London Letter." *Cambridge Daily News* 30 January 192[?]. Edy Craig Papers, Ellen Terry Memorial Museum.

Loraux, Nicole. *Tragic Ways of Killing a Woman.* Trans. Anthony Forster. Cambridge, MA: Harvard University Press, 1987.

Luhan, Mabel Dodge. *Movers and Shakers.* Albuquerque: University of New Mexico Press, 1985.

Lukács, Georg. "The Sociology of Modern Drama." Trans. Lee Baxandall. Dukore, *Dramatic Theory and Criticism.* 933–941.

Madden, Ed. "*The Well of Loneliness*: the Gospel According to Radclyffe Hall." *Journal of Homosexuality* 33.3 (June–July 1997): 163–186.

Manning, Susan. *Ecstasy and the Demon: Feminism and Nationalism in the Dances of Mary Wigman.* Berkeley, CA: University of California Press, 1993.

Manvell, Roger. *Ellen Terry.* London: Heinemann, 1968.

Marcus, Jane. *Art and Anger: Reading Like A Woman.* Columbus: Ohio State University Press, 1988.

"Britannia Rules *The Waves*." *Decolonizing Tradition: New Views of Twentieth-Century "British" Literary Canons.* Ed. Karen R. Lawrence. Urbana, IL: University of Illinois Press, 1992. 136–162.

"Elizabeth Robins." Diss. Northwestern University, 1973.

"Some Sources for *Between the Acts*." *Virginia Woolf Miscellany* 6 (Winter 1977): 1–3.

"Transatlantic Sisterhood: Labor and Suffrage Links in the Letters of Elizabeth Robins and Emmeline Pankhurst." *Signs* 3.3 (Spring 1978): 744–755.

Marshall, Gail. *Actresses on the Victorian Stage: Feminine Performance and the Galatea Myth.* Cambridge University Press, 1998.

Martin, John. "Isadora Duncan Danced Like a 'Puritanical Pagan.'" Rev. of *My Life*, by Isadora Duncan. *The New York Times Book Review* 8 January 1928: 3.

McDonald, Jan. "'The Second Act Was Glorious': The Staging of the Trafalgar Scene from *Votes for Women!* at the Court Theatre." *Theatre History Studies* 15 (June 1995): 139–160.

Melville, Joy. *Ellen and Edy: A Biography of Ellen Terry and Her Daughter, Edith Craig, 1847–1947.* London: Pandora, 1987.

Meredith, George. "An Essay on Comedy." Dukore, *Dramatic Theory and Criticism.* 618–624.

Meyer, Michael. *Ibsen.* Harmondsworth: Penguin Books, 1985.

Meyer, Michael. Introduction. *Plays: Two.* By Henrik Ibsen. Trans. Michael Meyer. London: Methuen, 1980. 11–21.

Plays: Four. By Henrik Ibsen. Trans. Michael Meyer. London: Eyre Methuen, 1980.

Michelson, Peter. *Speaking the Unspeakable: A Poetics of Obscenity.* Albany, NY: State University of New York Press, 1993.

Modleski, Tania. *Feminism Without Women: Culture and Criticism in a "Postfeminist" Age.* New York: Routledge, 1991.

Monroe, Harriet. "Golden Moments." *Poetry: A Magazine of Verse* 31.4 (January 1928): 206–210.

O'Neal, Hank. *"Life is painful, nasty & short . . . in my case it has only been painful & nasty." Djuna Barnes 1978–1981: An Informal Memoir*. New York: Paragon House, 1990.

Onions, C. T., ed. *The Oxford Dictionary of English Etymology*. Oxford: Clarendon Press, 1966.

Ortner, Sherry. "Is Female to Male as Nature is to Culture?" *Women, Culture and Society*. Ed. Michelle Z. Rosaldo and Louise Lamphere. Stanford University Press, 1974. 67–87.

The Papers of Henry Irving and Ellen Terry from the Bram Stoker Collection, Shakespeare Centre Library, Stratford-upon-Avon. Brighton: Harvester Microform, 1987.

Partridge, Eric. *Origins: A Short Etymological Dictionary of Modern English*. New York: Greenwich House, 1983.

Plumb, Cheryl J. Introduction to *The Dove. Modern Drama by Women 1880s–1930s: An International Anthology*. Ed. Katherine E. Kelly. London: Routledge, 1996. 299–302.

Pomeroy, Sarah B. "Images of Women in the Literature of Classical Athens." Drakakis and Conn Liebler, *Tragedy*. 214–232.

Powell, Kerry. *Women and Victorian Theatre*. Cambridge University Press, 1997.

Prins, Yopie. "Greek Maenads, Victorian Spinsters." *Victorian Sexual Dissidence*. Ed. Richard Dellamora. University of Chicago Press, 1999. 43–81.

"Pseudo-Freud, Neo-Shaw, Pre-Barrie in the Little Theatres." Rev. of *The Dove. New York Evening Post* 7 May 1926: 14.

Rev. of *Votes for Women*. *Irish News* 15 April 1907. Elizabeth Robins Papers, Fales Library, New York University.

Rich, Adrienne. "Compulsory Heterosexuality and Lesbian Existence." *Powers of Desire: The Politics of Sexuality*. Ed. Ann Snitow, Christine Stansell, and Sharon Thompson. New York: Monthly Review Press, 1983. 177–205.

    "When We Dead Awaken: Writing as Re-Vision." *On Lies, Secrets, and Silence: Selected Prose 1966–1978*. New York: Norton, 1979. 33–49.

Richman, David. "Directing *Freshwater*." *Virginia Woolf Miscellany* 2 (Spring 1974): 1–2.

Roach, Joseph. *Cities of the Dead: Circum-Atlantic Performance*. New York: Columbia University Press, 1996.

Roach, Joseph R., and Janelle Reinelt, eds. *Critical Theory and Performance*. Ann Arbor: University of Michigan Press, 1992.

Robins, Elizabeth. *Ancilla's Share: An Indictment of Sex Antagonism*. London: Hutchinson, 1924.

    Both Sides of the Curtain. London: William Heinemann, 1940.

    The Convert. London: Women's Press, 1980.

    Diaries. Ms. Elizabeth Robins Papers. Fales Library, New York University.

    Ibsen and the Actress. London: Hogarth Press, 1928; rpt. New York: Haskell House, 1973.

"On Seeing Madame Bernhardt's Hamlet." *North American Review* 171.6 (December 1900): 908–919.

"Oscar Wilde: an Appreciation." Ts. Elizabeth Robins Papers. Fales Library, New York University.

Raymond and I. London: Hogarth Press, 1956.

"Some Aspects of Henrik Ibsen." Ts. Elizabeth Robins Papers. Fales Library, New York University.

"Some Aspects of Henrik Ibsen: Lecture delivered before The Philosophical Institute, Edinburgh. October 27, 1908." Ts. Elizabeth Robins Papers. Fales Library, New York University.

Theatre and Friendship. New York: G. P. Putnam's Sons, 1932.

Votes for Women. How the Vote was Won and Other Plays. Ed. Dale Spender and Carole Hayman. London: Methuen, 1985. 35–87.

Way Stations. London: Hodder and Stoughton, 1913.

Whither and How. Ts. and ms. Elizabeth Robins Papers. Fales Library, New York University.

Robins, Elizabeth, and Florence Bell. *Alan's Wife.* London: Henry and Co., 1893.

Rolley, Katrina. "Cutting a Dash: the Dress of Radclyffe Hall and Una Troubridge." *Feminist Review* (Summer 1990): 54–66.

Rose, Phyllis. *A Woman of Letters: A Life of Virginia Woolf.* New York: Harvest–HBJ, 1978.

Rowell, George. "Misleading Ladies: Two Biographies of Ellen Terry." *Theatre Notebook* 42:3 (1988): 126–131.

Ruehl, Sonja. "Inverts and Experts: Radclyffe Hall and the Lesbian Identity." *Feminism, Culture and Politics.* Ed. Rosalind Brunt and Caroline Rowan. London: Lawrence and Wishart, 1982. 15–36.

Ruotolo, Lucio P. Preface. *Freshwater*, by Virginia Woolf. Ed. Lucio P. Ruotolo. San Diego: Harvest–HBJ, 1976. v–ix.

Ruskin, John. *The Shrine of the Slaves, St. Mark's Rest: The History of Venice.* First supplement. Orpington, 1877.

[Russell, Edward R.] An Old Hand. "*Macbeth* at the Lyceum." *Liverpool Daily Post* 31 December 1888. *The Papers of Henry Irving and Ellen Terry.* Reel 22, box 55, no. 54.

Edward R. Russell. "*Macbeth* Revisited." Programme for the 150th performance of *Macbeth* at the Lyceum, 1889. *The Papers of Henry Irving and Ellen Terry.* Reel 11, box 17, no. 5.

St. John, Christopher. *Ellen Terry: A Short Biography.* [London: Pelican Press], 1947.
   Introduction. *Four Lectures on Shakespeare*, by Ellen Terry. Ed. Christopher St. John. New York: Benjamin Blom, 1969. 7–21.

Sarris, Andrew. "Films: The Loves of Isadora." *The Village Voice* 10 July 1969: 43.

Saslow, James M. "'Disagreeably Hidden': Construction and Constriction of the Lesbian Body in Rosa Bonheur's *Horse Fair.*" *Queer Representations: Reading Lives, Reading Cultures.* Ed. Martin Duberman. New York University Press, 1997. 69–84.

Schneider, Karen. "Of Two Minds: Woolf, the War and *Between the Acts*." *Journal of Modern Literature* 16.1 (1989): 93–112.

Scott, Bonnie Kime, ed. *The Gender of Modernism*. Bloomington, IN: Indiana University Press, 1990.

    Refiguring Modernism. Vol. 1. *The Women of 1928*. Bloomington, IN: Indiana University Press, 1995.

Scott, James B. *Djuna Barnes*. Boston: Twayne, 1976.

Senelick, Laurence, ed. *Lovesick: Modernist Plays of Same-Sex Love, 1894–1925*. London: Routledge, 1999.

Sergeant, Elizabeth Shepley. "Heroic Isadora." Rev. of *My Life*, by Isadora Duncan. *The New Republic* 21 March 1928: 164–165.

Seroff, Victor. *The Real Isadora*. New York: Dial, 1971.

Sgarbi, Vittorio. *Carpaccio*. Trans. Jay Hyams. New York: Abbeville Press, 1994.

"Shakespeare as Suffragist." *The Vote* 4.92 (29 July 1911): 180.

Shaw, George Bernard. "Henry Irving and Ellen Terry." *Pen Portraits and Reviews*. London: Constable, 1932. 160–171.

    "Mr. Grundy's Improvements on Dumas." *Dramatic Opinions and Essays*. Vol. 2. London: Constable, 1912. 304–312.

    Preface. *Ellen Terry and Bernard Shaw: A Correspondence*. By Ellen Terry and George Bernard Shaw. Ed. Christopher St. John. New York: G. P. Putnam's Sons, 1931. vii–xxviii.

    The Quintessence of Ibsenism. New York: Brentano's, 1910.

    "The Technical Novelty in Ibsen's Plays." Dukore, *Dramatic Theory and Criticism*. 638–647.

Showalter, Elaine. *The Female Malady: Women, Madness, and English Culture, 1830–1980*. New York: Penguin, 1985.

    Sexual Anarchy: Gender and Culture at the Fin de Siècle. New York: Viking, 1990.

Siddons, Sarah. "Remarks on the Character of Lady Macbeth." *Life of Mrs. Siddons*, by Thomas Campbell. Vol. 2. London: Effingham Wilson, Royal Exchange, 1834. 10–39.

Silver, Brenda R. Introduction and commentary. "'Anon' and 'The Reader': Virginia Woolf's Last Essays." *Twentieth-Century Literature* 25.3–4 (1979): 356–441.

Sinfield, Alan. *Out on Stage: Lesbian and Gay Theatre in the Twentieth Century*. New Haven: Yale University Press, 1999.

Sontag, Susan. "Against Interpretation." *Against Interpretation and Other Essays*. New York: Farrar, Straus & Giroux, 1969. 3–14.

Spalding, Frances. *Vanessa Bell*. San Diego: Harvest–HBJ, 1983.

States, Bert O. *Great Reckonings in Little Rooms: On the Phenomenology of Theater*. Berkeley, CA: University of California Press, 1985.

Steegmuller, Francis, ed. *"Your Isadora": The Love Story of Isadora Duncan and Gordon Craig Told Through Letters and Diaries*. New York: Vintage, 1976.

Stein, Gertrude. "Orta or One Dancing." *Two: Gertrude Stein and her Brother and Other Early Portraits [1908–12]. The Unpublished Writings of Gertrude Stein*. Vol. 1. New Haven: Yale University Press, 1951. 286–304.

Stowell, Sheila. "Rehabilitating Realism." *Journal of Dramatic Theory and Criticism* 6.2 (Spring 1992): 81–88.

A Stage of Their Own: Feminist Playwrights of the Suffrage Era. Ann Arbor: University of Michigan Press, 1992.

Strindberg, August. "Preface to *Miss Julie.*" Trans. E. M. Sprinchorn. Dukore, *Dramatic Theory and Criticism.* 564–574.

"A Suffragette Play at the Court." *The Pall Mall Gazette* 10 April 1907: 2.

Templeton, Joan. "Fallen Women and Upright Wives: 'Woman's Place' in Early Modern Tragedy." *Reconfigured Spheres: Feminist Explorations of Literary Space.* Ed. Margaret R. Higgonet and Joan Templeton. Amherst, MA: University of Massachusetts Press, 1994. 60–71.

Ibsen's Women. Cambridge University Press, 1997.

Terry, Ellen. *Ellen Terry's Memoirs.* With preface, notes, and additional biographical chapters by Edith Craig and Christopher St. John. New York: Benjamin Blom, 1969.

Four Lectures on Shakespeare. Ed. Christopher St. John. New York: Benjamin Blom, 1969.

"More Reminiscences by Ellen Terry: Some Reflections on Shakespeare's Heroines." *McClure's Magazine* 36.1 (November 1910): 95–106.

In "Realism and the Actor: An International Symposium." *The Mask* 1.9 (November 1908): 178–179.

"Some Recollections." *The Tatler* 250, 11 April 1906: 44.

The Story of My Life. New York: Schocken Books, 1982.

"Stray Memories." Parts 1–3. *The New Review* 4.23, 4.24, 4.25 (1891): 332–341, 444–449, 499–507.

Terry, Ellen, and George Bernard Shaw. *Ellen Terry and Bernard Shaw: A Correspondence.* Ed. Christopher St. John. New York: G. P. Putnam's Sons, 1931.

Terry, Walter. *Isadora Duncan: Her Life, Her Art, Her Legacy.* New York: Dodd, Mead, 1963.

Thomas, Sue. "Sexual Matter and *Votes for Women.*" *Papers on Language and Literature* 33.1 (Winter 1997): 47–70.

Thompson, Alex. M. "Stageland. A Masterpiece of Stage Management." *The Clarion* 19 April 1907: 3.

Tickner, Lisa. *The Spectacle of Women: Imagery of the Suffrage Campaign 1907–14.* London: Chatto and Windus, 1987.

"Trafalgar Square Dramatised: Suffrage Play at the Court Theatre." *Daily Express* 10 April 1907: 5

Veltrusky, Jirí. "Man and Object in the Theatre." *A Prague School Reader on Esthetics, Literary Structure, and Style.* Trans. Paul L. Garvin. Washington, DC: Georgetown University Press, 1964. 83–91.

"*Votes for Women!*" *The Era* 13 April 1907: 13.

"'Votes for Women!' Extraordinary Play at the Court Theatre." *Daily Mail* 10 April 1907: 5.

"'Votes for Women!' A Suffragette Tract. Trafalgar Square on the Stage." *Daily News* 10 April 1907: 12.

"Warm Welcome for Miss Ellen Terry." *New York Times* 4 November 1910: 9.

Weeks, Jeffrey. *Coming Out: Homosexual Politics in Britain, from the Nineteenth Century to the Present*. London: Quartet, 1977.

West, Rebecca. "Concerning the Censorship." *Ending in Earnest: A Literary Log*. Garden City, NY: Doubleday, Doran, 1931. 6–12.

Weston, Olive. "Ellen Terry, the Woman." *Philadelphia Press* 12 May 1889.

Whitelaw, Lis. *The Life and Rebellious Times of Cicely Hamilton: Actress, Writer, Suffragist*. London: The Women's Press, 1990.

Whitman, Walt. "Song of Myself." *The Norton Anthology of Modern Poetry*. Ed. Richard Ellmann and Robert O'Clair. 2nd edn. New York: Norton, 1973. 22–35.

Wilde, Oscar. "The Decay of Lying." Dukore, *Dramatic Theory and Criticism*. 624–628.

Williams, Raymond. "Conclusion from *Drama from Ibsen to Brecht*." *Modern Drama: Plays/Criticism/Theory*. Ed. W. B. Worthen. Fort Worth: Harcourt Brace, 1995. 1170–1178.

"From *Modern Tragedy*." Drakakis and Conn Liebler, *Tragedy*. 147–179.

Winter, William. "*Ellen Terry*" ["*The Merchant of Venice*"]. *Shakespeare on the Stage*. First series. New York: Moffat, Yard, 1911. 217–222.

"Shadows of the Stage: Ellen Terry – Her Personality and Her Lectures." *Harper's Weekly* 17 December 1910: 18.

Wolff, Janet. "Reinstating Corporeality: Feminism and Body Politics." *Feminine Sentences: Essays on Women and Culture*. Cambridge: Polity Press, 1990. 120–141.

Woolf, Leonard. "The World of Books: 'I Remember' and Other Motives." Rev. of *My Life*, by Isadora Duncan. *The Nation & Athenaeum* 19 May 1928: 210.

Woolf, Virginia. "'Anon' and 'The Reader.'" Ed. Brenda R. Silver. *Twentieth-Century Literature* 25.3–4 (1979): 356–441.

Between the Acts. San Diego: Harvest–HBJ, 1941.

"*The Cherry Orchard*." *The New Statesman* 24 July 1920: 446–447.

The Diary of Virginia Woolf. Ed. Anne Olivier Bell, assisted by Andrew McNeillie, 5 vols. London: Hogarth Press, 1977–84.

"The *Dreadnought* Hoax." *Virginia Woolf: A Biography*, by Quentin Bell. Vol. 1. San Diego: Harvest–HBJ, 1972. 213–216.

"Ellen Terry." *Collected Essays*. Vol. 4. London: Hogarth Press, 1967. 67–72.

Freshwater. Ed. Lucio P. Ruotolo. San Diego: Harvest–HBJ, 1976.

"The Higher Court." *New Statesman* 17 April 1920: 44.

The Letters of Virginia Woolf. Ed. Nigel Nicolson and Joanne Trautmann. 6 vols. London: Hogarth Press, 1975–80.

"The Memoirs of Sarah Bernhardt." *Books and Portraits: Some Further Selections from the Literary and Biographical Writings of Virginia Woolf*. Ed. Mary Lyon. London: Hogarth Press, 1977. 201–207.

Orlando. San Diego: Harvest–HBJ, 1928.

"Professions for Women." *The Death of the Moth and Other Essays*. New York: Harcourt, Brace, 1942. 235–242.

"Rachel." *Times Literary Supplement* 20 April 1911: 155.

A Room of One's Own. San Diego: Harvest–HBJ, 1981.

"A Sketch of the Past." *Moments of Being.* Ed. Jeanne Schulkind. San Diego: Harvest–HBJ, 1985. 61–159.

"Speech Before the London/National Society for Women's Service, January 21 1931." *The Pargiters: The Novel–Essay Portion of "The Years,"* by Virginia Woolf. Ed. Mitchell A. Leaska. New York: New York Public Library, 1977. xxvii–xliv.

Three Guineas. San Diego: Harvest–HBJ, 1938.

"*Twelfth Night* at the Old Vic." *The Death of the Moth and Other Essays.* New York: Harcourt, Brace, 1942. 45–50.

The Voyage Out. San Diego: Harvest–HBJ, 1931.

Zola, Emile. "Naturalism on the Stage." Trans. Belle M. Sherman. Dukore, *Dramatic Theory and Criticism.* 692–719.

Index

Lightning Source UK Ltd.
Milton Keynes UK
UKOW04f1815070715

254762UK00001B/128/P